RED BULL RACING
F1 CAR

2010 (RB6)

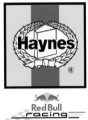

For Barbara, Tom and Emily

First published in July 2011
Reprinted in August 2011 and September 2011

A catalogue record for this book is available
from the British Library

ISBN 978 0 85733 099 4

Library of Congress control no. 2011923587

Design and layout: Lee Parsons,
Richard Parsons, Dominic Stickland

Published by Haynes Publishing,
Sparkford, Yeovil, Somerset BA22 7JJ, UK
Tel: 01963 442030 Fax: 01963 440001
Int. tel: +44 1963 442030
Int. fax: +44 1963 440001
E-mail: sales@haynes.co.uk
Website: www.haynes.co.uk

Haynes North America Inc., 861 Lawrence Drive,
Newbury Park, California 91320, USA

Printed and bound in the UK by Gomer Press Limited,
Llandysul Enterprise Park, Llandysul, Ceredigion SA44 4JL

Photograph Credits

All images copyright of **Red Bull Racing/Getty Images**
with the exception of the following:

John Colley: 22, 23 left, 28 top, 34, 36, 37 top, 38 top,
39, 40 bottom, 41, 42, 44, 46, 48 bottom, 50 bottom, 51,
52 top, 54 upper and bottom right, 56, 57, 62 bottom,
63 top, 66 middle right, 68 top, 69 bottom pair, 79 top,
84 top, 85 top, 87, 88 bottom, 89–91, 92 top, 93, 94 top
and bottom left, 100 left trio, 102, 104 top pair, middle
right and bottom left, 105, 111 top left, 112 left and
bottom right, 113 bottom, 116, 117, 119 bottom, 127,
134 bottom, 135 bottom, 143 left and middle, 145, 146
middle and bottom right, 153 upper pair, 156, 158 bottom

DPPI: 72–75, 76, 77 top, 78

Haynes Publishing: 35 top, 37 bottom, 40 top, 43 bottom,
45, 48 top, 49, 52 middle, 77 bottom, 106 bottom, 129

Moog: 108

Realise Creative: Front cover, 3, and 24–25 upper

Useful contacts

Red Bull Racing website: www.redbullracing.com
Red Bull Racing team merchandise: www.redbullshop/redbull/en/racing
Sebastian Vettel official website: www.sebastianvettel.de
Mark Webber official website: www.markwebber.com
Official Formula 1 website: www.formula1.com

RED BULL RACING
F1 CAR

2010 (RB6)

Owners' Workshop Manual

An insight into the technology, engineering, maintenance and operation of the World Championship-winning Red Bull Racing RB6

Steve Rendle

CONTENTS

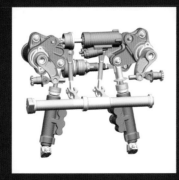

FOREWORDS

The 2010 season was incredible for Red Bull Racing. As a team we achieved four one–two finishes, nine wins, fifteen pole positions and two World Championships. The key element of our success was the RB6 – a great car that was designed and created by a committed group of people here in Milton Keynes and driven by two focused, talented drivers. We were delighted when Haynes approached us to take part in this project, I remember using a Haynes Manual for my first car, which was a VW Beetle. It's fantastic that there is now a Haynes Manual to represent the RB6, which was our most successful car to date.

I hope you enjoy reading it.

Christian Horner
Team Principal, Red Bull Racing

The RB6 was a good car that brought us two World Championships. Our pace of development in 2010 was phenomenal, with new parts going onto the car at almost every race. Pre-season testing revealed the car's potential, but the highly competitive nature of Formula One meant we couldn't stand still for a minute. As a team we concentrated on reliability and were constantly looking for ways to improve our overall package. I will always look back at the RB6 with fond memories and it's great that there is now a Haynes Manual to record it.

Adrian Newey
Chief Technical Officer, Red Bull Racing

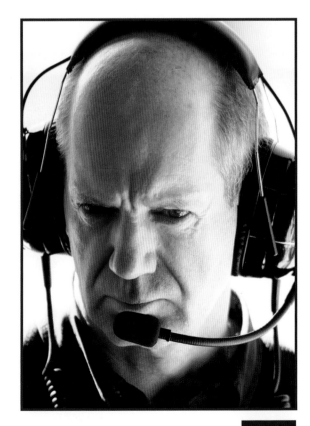

INTRODUCTION

The aim of this Haynes Manual is to provide a detailed insight into how one of the most technologically advanced machines on the planet is designed, built and operated. At the outset of the project, our goal was to explain how a leading F1 team designs, develops and races a competitive car. What transpired as the season progressed though, was that the project would become a behind-the-scenes look at the star car of one of the most hotly contested F1 championships for many years. A car that won the F1 Constructors' World Championship for Red Bull Racing and took Sebastian Vettel to the F1 Drivers' World Championship – the Red Bull Racing RB6.

During the early summer of 2010, when Red Bull Racing was lying second in the F1 Constructors' Championship, and its two drivers occupied third and fourth places in the Drivers' Championship, the seeds were sown that led to this Haynes Manual. The team's engineering, marketing and press departments gave their blessings to the project, and work began. As the season progressed, it became apparent that the team would be fighting until the end of the year for both World Championships, and yet the willingness of all involved to cooperate with the book remained undiminished. After winning both Constructors' and Drivers' titles with the RB6, the team's focus shifted to developing the RB7, the car that would defend its success in 2011. During this incredibly busy period, the team granted access to key staff, project cars and the Milton Keynes facilities to enable the writing project to continue. Meanwhile, the RB7 proved to be fast and reliable in testing, and took Sebastian Vettel to victory in the season's two opening races.

Designing, building and racing a successful F1 car requires a huge level of commitment from all those involved. During the 2010 season, Red Bull Racing employed 550 people, and every one of them made a contribution to the team's remarkable success over the year. The pace of development was astonishing, and Red Bull Racing pushed hard to stay ahead through innovation, determination and sheer hard work.

As I hope readers will appreciate, it has not been possible to provide details of the RB6's every last nut and bolt – a World Championship-winning team does not stay ahead of its rivals by publishing the blueprints to its car for all to see! Occasionally it has been necessary to use photographs and illustrations of previous Red Bull Racing designs to illustrate particular features, but wherever possible the RB6 appears throughout as the main project car.

Finally, I am grateful to have had the opportunity to write this book, which has been an exciting and rewarding experience. I can only hope that it does justice to the car and team that finished on top of the world in 2010.

ACKNOWLEDGEMENTS

As the author of this book, I owe a huge debt of gratitude to everybody at Red Bull Racing for lending their support to this project. Several people have helped beyond the call of duty. To everyone involved, I would like to express my heartfelt thanks for your help, and for making me feel so welcome during my visits to Milton Keynes. Red Bull Racing's reputation as the friendliest team in the paddock is well deserved, and I feel privileged to have had the opportunity of working with you.

I would like to say a special 'thank you' to a few people without whom this project would not have happened.

At Red Bull Racing: Rob Marshall, Dominik Mitsch, Wayne Greedy, Barbara Proske, Paul Monaghan, Katie Tweedle, Andrew Macfarlan, Josh Burgess, Henry Beggin, Dave Boys, Amelia Hooper, Mark Webber and Sebastian Vettel – and Christian Horner and Adrian Newey for giving their blessing to this project. At Renault Sport F1: Fabrice Lom and Lucy Genon. At Haynes Publishing: Iain Wakefield, Mark Hughes, Lee Parsons, Richard Parsons and Dominic Stickland. Thanks are also due to John Colley of John Colley Photography and Duncan Mills. There are undoubtedly other people who have made valuable contributions without my being aware, and I would like to express my thanks to them too.

Finally, thanks to my family for unwavering support and understanding – and for waiting!

Steve Rendle July 2011

← Sebastian Vettel crosses the line to take victory in the Malaysian Grand Prix on 4 April 2010 – the first race win for the Red Bull Racing RB6.

THE RED BULL RACING STORY

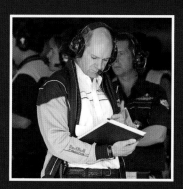

'Red Bull Racing is a strong, dynamic and very high-performing team, working hand in hand and in harmony, pulling together in one direction with the common dream and target, where everyone understands everyone else and the importance of his role'

Sebastian Vettel – 2010 F1 Drivers' World Champion

↑ The exterior of Building 1 at Red Bull Racing's Milton Keynes headquarters.

→ Austrian businessman Dietrich Mateschitz – the owner of the Red Bull energy drinks brand, parent company of Red Bull Racing.

The 2010 season was Red Bull Racing's sixth year in F1 as a manufacturer. In those six short years, the team made rapid progress, rising from a regular points finisher to reach the pinnacle of the sport, taking the Drivers' and Constructors' Championship double in 2010.

The 2010 success followed on the back of a very strong 2009, when Red Bull Racing finished a close runner-up in the Constructors' Championship, with Sebastian Vettel also second in the Drivers' Championship. At the time of writing, in late-July 2011, the team is mounting a strong defence of its World Championship titles, beginning where it left off in 2010, with six wins and three second places for Sebastian Vettel from the first ten races.

There are no miracles involved in this remarkable rise to prominence, and the team's achievements are due to ambition, commitment, hard work and, perhaps most importantly, effective teamwork, all cemented together by strong leadership. The team continues to project a hip and youthful persona off-track, and is undoubtedly one of the friendliest teams in F1, but there is an undiminished hunger to build on the spectacular success of 2010.

The Bull continues to charge.

TEAM HISTORY
The road to the top

The first chapter in the story of the team that became Red Bull Racing began in 1997, when former F1 World Champion Sir Jackie Stewart and his son Paul formed their own F1 team from scratch, with the backing of Ford. The Stewarts already had premises in Milton Keynes from which they had run

Formula Vauxhall Lotus, F3 and F3000 teams, and these premises were expanded to run the F1 operation. After three seasons, with highlights including a second place in the 1997 Monaco Grand Prix (for Rubens Barrichello) and three podiums during 1999, Ford bought out the Stewart Grand Prix team and the operation was rebranded as Jaguar Racing for 2000.

The Jaguar takeover came at a time of turmoil for the Ford brand. After a succession of team management and driver changes, five unremarkable seasons produced less than spectacular results, highlighted by three consecutive seventh-place finishes in the Constructors' Championship in the period 2002–2004. Towards the end of 2004, with its priorities changing to focus on its road-car business, Ford put the team up for sale.

Austrian businessman Dietrich Mateschitz was already involved in the sponsorship of a number of high-profile sports, promoting his Red Bull energy drinks company. The Red Bull sponsorship portfolio involved motor racing in various formulae, including F3000 (the feeder series for F1) and F1, and as part of this sponsorship plan Red Bull had in place a 'young driver' programme with the aim of nurturing and promoting new driving talent. During 2004 Red Bull had sponsored the Arden International F3000 team that took Vitantonio Liuzzi to the championship title under the leadership of team principal Christian Horner. In November 2004, Red Bull concluded a deal to buy the Jaguar team as a going concern, and the team was rebranded as Red Bull Racing.

By purchasing the assets of Jaguar Racing, Red Bull acquired the keys to the Milton Keynes factory, a core team of staff, and the early designs for what would have been the 2005 Jaguar, but which would now become the Red Bull Racing RB1, powered by a Cosworth V10 engine.

Christian Horner was recruited from the Arden International F3000 team to become team principal of the new F1 operation, and the experienced David Coulthard – already a multiple grand prix winner – was brought in to lead the team on the track. For the new team's 2005 debut season, the second car was shared between F3000 graduate Liuzzi and fellow Red Bull junior driver, Austrian Christian Klien. The new team made its race debut in Melbourne at the 2005 Australian Grand Prix, with both cars finishing in the points, in fourth and seventh places. The team finished its debut season in seventh place in the Constructors' Championship.

The new team brought a refreshingly youthful presence to the F1 paddock, and the three-storey

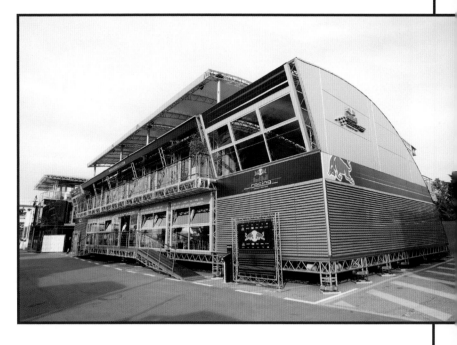

Red Bull Energy Station, which formed the team's circuit base for the European race weekends, caused an instant stir. The Energy Station set new standards for innovation in team hospitality, with catering by Michelin-starred chefs, music courtesy of guest DJs, top-quality table football and a fantastic roof garden. In the ever-competitive environment of F1, other teams soon raised their game and also produced impressive paddock hospitality suites and press centres.

↑ The Red Bull Energy Station caused a stir when it first appeared in the paddock in 2005.

↓ Adrian Newey was recruited as Chief Technical Officer ahead of the 2006 season.

↑ Team principal Christian Horner in discussion with David Coulthard at the 2006 Canadian Grand Prix.

→ David Coulthard at the wheel of the 2006 RB2.

↓ The RB3 was Adrian Newey's first design for Red Bull Racing.

↘ In 2008, Red Bull Racing pioneered the use of the 'shark-fin' engine cover on the RB4.

However, this outward sign of a relaxed atmosphere did not diminish the team's focus on winning on the track. Christian Horner, F1's youngest team principal, continued to bolster the team's technical resources ahead of the 2006 season, recruiting a growing band of proven championship-winning engineers and designers. Key among these new recruits were Adrian Newey, Peter Prodromou and Rob Marshall. Newey was already considered to be the most innovative designer in F1 as well as one of the world's leading aerodynamicists, Prodromou is also a

highly respected aerodynamicist, and Marshall was responsible for the mechanical design of the 2005 World Championship-winning Renault. As the team's new Chief Technical Officer, Newey joined with a legendary pedigree, having designed no fewer than six Constructors' Championship-winning F1 cars. Adrian explains what attracted him to the team: "It was a very young team, which offered me the opportunity to be centrally involved in developing not only the design of the car but the whole infrastructure of the engineering team."

Neither of the team's major new technical signings had any significant input into the 2006 RB2, which saw a change to Ferrari power as F1's 3.0-litre V10s made way for the new 2.4-litre V8s. In spite of a challenging year, the team achieved its first podium finish when David Coulthard drove a faultless race to take third place in Monaco.

The first fruits of the design team led by Adrian Newey appeared in 2007 in the form of the RB3. Australian Mark Webber joined David Coulthard on the driving strength, and another change of engine supplier saw the team switch to Renault, renewing a partnership between the French company and Newey that had dominated F1 for much of the 1990s. Although the season was marred by reliability problems, Mark Webber took third place at a rain-sodden Nürburgring, and confirmation that the team was making progress came with a climb to fifth place in the Constructors' Championship.

The 2008 RB4 built on the strengths of the RB3, with David Coulthard and Mark Webber continuing as drivers. At the first pre-season test, the RB4 caused a stir, running with a radical new 'shark-fin' engine cover – soon to be adopted by several other teams. The car proved consistent and reliable, and was a regular points scorer. David Coulthard scored another podium finish with an aggressive drive to third place at the Canadian Grand Prix, and at the British Grand Prix the popular Scot announced that he had decided to hang up his helmet at the end of the season. The scene was set for long-term Red Bull young driver protégé, and youngest-ever F1 race winner, Sebastian Vettel

↓ With a clean sheet of paper for 2009, the result of the design team's efforts was the highly successful RB5.

to make the step up from the Red Bull-owned Toro Rosso team to replace Coulthard for 2009, providing Red Bull Racing with one of the most dynamic driver pairings on the grid.

2009 – A PIVOTAL YEAR

Adrian Newey's new challenger for 2009, the RB5, provided the tool to transform the team from regular points-scorers to World Championship challengers. One of the key factors that brought about this new level of competitiveness was the introduction of a new set of F1 regulations aimed at improving the on-track spectacle. As a result, for the first time in its history, the team found itself on a level playing field with the established front-runners. With the regulation changes, Adrian Newey's design team was in its element, presented with an opportunity for its creative talent to flourish, as Adrian reflected at the beginning of 2010: "I do enjoy regulation changes such as those we had last year. They allow you to sit back with a clean sheet of paper and from first principles try to work out the best solutions to those regulations. Eleven years since a big change, and four years since any change

at all, meant F1 became quite repetitive. Nobody was coming up with new ideas; there were just lots of little alterations on existing, well-established themes… and I don't find that quite as interesting."

The RB5 started the season strongly in Australia and Malaysia, Sebastian Vettel qualifying third for both races, but posting two retirements, while Mark Webber finished sixth in Malaysia after the race was abandoned at 33 laps due to torrential rain.

At the third round of the championship, in China, Sebastian Vettel took the RB5 to its debut pole position, and led the race from start to finish.

↓ Sebastian Vettel took Red Bull Racing's first F1 victory at a rain-soaked 2009 Chinese Grand Prix.

↑ Mark Webber on his way to victory in the 2009 Brazilian Grand Prix.

Mark Webber, who started from third on the grid, followed Sebastian home to ensure that Red Bull Racing took its first win in emphatic style with a 1–2. The shape of things to come…

This result was a tribute not only to the design team and the drivers, but also to the team's mechanics and engineers who, after a month away from home at the season's first three 'fly-away' races, had put in a huge effort to get the cars ready for qualifying after a series of driveshaft problems.

When the teams returned to Europe in May for the Spanish Grand Prix, a series of strong performances had established Red Bull Racing as a serious championship contender. The success continued, with Vettel winning the British Grand Prix at Silverstone and Webber taking his maiden F1 victory at the German Grand Prix.

After two more podiums, for Webber in Hungary and Vettel in Belgium, the team returned to the top step to win the final three races. Vettel won in Japan and Webber in Brazil, and then the young German ended the year on a high with a win in Abu Dhabi, securing second place in the Drivers' Championship and confirming Red Bull Racing's second place in the Constructors' Championship.

The team had come of age and, with limited rule changes for 2010, was expected to be a serious contender for championship victory the following season. Expectations were high…

THE 2010 WORLD CHAMPIONSHIP-WINNING SEASON

For 2010, the Red Bull Racing design team honed the successful RB5, building on its strengths and designing the new car, the RB6, around a

← The 2010 RB6 – the car that took Red Bull Racing to double World Championship victory.

double diffuser. This was a feature that was never optimised to the team's satisfaction on the RB5, as a double diffuser was only adopted in response to its use by rival teams, after the fundamental design work on the car had been completed.

The RB6 made its debut later than some of its rivals, at the second pre-season test session at Jerez in Spain. By the third pre-season test session, also at Jerez, the new car was setting the pace.

At the season-opening Bahrain Grand Prix, Sebastian Vettel carried on where he'd left off in 2009, qualifying in pole position and leading the race until an electrical problem slowed the car, dropping him to fourth place at the finish.

In Australia Red Bull Racing continued to show their intent, with Vettel once again taking pole, this time just pipping team-mate Mark Webber to give the team a front-row lock-out. Unfortunately, more misfortune intervened, Vettel spinning out due to a loose wheel nut, while Webber finished ninth after an unfortunate roll of the dice with the safety car and pit-stop strategy.

Everything came good at last in Malaysia, with Webber taking pole, and Vettel starting third. After a hard-fought battle between the two team-mates during the first lap, Vettel seized the initiative and from then on the two Red Bull Racing drivers put on a dominant display for their first 1–2 finish of the season.

The team was now hitting its stride. Another front-row lock-out in China was followed by frustration in the race after the changing conditions once again played havoc with pit stops, Vettel finishing sixth and Webber eighth. The Australian made up for that disappointment in China with another win in Spain, followed by a

flawless display to take victory again a week later in the confines of the Monaco street circuit. Sebastian Vettel finished third in Spain and then second in Monaco, giving the team plenty to cheer about in the historic Principality with another 1–2. The team quite literally made a splash with their celebrations, the two drivers, Adrian Newey and Christian Horner precipitating a mass jump into the team's Energy Station pool.

The Turkish Grand Prix saw an unfortunate collision between the two Red Bull Racing drivers when battling for the lead, Mark Webber recovering to take third. At the following race in Canada, a tricky tyre-strategy decision didn't go the way of the Milton Keynes team, as they salvaged points with fourth and fifth places.

Two more wins followed at the European Grand Prix in Valencia, and then at Silverstone for the British Grand Prix. Vettel won in Valencia, and Webber took victory at Silverstone, following a frightening retirement in the European race after

↑ The RB6s led from the front in 2010, taking four 1–2 finishes during the season. Here Mark Webber heads Sebastian Vettel during the early stages of the Spanish Grand Prix.

← The RB6 featured extremely tight packaging – its rear end was noticeably more compact than all of its rivals.

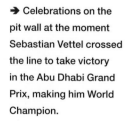

↑ Team members hold Sebastian Vettel aloft after his – and the team's – first victory of 2010, at the Malaysian Grand Prix.

➔ Cooling down in the Energy Station pool following the sensational result in the Monaco Grand Prix.

➔ Adrian Newey and Christian Horner are sprayed with champagne after the team's victory in the Constructors' Championship in Brazil.

➔ Celebrations on the pit wall at the moment Sebastian Vettel crossed the line to take victory in the Abu Dhabi Grand Prix, making him World Champion.

hitting the back of Heikki Kovalainen's Lotus and becoming airborne.

The team had now reached a level from which a third and sixth place at the German Grand Prix seemed disappointing. That disappointment was short-lived, as Mark Webber took an emphatic victory at the Hungarian Grand Prix, moving himself to the head of the Drivers' Championship and the team to the head of the Constructors' Championship for the first time in its history.

Second place for Mark Webber at Spa in Belgium was followed by a troubled weekend at Monza in Italy that nevertheless earned more points for fourth and sixth places to keep the team at the head of the Constructors' Championship.

In Singapore the two RB6s were beaten home by Alonso's Ferrari, but second and third places for Vettel and Webber extended the team's lead in the Constructors' Championship and moved Mark Webber 11 points clear at the head of the Drivers' Championship. The Suzuka circuit, home of the Japanese Grand Prix, suited the RB6. After qualifying on pole, Vettel controlled the race from start to finish, with Webber close behind – the team's third 1–2 of the season.

Going into the Korean Grand Prix weekend, five drivers still had a mathematical chance of winning the World Championship, with Webber heading the challenge from Alonso, Vettel, Hamilton and Button. Red Bull Racing made the front row its own again in qualifying, with Vettel taking pole. After the elation of Japan, the Korean race was a huge disappointment, the team posting its only double retirement of the season. A slippery kerb caught out Webber in difficult conditions, and Vettel retired with engine failure, while another win for Alonso gave him the lead in the Drivers' Championship.

Both championships were now entering their concluding phase, and the pace of development at Red Bull Racing was relentless, a number of new aerodynamic developments appearing on the RB6s in Brazil. In tricky qualifying conditions, Williams driver Nico Hulkenberg took a well-judged pole position, with Vettel and Webber lining up behind him. Another 1–2 finish in the race, Vettel ahead of Webber, sealed the Constructors' Championship for the team, to scenes of elation – just reward for the huge commitment and the relentless hours put in by all the team personnel during the season.

Christian Horner summed up after the Brazilian Grand Prix: "It is unbelievable. To see the joy on the faces of so many guys, who have put so much time in. All the all-nighters, all the hours and hours of work – not just here, but back in Milton Keynes.

Sebastian Vettel soaks up the atmosphere on the Abu Dhabi podium after winning the race and becoming the youngest-ever World Champion.

The realisation of six years of hard work. The Constructors' World Championship trophy in the team's trophy cabinet at Milton Keynes.

What has gone on this year, I don't think there is a more dedicated and committed team in the pitlane. To have achieved what we have is very much a dream come true."

There was much partying, both in São Paulo and Milton Keynes, but the final race of the season was only seven days away, so the celebrations soon gave way to more hard work as the team prepared for the Drivers' Championship showdown in Abu Dhabi.

By finishing third behind the RB6s in Brazil, Alonso now led the Drivers' Championship by eight points, with Webber second and Vettel third, a further seven points behind. Alonso was now the clear favourite for the title, only needing to finish in fourth place or higher in Abu Dhabi to take the championship, regardless of the finishing positions of his rivals.

As the showdown commenced, a cool-headed Vettel took pole position, ahead of Hamilton, Alonso, Button and Webber. Sebastian led away from the start, relinquished the lead temporarily to Button after making his tyre stop, and regained the lead when the Englishman pitted 15 laps later. Behind the leading RB6, Ferrari made a tactical error by pitting Alonso to cover Webber's stop. This dropped Alonso to seventh place, unable to pass the cars ahead. As the sun set over the season finale, Vettel took the chequered flag to win the race from Hamilton and Button. With Alonso and Webber finishing seventh and eighth respectively, the young German took the World Championship by four points from Alonso, becoming the sport's youngest-ever World Champion.

Sebastian recounted his feelings at the end of the race: "It was funny when I crossed the line. I was waiting for my engineer to call me, then he came on the radio and said 'OK' and I thought 'hmmm, it didn't work'. Then he said we had to wait for the other cars to cross the line and I then knew exactly what he was talking about, I knew he was going through the positions. And all of a sudden he was starting to scream 'World Champion' and everything just stopped. I was just happy in this moment, totally out of my mind. When I heard the recording of myself on the radio, initially I was a bit embarrassed because I sounded like a little kid or baby girl screaming. For the guys [in the garage], they share emotions together, and I gave them those words. It was funny for me to hear it for the first time. It was very special because immediately you have the situation again in your head and all the good stuff is coming up again – it was an incredible feeling."

↑ Teamwork is everything in F1. Here the race team assemble for a team photograph at the 2010 Abu Dhabi Grand Prix.

In spite of the increased media attention, and the responsibilities that come with the role of World Champion, Sebastian's outlook on life does not seem to have changed: "Not at all. For sure I had to attend a lot of functions and events after the win but after Christmas everything calmed down and I had the chance to spend time on my own and with my family and friends, which was important. For me life hasn't changed so far, only that I received a nice Trophy with my name on it."

And so, after six years of highs and lows, unwavering commitment from everybody in the team and, above all, highly effective teamwork, Red Bull Racing finished 2010 as double World Champions.

2010 SEASON STATISTICS

Races	19
Race laps completed	2109
Laps led	699
Wins	9
1–2 finishes	4
Podiums	20
Fastest laps	6
Pole positions	15
Front-row lock-outs	8
Front-row starts	26
Points scored	498

RACE — SEBASTIAN VETTEL — MARK WEBBER

RACE	SEBASTIAN VETTEL		MARK WEBBER	
	Qualifying	Race	Qualifying	Race
Bahrain	Pole	4th	6th	8th
Australia	Pole	Rtd	2nd	9th, FL
Malaysia	3rd	1st	Pole	2nd, FL
China	Pole	6th	2nd	8th
Spain	2nd	3rd	Pole	1st
Monaco	3rd	2nd, FL	Pole	1st
Turkey	3rd	Rtd	Pole	3rd
Canada	2nd	4th	7th*	5th
Europe	Pole	1st	2nd	Rtd
Britain	Pole	7th	2nd	1st
Germany	Pole	3rd, FL	4th	6th
Hungary	Pole	3rd, FL	2nd	1st
Belgium	4th	15th	Pole	2nd
Italy	6th	4th	4th	6th
Singapore	2nd	2nd	5th	3rd
Japan	Pole	1st	2nd	2nd, FL
Korea	Pole	Rtd	2nd	Rtd
Brazil	2nd	1st	3rd	2nd
Abu Dhabi	Pole	1st	5th	8th

Pole = Pole position   Rtd = Retired   FL = Fastest lap   *5-place grid penalty due to gearbox change

2011 – THE NEXT CHAPTER

Since late summer 2010, in addition to working continually on development of the RB6, the Red Bull Racing design team had been hard at work on its successor for the 2011 season, the RB7.

The RB7 made its debut at the first pre-season test, at Valencia in February 2011. As testing got underway, the team's new challenger appeared to be quick and reliable, although it was difficult to draw direct comparisons with the cars of rival teams, due to uncertainty about the fuel load each car was carrying. At the final pre-season test session at Barcelona in early March, the car continued to perform well, and the scene was set for the team's world title defence.

At the time of writing, in late-July 2011, Red Bull Racing are mounting a successful defence of both World Championship titles, the team leading the Constructors' Championship and Sebastian Vettel leading the Drivers' Championship, with six wins and three second places from the first ten races.

⬆ Red Bull Racing's 2011 challenger, the RB7, at the Australian Grand Prix. Sebastian Vettel carried on where he left off in 2010, taking a dominant win.

⬇ The RB7 launch in Valencia featured a Press Kit styled as a Haynes Manual. Wayne Greedy, who helped extensively with this book, is 'Monsieur Mécanicien'!

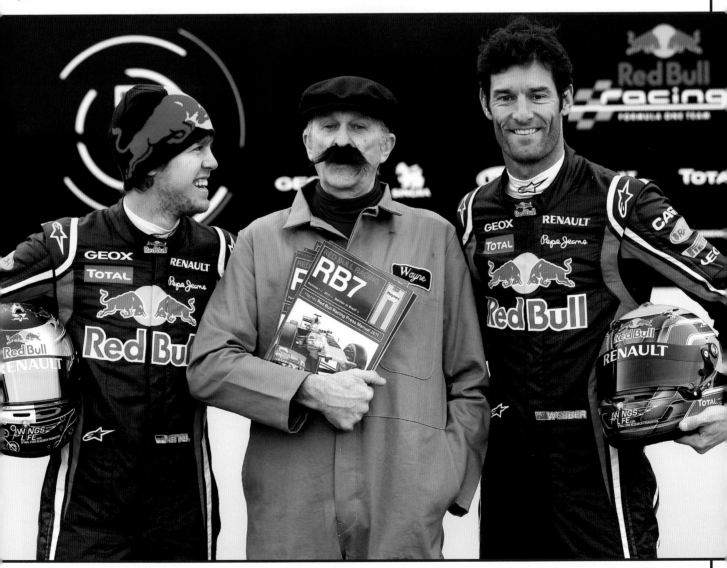

THE ANATOMY OF THE RED BULL RACING RB6

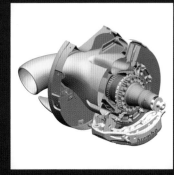

'A beautiful car, but most important it was bloody quick, one of the best on the grid, and fun to drive.'

Sebastian Vettel – 2010 F1 Drivers' World Champion

INTRODUCTION

↑ A cutaway view providing a glimpse under the skin of the superbly engineered RB6.

→ Every single component of an F1 car is painstakingly designed and crafted using cutting-edge technology. This view shows the major components of an RB5.

A modern F1 car is arguably the pinnacle of engineering excellence – a work of art created by a hand-picked team of engineers and craftsmen and craftswomen, all of whom are at the top of their profession. The essence of F1 is to provide the ultimate challenge for man and machine on the track and, by its very nature, F1 racing pushes the limits of both human and mechanical endurance.

To illustrate just how competitive F1 now is, over the 19 races of the 2010 season, the average gap in qualifying between pole position and sixth place on the grid was exactly 1.0 second – remarkable when

you consider the variables of track configuration and weather conditions, not to mention the seven different teams and 12 different drivers who qualified in the top six during the season. But mere statistics don't do justice to the challenge and engineering expertise involved in putting together a winning F1 car, and during the 2010 season there was no better example of how a team successfully tackles that challenge than the double-championship-winning Red Bull RB6.

Mark Webber gives his opinion of the car: "Off the back of its predecessor, the RB5, the RB6 became

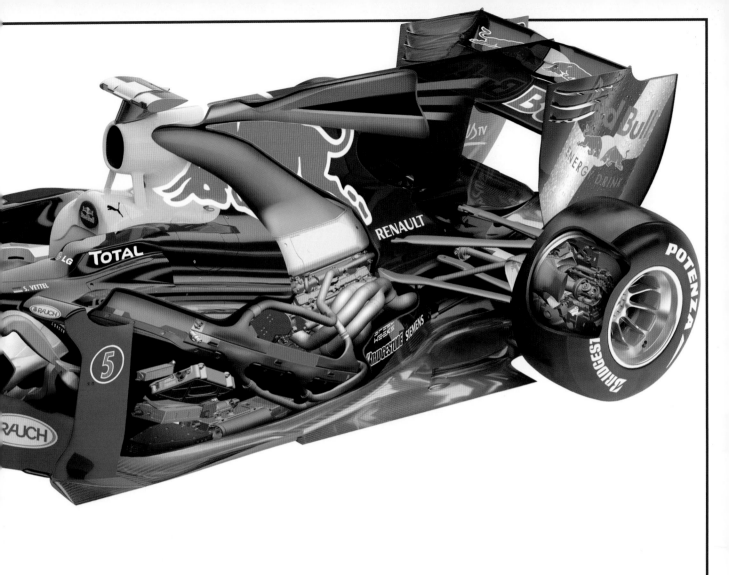

an incredibly versatile car. In terms of the car and performance, we designed one of the most versatile and complete racing cars that I've ever driven. It was fast on every track, it had no real vices, we made it good over the bumps, good through slow-speed corners and fast corners, so it was a real testament to the guys that we could turn up at most venues, irrespective of what the track layout was, and our car was going to be pretty quick."

So, let's take a closer look under the skin of the car that was the envy of the paddock during the 2010 season.

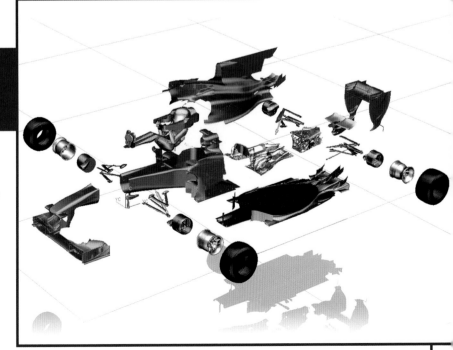

CHASSIS ('TUB')

↑ The chassis is the core of the car, providing protection for the driver, and a stiff structure capable of dealing with enormous aerodynamic and mechanical loads.

The chassis, or 'tub', is the backbone of the car, to which all the other components are attached. It must provide an enormously strong, stiff structure, capable of dealing with the loads transferred to it from the suspension, steering, engine, transmission and various aerodynamic components. The chassis also forms a survival cell that must protect the driver from injury in the most severe of impacts. Additionally, the chassis also houses the fuel tank, and is designed very much with aerodynamic performance in mind – the team's aerodynamicists are able to outline the optimum shape they require to execute their design concept for a new car, and the chassis-design team then aims to accommodate the necessary components within the preferred outline with minimal compromise to the overall packaging. As we'll discover later, aerodynamic efficiency is the primary parameter dictating the design of the car.

The chassis is instrumental to the performance and 'feel' of the car, as ultimately it provides the link between all the other components of the car and the driver. An F1 driver drives the car quite literally 'by the seat of his pants' – and, when he is driving the car, the seat of his pants is firmly attached to the chassis, albeit via an anatomical seat, so that he can feel every twitch and bump as the car rides over the track surface.

The chassis is of monocoque construction, and is designed to conform to FIA regulations which stipulate fundamental parameters such as minimum dimensions and the locations of the roll structures in relation to the driver. One of the main FIA rule changes for the 2010 F1 season was to ban refuelling during the race. This meant that the car had to carry sufficient fuel for the entire race, which in turn dictated a larger fuel tank and so a longer, and therefore heavier, chassis to accommodate it. The FIA also stipulates various impact tests, roll-structure tests and static 'squeeze' tests which must be carried out to prove the integrity of the chassis's integral survival cell. These tests are carried out on a 'reference chassis' prior to the start of the season, and all the tests must be passed, without damage to the main structure, before the chassis is homologated and the completed car is allowed to race. During

2010, the regulations did not allow for any redesign of components or structures where homologation was required, which effectively meant that the chassis (and other homologated structures such as the gearbox casing) could not be modified structurally during the season, once inspected and homologated by the FIA. See 'FIA crash tests' on pages 176–177 for full details of the various FIA requirements.

DESIGN AND MANUFACTURE

Because the chassis forms the car's backbone, it is the starting point for the design of the whole car, and so chassis design occupies a significant amount of the design team's time. Typically, work on the design of the chassis for a new car starts in July of the preceding season, and the first completed chassis will be presented to the FIA for crash testing the following February, often only four to six weeks before the first race of the season.

The chassis is manufactured from carbon-fibre composites, which provide remarkable strength for a very low weight when compared to alternative materials, such as the aluminium tube and sheet structures that preceded the use of carbon-fibre in F1 chassis design. Owing to the use of CAD (Computer Aided Design) and CNC (Computer Numerically Controlled) tooling in the carbon-fibre chassis design and manufacturing process, every detail of the process can be repeated extremely accurately, which means

that there is a very high level of consistency between individual chassis in terms of their dimensions and stiffness. The practical benefit of this is that the mechanical and aerodynamic set-up of one team car should be consistently repeatable on another car with a similar chassis, as Sebastian Vettel confirms: "I don't really have a favourite chassis. Basically the cars are the same, we don't change chassis too much over the season, maybe twice and mainly when there is some damage that we struggle to repair. We do not have many spare chassis anyway."

The chassis-manufacturing process is detailed in the section on pages 28–30.

SURVIVAL CELL

The driver survival cell is integral with the chassis. As well as providing an extremely strong cocoon around the driver, the survival cell incorporates impact and rollover structures. The survival cell also features side-impact-protection panels to reduce the chances of parts of another car, or trackside structures, punching through the side of the chassis during an impact and causing potentially serious injury to the driver. The survival cell must be designed to conform to FIA regulations regarding dimensions and side-impact-protection panel specifications, and the finished prototype chassis must be subjected to a programme of rigorous impact tests to ensure the integrity of the survival cell.

⬇ The finished prototype chassis is subjected to a programme of FIA crash tests to prove its integrity. Here a chassis, with nose fitted, is about to undergo a front impact test. In order to pass the test, the chassis must sustain no damage.

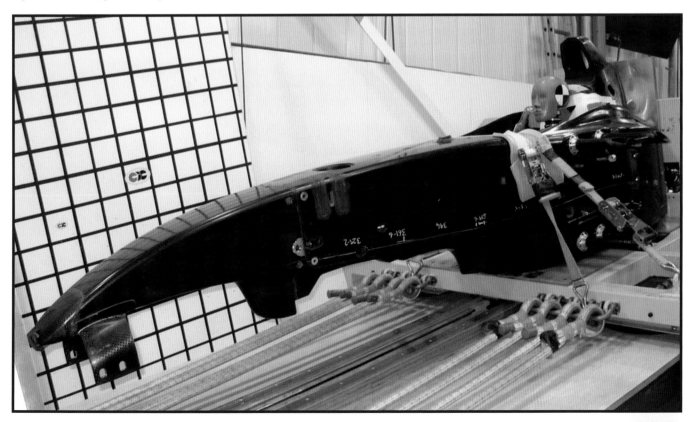

1 The chassis is designed, analysed and refined using CAD and Finite Element stress Analysis (FEA) software.

2 Solid epoxy patterns for the chassis are cut using five-axis milling machines, which read data from the CAD design file in order to faithfully replicate the required dimensions and contours on the patterns. Any defect present on the patterns will be reproduced on all the chassis produced from them, so it is vital that the machining is accurate to ensure that all the contours of the patterns are perfect. The finished patterns are accurate to ±0.05mm. Rather than metal, epoxy is used for the patterns to ensure that when the moulds (see next step) are undergoing curing at high temperatures (in excess of 130°C) the effects of thermal expansion are minimised – ie, the patterns and moulds expand at similar rates.

→ This view shows an epoxy pattern being cut by a five-axis milling machine. A filtered extraction system is used to deal with the fine dust produced.

↘ This image shows the graphical output from a Finite Element stress Analysis (FEA) of the RB2 chassis. The areas coloured green indicate highly stressed areas that need reinforcement.

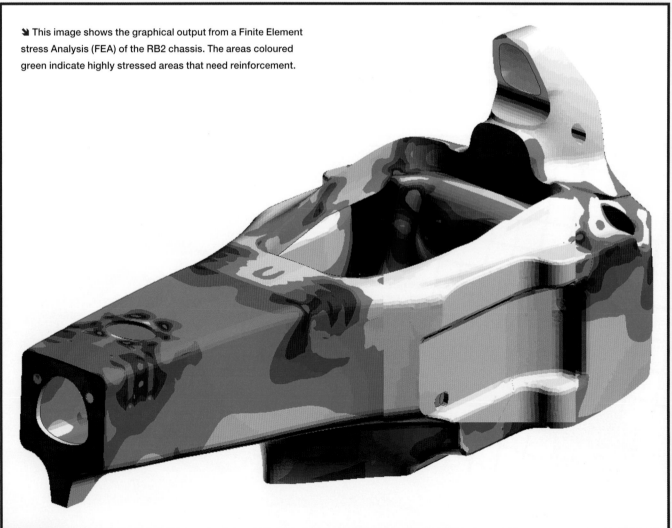

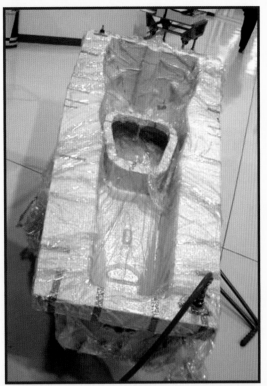

← ← Carbon-fibre plies being laid up in a mould.

← An upper chassis half mould, laid up with carbon-fibre plies ready for thermal curing.

3 Female moulds are made from the patterns. This work is carried out in the 'clean room', which is effectively a room sealed off from the surrounding areas of the factory using double-door airlocks. Inside the clean room, the pressure, humidity and temperature are carefully controlled, and the staff wear special overalls and footwear at all times. The moulds are made from carbon-fibre, and their construction involves several stages, with a number of vacuum treatments, layering and thermal curing ('cooking') processes. Upper and lower moulds are produced, as the chassis itself is manufactured in upper and lower halves that are later bonded together. Great care must be taken to avoid damage when removing the moulds from the patterns.

4 The exterior surfaces of the finished moulds are machined to remove any sharp edges, and these moulds are then used to manufacture all the chassis required for the season.

5 The chassis themselves are manufactured from layered carbon-fibre cloth. Several different types of carbon-fibre cloth are used, and the orientation of the fibre 'plies' (layers) in the cloth is critical – the plies must run in specific directions according to the required stiffness properties and directional loading that the relevant area of the chassis will be subjected to. Several hundred carbon-fibre plies are used in each chassis, comprising numerous different shapes to produce the desired properties throughout the chassis. These various shapes

← The autoclaves are large enough to accommodate a complete chassis. These units are essentially large and very precisely controlled pressure cookers.

are machine-cut to ensure accuracy and repeatability from one chassis to another.

6 The number of plies and their orientation varies at different locations around the chassis, for example around mounting points for the suspension or engine, where increased strength is required. The layering of the various carbon-fibre plies is known as the 'lay-up', and the orientation and exact positioning of each ply is critical. To ensure that the plies are correctly positioned, the staff (laminators) carry out the lay-up work with reference to printed manuals containing annotated visual descriptions of the exact process to be followed for each ply. Once laid-up, every ply must be checked against the relevant manual and signed off by an inspector before the next ply can be added.

↑ A completed upper chassis half ready for bonding together with the lower half before machining and finishing.

↓All composite components undergo final trimming and inspection in a 'clean' area.

7 After laying up the plies in the mould, the whole assembly is placed in a vacuum bag and pushed into an autoclave (a large oven that provides a thermal curing process with precise control of temperature and pressure). The bag is vacuumed down to squeeze the plies against one another. High temperatures in the autoclave cause pre-impregnated resin (that lies within each ply) to flow evenly throughout the material. The resin then cures (becomes solid), thus fusing all the plies together to create a single solid half of the chassis.

8 During the lay-up, it is possible to integrate certain other components into the structure, such as metal inserts and fixing studs, to act as mountings for various components later attached to the chassis.

9 The completed chassis halves are removed from the moulds, and bonded together to form the final monocoque. Bulkheads are bonded into the chassis to supply mounts for the front suspension rockers and driver's seat back. The surfaces to be bonded together must be meticulously cleaned, as no mechanical fasteners are used to supplement the bonding on the finished chassis. Specially produced jigging is used when bonding the chassis halves together to ensure repeatable accuracy.

10 Final machining and trimming of the finished chassis is carried out to produce any required detailing and to accommodate suspension pick-up points, component mountings, etc. Again, jigs are used for some of these processes to ensure accuracy.

11 Throughout the preceding steps, a rigorous inspection procedure is followed at every stage. Red Bull Racing have a Composite Inspection Department where all the parts and bonded assemblies are inspected after curing before they are released for the next stage of manufacture, or for final use on the car. Parts are also returned for inspection between on-track events (testing, races, etc), and many parts have a specified inspection/service schedule which may include Non-Destructive Testing (NDT) of bonded joints and the condition of laminates, stiffness testing, visual checking, and cleaning/tidying up processes.

NOTE Although these steps provide a simplified overview of the carbon-fibre chassis-manufacturing process, the same basic principles and procedures apply to the manufacture of all the carbon-fibre components used on the car.

There are two elements to the side-impact protection:

- The chassis sides are fitted with crushable side-impact structures (see pages 176–177) that must pass a crash test.
- FIA-specified panels, manufactured from a particular weave of carbon-fibre known as Zylon, which are bonded to the sides of the finished, homologated chassis. The location, thickness and size of the Zylon panels must conform to FIA regulations.

The FIA regulations stipulate that the survival cell must incorporate three FIA-supplied transponders, which must be fitted in specified locations – one either side of the cockpit opening, and one at the front of the chassis in line with the front-wheel axle centreline. These transponders must be accessible to FIA inspectors at any time, and are used to confirm the identity of individual chassis and to record various data.

ROLL STRUCTURES

In order to protect the driver from the risk of injury if the car becomes inverted during an accident, FIA regulations state that two roll structures must be incorporated into the structure of the chassis. The driver's helmet and his steering wheel must be a specified distance below a line drawn between the highest points of the two roll structures. Both roll structures are subjected to load tests on the prototype chassis as part of the FIA chassis-homologation procedure.

The rear roll structure is formed by a roll hoop attached to the highest point of the chassis behind the driver's head. On the RB6, the rear roll hoop is a separate carbon-fibre component, bonded to the

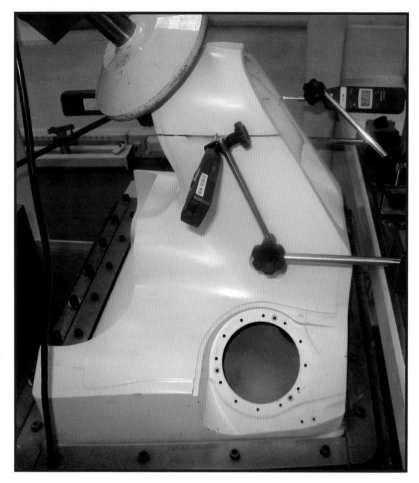

chassis, although some teams choose to design a roll hoop that is integral with the chassis. The roll hoop incorporates an aperture that forms part of the inlet for the engine air box. The biggest challenge in designing the roll hoop is making it as light as possible while still providing the required strength.

The front roll structure takes the form of an internal bulkhead above the driver's knees.

↑ A typical rear roll structure undergoing an FIA 'push' test. The load is applied via a pad under controlled conditions (see pages 176–177).

⬇ The driver's helmet and steering wheel must fall below a line drawn between the two roll structures.

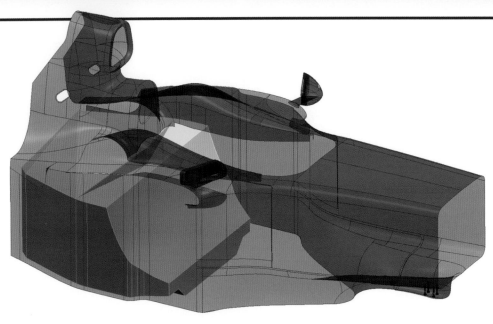

→ A bespoke bladder-
type fuel cell is used,
shaped to fit the chassis.

FUEL TANK

The fuel tank is located in the chassis to the rear of
the cockpit, behind the driver's seat, and is separated
from the driver by a bulkhead that must conform
to FIA specifications.

The fuel tank takes the form of a bespoke bladder-
type cell, supplied by specialist manufacturers ATL.
The cell is made from an elastomer-impregnated
Kevlar material, which is light, but extremely flexible.
The fuel cell is designed to deform if subjected to a
high-energy impact, and is also highly resistant to
ripping, penetration and gouging, to minimise the
chances of fuel leakage in the event of an accident.
The pliable nature of the finished fuel cell enables it to
be installed, and if necessary removed, relatively easily
through an aperture in the chassis that is significantly
smaller than the fuel cell itself.

An internal baffle is fitted to the fuel tank, again
made from specialised lightweight fabrics, to help
to reduce fuel slosh inside the tank under extreme
acceleration, deceleration and cornering forces, and
to ensure a constant supply of fuel to the engine. The
fuel pumps are carefully designed to optimise fuel
scavenge – ie, to make sure that the fuel system is able
to pick up almost every last drop of fuel inside the tank
– in order that the car need not carry any more fuel
than is absolutely necessary.

BALLAST

For the 2010 season, the FIA specified a minimum
weight limit for the car of 620kg with the driver on
board and cameras fitted. For the 2011 season, with
the addition of the KERS system, this minimum weight
increased by 20kg to 640kg.

The design team aim to produce a car that is under
the minimum-allowable weight, to allow them to ballast
the car up to the minimum weight. This enables the team
to place the ballast in the optimum longitudinal (front/rear)
position to aid the set-up of the car (in 2010 there were
no FIA restrictions on where the ballast could be located,
provided it was securely attached). Generally, the ballast
is placed as low on the car as possible, in order to keep
the car's centre of gravity (C of G) as low as possible.

Optimum weight distribution can only be accurately
determined by testing the car on-track, so the ability to
move the ballast in order to adjust weight distribution
is important. Altering the weight distribution is one of
the most fundamental tuning devices for adjusting the
handling performance parameters of the car.

Although there are no restrictions on the materials
that can be used for ballast, Red Bull Racing made
use of tungsten for the RB6. Tungsten has a very high
density (71% more dense than lead), which means
that its use enables a part to be physically smaller for
a given weight, allowing more flexibility in its location
on the car. Most F1 cars are extremely sensitive to a
change in weight distribution, and changes may be
made in steps of as little as 500g.

CRASH TESTING OF CHASSIS

Details of the various crash tests that must be carried
out on the chassis are given in the 'FIA crash tests'
section on pages 176–177.

→ A tungsten ballast block,
shaped to suit the required
fitting location.

AERODYNAMICS

It is often quoted that a modern F1 car produces sufficient aerodynamic downforce to enable it to drive upside-down across a ceiling. Fact or fiction? Well, the downforce produced by an F1 car is dependent on its speed, and at maximum speed the downforce produced by the car is far in excess of its weight. So, in theory, yes, if the straight at Monza, for example, could be turned upside-down once a car was running on it at maximum speed, the car would not fall off!

To give a better idea of the forces involved in F1 aerodynamics, when the car is travelling at maximum speed a typical front wing produces over 500kg of downforce. This downforce allows a modern F1 car to generate a lateral cornering force of up to 5g (five times its own weight).

On a contemporary F1 car, aerodynamic performance is absolutely critical. It is the most important single element in the performance of the car, and the driving force behind the design of the whole car. It is also the dominant factor during the racing season, when the majority of the development work carried out on the car revolves around improving aerodynamics. The aerodynamicist's two main priorities are to create the maximum possible level of downforce, and to minimise drag. Essentially, downforce pushes the car's tyres on to the track, which helps to improve cornering forces, allowing the car to corner faster. Aerodynamic drag is the force that opposes the motion of the car through the air. Both downforce and drag are dependent on speed – as the speed of the car increases, both downforce and drag increase disproportionately (if the car's speed doubles, the aerodynamic forces increase fourfold). To give an idea of the level of drag acting on the car, at maximum speed the car's total drag with a high-downforce set-up will produce over 1g of deceleration simply when the driver lifts off the throttle, before he even touches the brakes.

The primary tools used for aerodynamic development are the wind tunnel and Computational Fluid Dynamics (CFD) analysis software – theses two tools complement each other, and both have useful roles to play. Further details of CFD and the wind tunnel are provided in 'The Designer's View' Chapter on pages 131–135.

↑ The rear wing is the most visibly obvious aerodynamic device on the car, and produces approximately a third of the car's downforce.

↗↓ Every surface of the car is designed with aerodynamic performance in mind, and the aesthetic lines are purely coincidental.

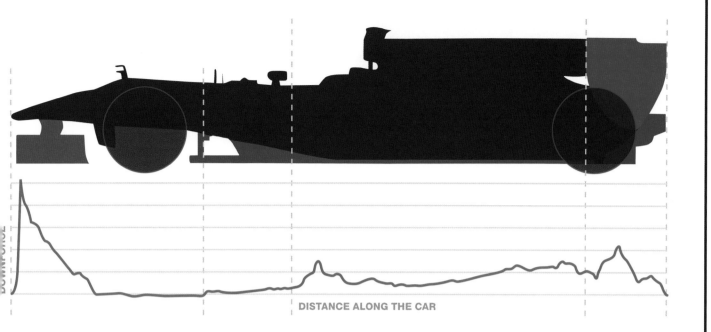

DOWNFORCE

DISTANCE ALONG THE CAR

⬆ The typical distribution of downforce on the car.

⬇ Low-downforce (Monza, top) and high-downforce (Monaco, bottom) RB6 aerodynamic packages. Note the obvious difference in rear wing configuration.

Although some parts on the car – such as the front and rear wings, turning vanes and rear diffuser – are fitted for purely aerodynamic reasons, every external part is designed with aerodynamic performance in mind, and all the aerodynamic components on the car interact. For instance, the floor cannot work to produce downforce without the front wing, the rear wing does not work as well without the floor, and the floor does not work as well without the rear wing. In practical terms this means, for example, that when designing the car, the floor is shaped to deal with the wake from the front wing, and the diffuser and rear wing are designed to take into account the upwash from the rear wing, which can be used to help both components work more efficiently.

The overall aerodynamic package on the car requires setting up for a particular circuit in conjunction with the mechanical set-up, although aerodynamic efficiency – essentially downforce versus drag – is the primary factor in both aerodynamic and mechanical set-up. Some circuits require a fundamentally different package to others: for example, Monza is a low-downforce circuit, Monaco is a high-downforce circuit, and a number of others, such as Spa-Francorchamps (Belgium) and Montréal (Canada), require a medium-downforce set-up.

The main components influencing the aerodynamic performance of the car are described in further detail in the following sub-sections.

The front wing consists of five main components
– all manufactured from carbon-fibre:

1 **Mainplane** The main front wing element (aerofoil section),
which is secured directly to the nose.

2 **Endplates** The vertical plates secured to each end of the wing
assembly. The endplates perform two important functions:
helping to control the airflow over the front wing mainplane and
flaps by preventing the air from spilling over the sides of the
wing, and helping to direct turbulent air outboard of the car,
rather than allowing it to flow to the floor and diffuser.

3 **Main flap** The adjustable element fitted behind the mainplane.
This is the element that was adjustable by the driver from the
cockpit during 2009 and 2010. For the 2011 season, this element
can only be adjusted manually with the car at rest. The trailing
edge of the flap has various trim options to allow fine tuning.

4 **Upper flaps** Various flaps are fitted above the mainplane and
inboard of the endplates.

5 **Turning vanes** Various turning vanes are located under the
wing assembly to fine-tune the airflow.

↓ The complex shape of the RB6
front wing, showing the main
components (see text).

FRONT WING

The front wing is the most important
aerodynamic component because it precedes
every other part of the car over which its wake
will flow. The front wing has such a major effect
on overall aerodynamic efficiency that the
downforce it generates (around a third of the
total downforce produced on the car) is not
always the primary consideration – front-wing
downforce may be compromised in order to
optimise the airflow over other areas of the car.

The detailing and finish of the front
wing components are critical to the wing's
performance, and so a considerable amount
of time is spent on front-wing design
and development, using both CFD and
wind-tunnel simulation.

The RB6's front wing evolved constantly
during the season, and detailed changes
were made for almost every race.

The RB6 front wing also proved controversial,
rival teams suggesting that the wing flexed at
high speed, beyond the limit permitted by the
FIA regulations, moving closer to the track. The
regulations stated that with the car at rest, the
lowest surface of the front wing assembly must
be no lower than 75mm above the 'reference
plane' – the flat plane running through the

car's floor undersurface. A degree of flexing is permitted under load, as in practice it would be impossible to design a wing assembly that did not flex at all under the substantial aerodynamic loads acting on it at high speed. Prior to the controversy, the legality of the front wing on all the cars was checked by applying a specified load (50kg) to the top of each wing endplate. Under this load the wing was permitted to flex linearly in a vertical direction by a maximum of 10mm. To calm the controversy, from the 2010 Belgian Grand Prix onwards, the FIA decided that the test load should be doubled (to 100kg), along with the permitted flex (to 20mm). The RB6 front wing passed the new test without problem.

➜ The front wing endplates help to control the airflow over the wing itself, and direct turbulent airflow away from the car's floor.

⬇ The FIA introduced a new front-wing load test from the Belgian Grand Prix (see text).

100kg

(50kg)

75mm

20mm (10mm)

➜ During 2010, the driver could change the angle of the front-wing main flap (arrowed) using the adjuster.

Driver-adjustable front-wing main flap

For the 2009 and 2010 F1 seasons, the FIA introduced a regulation to allow adjustable front wings. The idea behind this was to improve overtaking opportunities by providing the driver with the ability to change the angle of the wing main flap a maximum of twice per lap.

When a car is following another closely, the overall air pressure ('total head of pressure') acting on the following car is reduced, because effectively the following car is caught in the hole in the air (low-pressure area) created by the car in front. This reduces the downforce available to the following car, and the front wing is particularly susceptible to this effect because of the upwash of air from the leading car – a substantial amount of the air which would normally flow over the following car's front wing 'misses' it, because it is deflected upwards by the leading car's rear wing.

The adjustable front wing allowed the driver to increase the angle (incidence) of the front wing main flap in order to recover some of the lost downforce, so maintaining the balance of the

⬇ The hydraulic front wing main-flap adjuster mechanism cover removed to show the location of the components in the endplate.

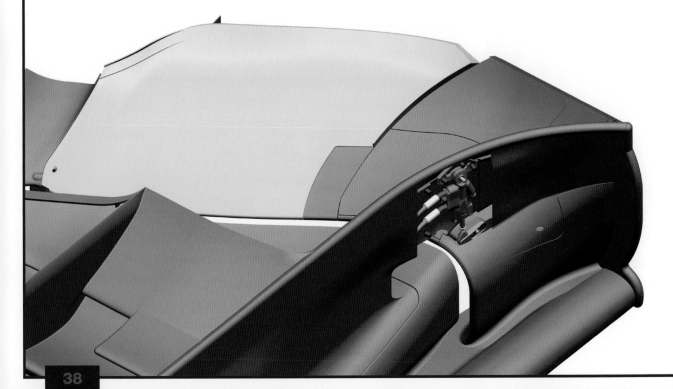

car and allowing it to close up on the leading car in a high-speed corner.

As explained previously, in the wake of another car, the following car suffers a loss of downforce, but as a result its drag is also reduced, which is why the following car picks up a tow from the car in front, as Sebastian Vettel describes: "You can feel the slipstream once you get really close enough – it's quite powerful and starts sucking you towards the other car."

On the RB6, the front wing adjustment mechanism was hydraulically operated, with the actuators and mechanism housed in the endplates during the early season, and in the wing itself later in the year. Some other teams used electro-mechanically operated systems.

NOSE

The nose is essentially a removable extension of the chassis, which forms the front crash structure and a mounting for the front wing assembly. The main part of the nose is a one-piece carbon-fibre moulding, and the wing support struts are bonded to the nose. The FIA regulations stipulate that two camera housings must be fitted to the nose (for more details refer to 'Cameras' on pages 103–104).

As with all other components, the design of the nose on an F1 car tends to vary from team to team, but generally speaking there are two fundamental concepts – the 'high' nose and 'low' nose. The RB6 features a high-nose design. With the high-nose concept, the lower surface of the nose runs almost horizontally forwards from the chassis, with the front-wing assembly suspended well below the lower edge of the nose. With the low-nose concept, the nose slopes down so that the front of the nose is very close to the wing assembly.

Because the nose incorporates the front crash structure, it must be subjected to FIA crash-testing, and homologated as per the chassis. Details of the crash structures are given on pages 176–177.

Because the nose serves as the mounting for the front wing, which is easily damaged during a race, the nose is secured to the chassis using quick-release fittings, to enable it to be replaced relatively quickly during a pit stop. The nose locates on four pegs on the front of the chassis, and is secured via a half-turn catch on either side, which can be released using an Allen key. The electrical connection for the camera(s) and the hydraulic connection (dry-break) for the front wing flap adjustment mechanism are made at the nose joint to ease disconnection.

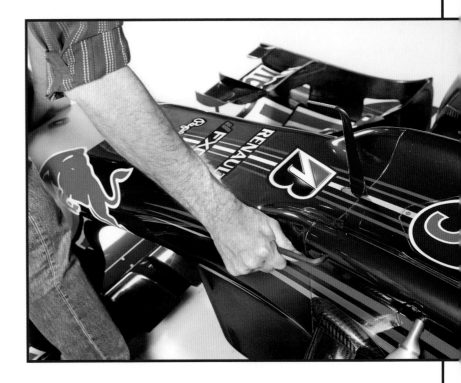

↑ The nose assembly is secured by a single half-turn catch on each side to allow quick removal and refitting.

↓ Once the catches have been released, the nose/front wing assembly can be lifted clear.

High Nose

Low Nose

↑ A schematic showing the difference between the high (top) and low (bottom) nose concepts.

↓ The two turning vanes on each side of the sidepod are designed to turn the airflow around the car.

THE CHASSIS

Although not an aerodynamic component in its own right, the chassis is designed to take account of aerodynamic considerations. The cross-sectional shape of the chassis, when viewed from the front, forms a complex V-section, which is designed to optimise the airflow around the sides of the chassis in order to help the front and rear wings, floor and diffuser to work to best effect.

TURNING VANES ('BARGE BOARDS')

Turning vanes, the vertical plates, usually curved, mounted on either side of the chassis between the front wheels and the sidepod air intakes, first appeared on F1 cars in the early 1990s. In the late 1990s and early 2000s, they became very complex devices, often with multiple elements, and during this period cars also sprouted turning vanes in various other positions around the car, such as on the edges of the sidepods and under the nose.

FIA regulation changes introduced for 2009 resulted in simpler turning vanes and restricted their positioning, but they are still important aerodynamic devices.

Turning vanes are so-called because they are designed to turn the airflow around the car. The turning vanes have multiple functions, but are used predominantly to help to control the turbulent wake from the front wheels, and to scavenge air from the front wing and under-chassis area, turning the airflow towards the sidepods, floor and diffuser.

On the RB6, the main turning vanes are located forward of the sidepods, below the air intakes. Additional tall, thin vanes are positioned at the outboard front edges of the sidepods, attached at their bases to the floor, and supported by struts attached to the edges of the sidepods. For the first three races of the 2010 season, the RB6's mirrors were mounted on the top of these turning vanes, the idea being to reduce the effect of the drag of the mirrors by placing them in the already turbulent airflow coming off the front tyres. From the Spanish Grand Prix outboard mirrors were banned, and the mirrors were moved to their previous positions on the sides of the chassis.

SIDEPODS

The sidepods house the engine coolant radiators, the engine and gearbox oil coolers, the hydraulic fluid cooler, and the car's side-impact structures. On the RB6, most of the electronic control units (ECUs) on the car are also housed in the sidepods beneath the radiators. Ducting within the sidepods feeds air to the various radiators and coolers, and to the various ECUs. The ducting provides support for the considerable weight of the various fluid-filled radiators and coolers, which are mounted directly in the ducting. Both the ducting and the various brackets and trays supporting the components mounted inside are manufactured from carbon-fibre.

The sidepods and radiator ducts are normally

bonded, or sometimes bolted, to the sides of the chassis, although when a new car is designed, the design team may adjust the way in which the bodywork components are split in order to suit specific requirements.

The contours of the sidepods are very carefully designed in order to help control the airflow to

↑ The lower, front section of the chassis (arrowed) forms a complex V-section to aid aerodynamics.

← The sidepods are packed with equipment, housing radiators and oil coolers and a number of electronic control units (several removed in this view).

↑ The heavily sculpted sidepods are one of the RB6's defining features.

the rear end of the car, around the wheels, and to the diffuser and rear wing. The RB6's sculpted sidepods, which are particularly low at the rear, are one of the defining characteristics of the car. When viewed from above, the sidepods have a pronounced curve inwards, to give the car a very narrow rear end – often referred to as the 'coke bottle' rear end. This narrow rear bodywork is designed to minimise drag and optimise the airflow between the rear wheels, helping to draw more air through the diffuser and improving airflow to the rear wing.

→ The car has a very narrow rear end, with several close-fitting panels covering the gearbox and rear suspension, to optimise the airflow at the back of the car.

FLOOR

The floor, a very complicated structure, is the most efficient downforce-producing component on the car, providing a high level of downforce for a minimal drag penalty.

An important point to note is that the floor of a current F1 car is stepped. This is to meet an FIA regulation which was introduced in 1995 to reduce the levels of downforce available. In simplified terms, the rules state that:

- All the parts of the car from a point 330mm behind the front wheel centreline to the rear wheel centreline must lie on one of two parallel planes – the 'reference plane' and the 'step plane'.
- The reference plane dictates the lowest surface of the car (the surface closest to the track). Without the FIA regulation 'plank' fitted, the lowest surface of the car is on the reference plane.
- The step plane must be 50mm above the reference plane.
- The parts lying on the reference plane must extend from a point lying 330mm behind the front wheel centreline to the rear wheel centreline, and must have a minimum overall width of 300mm and a maximum overall width of 500mm and must be symmetrical about the car centreline.

In practice, this means that current cars have a low central rectangular surface, running from behind the front wheel centreline to the rear wheel centreline, to which the 'plank' is fitted, and the surfaces either side of that rectangular surface are positioned 50mm higher, resulting in a stepped floor.

It may seem odd that the floor of the car can be used to produce downforce, so let's look at how this is achieved.

In conjunction with the front wing and the rear diffuser (and to an extent the rear wing), the floor forms a venturi. In its simplest form, a venturi is a tube with a constriction part-way along its length. The area where the fluid (air is a fluid) enters and flows into the tube, before it passes through the restriction, is known as the 'inlet', the restriction is known as the 'throat' and the area downstream of the throat is known as the 'diffuser'. When a fluid flows through a venturi, the fluid accelerates as it passes through the throat, and as the fluid is accelerated, its pressure drops.

If we apply the venturi principle to the floor of an F1 car, what we actually have is a venturi tube with a flat bottom, formed by the surface of the track. The area ahead of the front of the floor (where the airflow is controlled mainly by the front wing) is the 'inlet', the area under the floor is the 'throat', and the area behind the flat floor

⬇ A schematic of the venturi principle, showing how the area around the front wing forms the 'inlet', the floor the 'throat' and the diffuser its namesake.

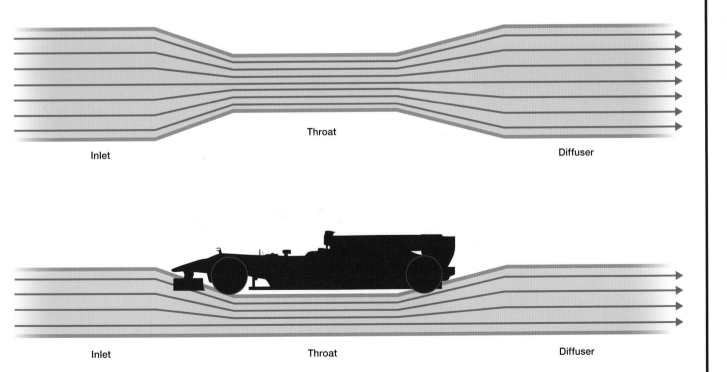

Inlet — Throat — Diffuser

Inlet — Throat — Diffuser

(where the airflow is controlled by the diffuser and rear wing) is the 'diffuser' – which is why the diffuser is so-named.

If the air pressure under an F1 car is lower than the pressure of the air acting on the upper surfaces of the car, then we have effectively generated downforce. So, by controlling the airflow upstream and downstream of the floor, to accelerate the air under the car as much as possible, high levels of downforce can be produced.

In isolation, the floor would generate little downforce – the front wing, diffuser and rear wing allow it to work effectively. For the floor to work effectively, the maximum amount of clean air must be directed under the car, and this air must be accelerated as much as possible. One way of increasing the venturi effect is to run with the floor inclined upwards towards the rear, and this is why, for the past few seasons, some cars have run with the rear ride height noticeably higher than the front.

The floor is shaped to deal with the wake from the front wing, and to interact efficiently with the diffuser and rear wing. With the RB6, Red Bull Racing discovered that the introduction of the double diffuser actually improved the downforce available from the forward floor, by allowing the front of the

floor to work harder due to the improved airflow beneath it. This helped to maintain the aerodynamic balance of the car, as, without this effect, the double diffuser would have resulted in a large increase in downforce at the rear of the car, with no corresponding increase forward of the diffuser.

The floor extends from a point 330mm behind the centreline of the front wheels to almost all the way to the back of the car. The forward section of the floor, which extends forward from the sidepod area under the chassis, is known as the 'tea tray'.

The FIA regulation skid block ('plank') is attached to the bottom of the floor, and must extend longitudinally from a point lying 330mm behind the front wheel centreline to the rear wheel centreline. The plank must be 300mm (± 2mm) wide and 10mm (± 1mm) thick along its entire length when new, and must be a minimum of 9mm thick at the end of the race. The plank therefore dictates the minimum possible ride height of the car. The plank has holes cut in it into which FIA scrutineering gauges can be fitted to check the minimum thickness. The plank is manufactured from beechwood, and comprises thin veneers bonded together with a high-strength resin. The manufacturing process is carefully

⬇ The forward section of the floor (arrowed), at the front of the chassis, is known as the 'tea tray'.

5mm ↑

200kg

controlled to ensure that each finished plank is identical in terms of wear rate and material density.

As it is theoretically possible to gain an aerodynamic advantage from a flexible floor – specifically in the tea-tray area – the FIA limit for the flexing of the floor was revised at the 2007 Spanish Grand Prix after a controversy surrounding Ferrari's floor design. The test involved applying a 200kg vertical load to the centre of the tea tray using a piston (effectively a jack under the floor). The floor was permitted to flex by a maximum of 5mm. After further controversy in 2010, the tea-tray test was revised for the Italian Grand Prix. With the same 200kg load applied 100mm either side of the tea-tray centreline, the permitted flex remained 5mm maximum. This prevented teams using a tea tray that could twist under aerodynamic load.

EFFECTS OF WHEELS

The wheel and tyre assemblies produce over a third of the total drag of a modern F1 car, and have a significant effect on the aerodynamics. The front wheels are particularly important, as they influence the airflow over all areas of the car in their wake. As a result, the wheels have a considerable influence on the design of many of the aerodynamic devices on the car. In particular, the front wheels affect the design of the front wing, turning vanes and sidepods, all of which can be used to modify the wake from the wheels. Similarly, the rear wheels influence the design of the diffuser, rear floor and rear wing.

The effect of the wheels on the airflow is complicated by the fact that the wheels rotate, the tyres deform under load and, in the case of the front wheels, their angle to the oncoming airflow varies with steering angle.

Within the regulations, the design of the wheels themselves can take into account aerodynamic factors, but wheel design is also influenced by weight considerations and the need for brake cooling.

During 2009 a number of teams used sometimes complex 'spinners' on the outer faces of the wheels, and these proved to be a significant contribution to aerodynamic efficiency. For the 2010 season, these spinners were outlawed.

↑ The FIA introduced a new 'tea-tray' test from the Italian Grand Prix of 2010 (see text).

SUSPENSION COMPONENTS

The suspension components are designed to minimise drag.

The overall design of the suspension layout is heavily dictated by aerodynamic considerations, and probably the best example of this on the RB6 is the rear suspension. The requirement to have the largest possible double diffuser meant that it was necessary to compromise the location of the lower rear wishbone, forcing it as high and as far forward as possible. Ideally, in order to achieve optimum suspension stiffness, the upper and lower wishbones should be positioned as far apart as possible. If the lower wishbone is raised towards the top one – as on the RB6 – the stiffness of the suspension drops off very rapidly, a compromise that the design team felt was worth adopting for the 2010 season. The 2009 RB5 was originally designed without a double diffuser (as the team had not considered using such a component during the original design process) and so the rear wishbones were well spaced for optimum stiffness. Although the fundamental principles of

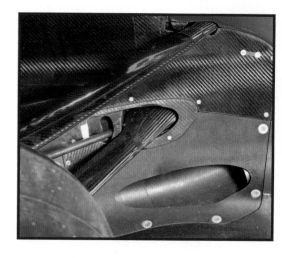

the RB5 rear suspension were retained for the 2010 RB6, which was designed from the outset with a double diffuser, the lower wishbone was moved much higher, and its rear leg was swept forwards to what was a structurally disadvantageous position. This was because aerodynamic gain from the double diffuser far outweighed the compromised suspension stiffness.

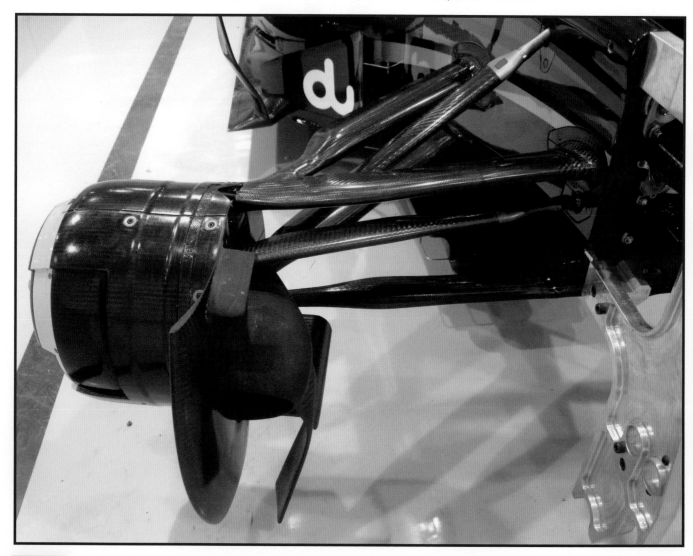

← A view of the rear of the car showing the layout of the double diffuser. The upper diffuser (arrowed) is fed by holes in the floor.

DIFFUSER

Made from unpainted carbon-fibre, the diffuser is the component at the rear of the floor that curves upwards from floor level towards the rear wing.

The diffuser is so-called because its main purpose is to act as the diffuser in a venturi system – this is explained in more detail on pages 43–44 under the 'Floor' heading. Essentially the diffuser allows the accelerated, low-pressure air from beneath the floor to decelerate and return to its 'normal' (ambient) pressure. The diffuser slows the air by effectively increasing the distance between the track surface and the floor, and this is why the diffuser curves upwards quite steeply. The way in which the airflow is decelerated and directed towards the rear wing and the back of the car is very important, and so great attention is paid to the design of the diffuser.

In essence, the diffuser is designed to draw the air from under the floor of the car, and the more air that it can draw, and the faster that air can be made to flow, the lower the pressure created, and hence the higher the downforce. An efficient diffuser can produce around 30–40 per cent of the total downforce on the car.

When the diffuser is viewed from the rear, a number of vertical strakes can be seen, and these are designed to clean up the airflow and make sure that it exits the rear of the car as smoothly as possible to maintain aerodynamic efficiency.

Unlike the front and rear wings, the diffuser is not adjustable, and although small changes to

strakes or gurney flaps (small rigid, adjustable trim tabs) may be made to adjust trim, the main set-up parameter for the diffuser is the car's rear ride height. The front wing and front/rear ride height all affect the performance of the diffuser, and a tiny ride-height change, to adjust the attitude (angle) of the floor, can have a significant effect on the performance of the diffuser.

Double diffuser

The controversial double-diffuser concept was pioneered at the beginning of the 2009 season by Williams, Brawn GP and Toyota, and was later adopted by Red Bull Racing and most other teams. The concept proved controversial because it exploited a loophole in FIA regulations. For the 2009 season, the FIA introduced significant changes to the regulations concerning the front and rear wings, the diffuser and also other aerodynamic appendages, with the aim of reducing downforce and improving overtaking opportunities. These new rules resulted in a significant reduction in the downforce produced by the front and rear wings and the diffuser, so the teams' designers, as is always the case in F1, searched for new ways to recover some of the 'lost' downforce.

The new regulations for 2009 reduced the size of the diffuser. Prior to 2009, the front edge of the diffuser could be placed in line with the front line of the rear wheels, but from 2009 the front edge of the diffuser was moved back, and could only

STANDARD DIFFUSER

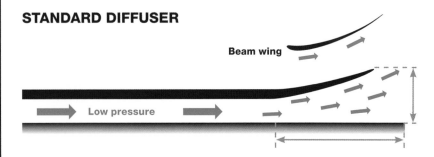

Beam wing

Low pressure

DOUBLE DIFFUSER

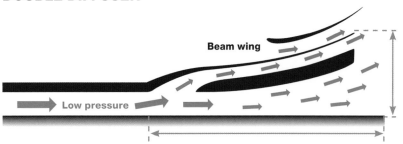

Beam wing

Low pressure

⬆ A schematic showing the airflow through standard and double diffusers. Note the comparison in effective height and length

⬇ The position of the exhausts and the shape of the surrounding floor panels create a 'blown diffuser', increasing downforce.

start at the centreline of the rear wheels. The permitted overall dimensions of the diffuser were also reduced, and the regulations stated that the maximum height of the diffuser must be no more than 175mm above the 'reference plane' (see 'Floor' on page 43).

Basically, the double-diffuser comprised two additional tunnels alongside the gearbox.

The double diffuser tunnels were fed from holes in the floor, where the 'reference plane' meets the 'step plane', at the point where the floor kicks up at the start of the 'main'

diffuser. The inlet holes stretched forward at the front edge of the main diffuser, effectively creating a much larger, deeper and more powerful aerodynamic device. This is where the controversy arose, because many of the teams interpreted the rules as legislating against these holes.

The teams running double diffusers appeared to have an advantage at the start of the season, and after protests from several of the 'non-double-diffuser' teams, the concept was deemed by the FIA to be legal. Teams without a double diffuser were forced to develop the concept as quickly as possible to ensure that they remained competitive.

Red Bull Racing first ran a double diffuser on the RB5 at the 2009 Monaco Grand Prix. It was found that the double diffuser improved downforce all the way along the floor, rather than just at the rear, which would have led to balance problems. The upper diffuser effectively increased the flow through the diffuser as a whole, increasing the speed of the air flowing under the car, lowering its pressure and increasing downforce. The overall increase in downforce from the double diffuser was huge in F1 terms.

The RB6 was designed from the outset with a double diffuser, which allowed the concept to be integrated into the design. A new gearbox, mounted higher than the RB5's, and with a new longer casing, and revised (but still pull-rod) suspension, enabled the design team to optimise the double diffuser right from the start of the 2010 season.

Blown diffuser

As well as integrating the double diffuser into the design of the RB6, Red Bull Racing also made use of a 'blown diffuser' – a system where hot exhaust gases are blown onto the rear of the floor, to increase downforce. Although not new to F1, having been used to good effect in the 1980s and '90s, the blown-diffuser concept was different in detail in 2010. Earlier systems worked by positioning the exhausts under the floor of the car to blow directly into the diffuser. The system developed for the RB6 blows exhaust gases over the top of the floor, and through slots (inboard of the rear wheels) that direct the gases into the double diffuser tunnels. The flow of high-speed, high-pressure exhaust gases adds energy to the air passing through the diffuser, stabilising the flow and enabling higher downforce levels to be attained without the diffuser stalling.

NO EXHAUST BLOWING

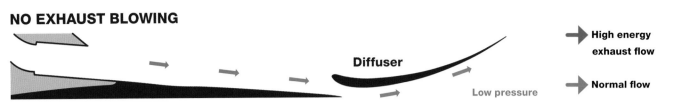

Diffuser

Low pressure

High energy
exhaust flow

Normal flow

EXHAUST BLOWING

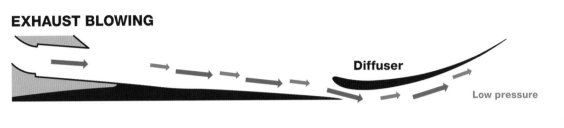

Diffuser

Low pressure

← A schematic showing
the airflow through a
blown diffuser.

The most obvious visual clue to the use of a blown diffuser is the very low exhaust outlet position at the rear of the car, only just above the upper surface of the floor. The position and angle of the exhaust outlets are critical.

One of the challenges with the blown diffuser is to avoid overheating any of the components surrounding the exhaust exits – particularly the tyres and suspension components. This is one area where Computational Fluid Dynamics (CFD) analysis proved to be a very useful tool, as it enabled the design team to investigate how the airflow over the car at speed would affect the position of the exhaust plumes. The CFD analysis was then backed up by running the RB6 in testing with a temperature-sensitive coating applied to the critical components.

Although the exhaust plumes do not run particularly close to the rear tyres, they are closest before and during a race start, when there is no air blowing at the sides of the car, and the exhaust plumes are expanding. Once the car is moving, the exhaust plumes narrow due to the movement of the surrounding air over the car, directing the flow clear of the tyres and temperature-sensitive suspension components.

Because the blown diffuser relies on engine exhaust gases, its effect is throttle-sensitive, which means that the level of additional downforce produced varies according to how much throttle the driver is applying at the time.

Owing to this throttle sensitivity, a car with a blown diffuser can be tricky to drive on the limit. If a car oversteers through a corner, the driver's instinctive corrective action is to apply opposite lock and lift off the throttle, but lifting off in a car with a blown diffuser will reduce rear downforce and exacerbate oversteer. On the RB6, this potential throttle-sensitivity problem is reduced because, with a double diffuser, a higher proportion of the downforce produced by the diffuser is generated at the point where the airflow enters the double diffuser tunnels, and the entry holes to this device are further forward on the car. This means that there is less of a change in aerodynamic balance than would be the case if the diffuser's downforce acted at the very back of the car.

Mark Webber provides a driver's perspective on the effect of the blown diffuser: "The blown diffuser gave you incredible confidence with the rear of the car. We have probably the best aerodynamic department in the world under Adrian Newey, and that helped us get a huge amount of rear grip from the car, so the drivers had to do their best to exploit that. It was a beautiful feeling in some of the fast corners, or any corner – the amount of grip that the RB6 had was really phenomenal. That gave us tremendous confidence to trust the car, so sometimes it really was a shock how quickly you could drive it, and that was testament to the aerodynamic upgrades."

But did the driver have to change his driving style to suit the blown diffuser? Again, Mark Webber gives his view: "Not really, because it was balanced. You can't just have an incredible rear end and not match that with front performance, so you need a car which is balanced, and that's where our guys were good in understanding that to get the most out of one end you need to make sure the car's balanced."

← An engine cover and upper bodywork for Red Bull Racing's 2011 challenger, the RB7, undergoes spraying in the paint booth.

↑ A rear wing assembly being subjected to load testing on a specially designed test rig, to simulate the loads it will encounter during a race.

ENGINE COVER AND UPPER BODYWORK

The engine cover is the largest piece of bodywork on the car. The shape and structure of the engine cover varies significantly from team to team, but generally it forms a cover over the airbox, engine, gearbox and sidepods, and its shape is critical to the aerodynamics of the car.

The upper bodywork is made up of several separate, removable panels to enable access to various components and systems such as the engine, gearbox and suspension parts. The way these panels fit together is very important, as any gaps or disruption to the airflow around the joints would have a negative effect on the aerodynamics of the car. The panels have to be designed to minimise the use of fasteners, as each fastener adds more weight. As with a high-quality road car, the 'shut lines' between the panels need to be highly accurate and as tight as possible.

Because the engine cover is so large, and so high up on the car, it has a significant (and undesirable) effect on the car's centre of gravity. In order to minimise this effect, and to save weight overall, the engine cover is designed to be as light as possible. Compared to many of the other carbon-composite components on the car, it uses very lightweight construction, as durability is not such an issue. As a result, the components need to be renewed regularly, and certain panels are disposable after each race. Although this may sound wasteful, the parts concerned are often updated in any case as part of the ongoing development process, and become superseded.

Many of the bodywork components and covers are secured using spring-loaded, threaded fasteners, which provide a secure, spring-loaded fixing, to prevent them from working loose under severe vibration, and are quick to do up.

↓ Most of the major body panels are secured by spring-loaded fasteners.

REAR WING

The rear wing produces approximately a third of the car's downforce, and is critical to the aerodynamic performance of the car. The biggest single downforce-generating component used on the RB6 during the 2010 season was the Monaco rear wing, which generated over one tonne of downforce with the car running at maximum speed.

The rear wing works in the same way as an aircraft wing, but it is mounted upside-down to generate downforce rather than lift. Owing to its shape, the wing generates downforce because the air flowing underneath it has further to travel than the air flowing over the top of it. This means that it has to travel more quickly, which causes the pressure on the underside of the wing to drop, effectively sucking the wing down.

As the air flows over the surface of the wing, it has a tendency to separate from the lower surface of the wing. To begin with, this 'flow separation' adds to the drag of the wing, but eventually the airflow breaks up completely, and the wing 'stalls'. When a wing stalls, it loses most of its ability to generate both downforce and drag. In a normal situation on an F1 car this is very undesirable, as a sudden loss of downforce will have a drastic effect on the handling of the car.

The steeper the angle of the rear wing, the more downforce it will produce, but the greater the chance of flow separation, so the greater the chance of the wing stalling. To reduce the tendency of the wing to stall, the airflow over the undersurface of the wing must be speeded up. This can be achieved by splitting the wing into two elements, with a slot between them. High-pressure air from the top of the main wing element can then bleed through the slot, helping to speed up the airflow

An innovation that was pioneered by Red Bull Racing at the beginning of the 2008 season, on the RB4, was the 'shark-fin' engine cover. This feature was carried over to the RB5 and the RB6, and adopted by many other teams, with varying success.

The 'shark-fin' significantly increases the surface area of the engine cover, and influences the airflow over the rear wing. Its effect on the rear-end aerodynamics of the car is quite complicated, and not all other teams have been able to fully exploit the benefits. On the RB6, the primary purpose of the 'shark-fin' is to improve rear-end stability, particularly in a crosswind and under braking. Whether or not a 'shark-fin' is desirable depends on the car's yaw sensitivity and the position of the car's centre of pressure (C of P). The car's yaw sensitivity is a measure of how sensitive the car's aerodynamics are to oncoming airflow at an angle to the direction in which the car is pointing, and the C of P is the point on the car through which the sum of the aerodynamic forces acts – for a car with neutral handling it is desirable for the C of P to be as close as possible to the centre of the car.

In a crosswind, the car's yaw angle (the angle between the direction in which the car is moving and the direction in which it is pointing) decreases with speed, so in a low-speed corner the car effectively has to turn at a greater angle to drive round the corner. Medium-speed corners are still yaw-sensitive, but the effect is much lower in a high-speed corner where the yaw angle is very low. The worst-case scenario would be in a low-speed corner with a significant crosswind, which will tend to push the whole car. With the RB6, the 'shark-fin' proved to be beneficial in 'weathervaning' the car to help it turn.

⬇ The 'shark-fin' engine cover was pioneered by Red Bull Racing on the RB4, and continued to feature on the RB6.

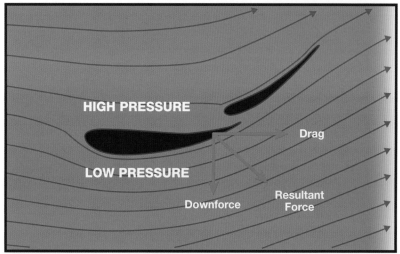

underneath the element. Generally speaking, the more slots (and so wing elements) used, the steeper the angle of the main element can be, and so more downforce can be generated.

In the 1990s, on 'high-downforce' circuits, teams would often use multi-element rear wings. In more recent years, FIA regulations aimed at reducing levels of downforce have been brought in to outlaw the use of multi-element rear wings and, from 2004, the regulations have stipulated just two elements.

The rear wing endplates are designed to optimise the airflow over the wing elements, and also to minimise the formation of vortices, which create drag. The RB6 has very tall endplates, which extend down to the level of the rear floor. This is beneficial because it effectively extends the effect of the diffuser beyond the point at which the rear of the diffuser finishes. The bottoms of the endplates themselves also act as additional vertical strakes for the diffuser to aid its efficiency.

Until the 2010 season, the rear wing was more or less an independent component, comprising two wing elements attached via endplates to a lower structural 'beam wing' which acted as the main wing mounting, attached to the top of the gearbox or rear crash structure. Some teams use an alternative mounting system where the wing is supported by a pylon or twin pylons close to the centreline of the car.

During the 2010 season, with the adoption of the F-duct system, rear wing design became much more complex, and the wing was integrated into the rear end of the car, requiring significant redesign work.

⬆⬆ On the RB6, the rear wing was integrated with the diffuser and rear bodywork.

⬆ A schematic showing the principle of operation of the rear wing, and how it generates downforce and causes drag.

➜ The effectiveness of the rear wing can clearly be seen in rainy conditions, when the wing throws up a 'rooster tail' of spray high into the air behind the car.

F-DUCT

The F-duct was an innovation for 2010, and was first developed by McLaren, who used it from the start of the season. The system appeared on the RB6 for the first time at the Turkish Grand Prix in May. Adrian Newey explains the system's origins: "Really it was experimentation. The F-duct technology actually stems from the Cold War in the 1950s, when the Americans were worried the Russians would develop ways of jamming the electronics on their fighter aircraft, and so they developed, effectively, a pneumatic version of electronics. So an F-duct is actually a transistor, but using air rather than electricity."

Although a high level of rear downforce is desirable under certain circumstances (generally on slower, low-grip circuits and when cornering), on a high-speed straight ultimate speed is compromised by a high level of downforce, as a high-downforce rear wing also produces a high level of drag.

The idea behind the F-duct was to provide the car with a straightline speed boost by temporarily reducing the drag created by the rear wing. As previously explained in the 'Rear wing' section, two elements are used on the

1 Intake duct in LH sidepod
2 Snorkel in cockpit
3 Intake duct in engine cover
4 Exit under rear wing
5 Exit into wing element void to stall the rear wing

For the 2011 season, a change in the FIA regulations permitted the use of an adjustable rear wing. This system allows the driver to significantly reduce drag by increasing the gap between the two rear wing elements from the usual 10–15mm to 50mm. The use of the system is governed by the FIA, and it can be employed at any time during practice and qualifying. During a race the system can only be used at predetermined positions on the track, when a car is following within one second of the car in front. Once the driver hits the brakes, the system is deactivated, and the wing element returns to its 'normal' position. The idea behind the system is to improve overtaking opportunities.

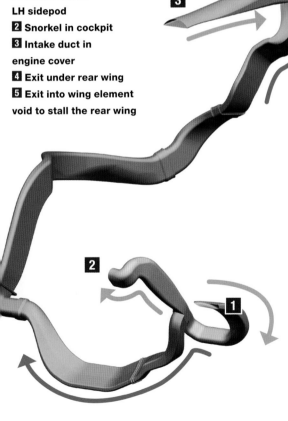

← Default airflow

← Activated airflow

rear wing to prevent the wing from stalling, by creating a slot to allow high-pressure air to bleed through. So, if this effect can be reversed, and the wing can be deliberately stalled, drag (and downforce) will be reduced and straight-line speed increased. Of course, this is only desirable in a situation when downforce is not so important – such as on a long straight – so the effect needs to be temporary, or 'switchable'.

An attempt to achieve this effect was first made during the 2004 season, when several teams used 'flexible' rear wings, which allowed the slot between the two elements to close up under high load (for instance on a high-speed straight), stalling the wing. From the 2006 Canadian Grand Prix, FIA regulations were changed, and rigid separators had to be fitted between the wing elements to prevent them from flexing.

The F-duct achieved the same effect as closing up the slot between the wing elements, by temporarily allowing extra air to flow over one of the elements, causing the airflow to separate from it (flow separation) and hence stall it. It was found that this system was well worth

↑ A schematic showing the principle of operation of the RB6 F-duct.

→ The driver operates the F-duct by placing his left hand over the snorkel (arrowed) in the cockpit.

↓ The engine cover removed to show the F-duct air ducting. The intake duct for the stall air is arrowed. In the default position, the lower duct (A) routes air under the rear wing. When the system is activated, the upper duct (B) routes air to the rear wing element.

↘ The rear of the car viewed with the engine cover in place, showing the lower duct (A) and rear wing void (B).

developing, as it could be used to gain a top-speed increase of up to 4mph – sufficient to aid overtaking opportunities on a long straight.

The key to optimising the F-duct system was to develop a rear-wing design that stalled under the influence of the F-duct, but did not compromise downforce when the system was not in operation. The RB6's system took time to develop, and initially the air from the F-duct was blown over the wing upper element – a reasonable stall was achieved, but at the expense of a small reduction in rear-wing performance when the system was not being operated. The system was developed and improved during the season, and at the Japanese Grand Prix a major revision appeared, with the air from the F-duct being blown over the main wing element rather than the upper element.

The switching of the airflow from the lower to the upper duct in the engine cover is achieved by using a 'fluid switch' operated by the driver. The basic method of operation is as follows:

■ 'Control' air flows into the system ducting through an intake in the right-hand sidepod. In the 'default' position, this air flows out through the 'snorkel' on the left-hand side of the cockpit.
■ 'Stall' air flows into the ducting from an intake in the bodywork above the driver's head, above the main engine air intake. In the default position, this air flows out through the outlet in the rear bodywork below the rear wing lower element.
■ The driver places his hand over the snorkel to activate the system.
■ The 'control' airflow is diverted along the ducting inside the engine cover, where it deflects the 'stall' airflow upwards so that it exits through the void in the rear wing upper element (early season) or over the main wing element (late season). This stall airflow creates turbulence at the rear of the wing element, stalling the airflow.

The effect of the F-duct was significant enough for the driver to feel it in action, as Mark Webber explains: "The F-duct was a bit awkward for us to start with, because the car wasn't designed with this in place, so the guys had to do something. When it comes to tight packaging, to try and incorporate something it's quite a challenge – it wasn't easy. I just had to be able to use the system by putting my hand over the snorkel on the straights. You felt a slight surge in acceleration and less drag, particularly if you put it on late, but we would generally put in on very, very early, so you wouldn't feel it quite as much."

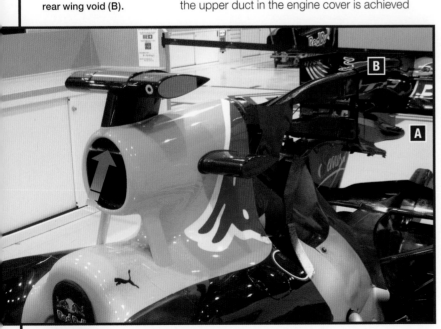

APPENDAGES

Until the end of the 2008 season, F1 cars had sprouted a number of appendages to aid aerodynamic efficiency, including various winglets, sidepod scallops, 'chimneys' and complex turning vanes. FIA regulation changes for the 2009 season, aimed at reducing downforce, effectively outlawed these appendages by introducing new rules relating to bodywork dimensions.

Although additional aerodynamic appendages are no longer allowed, every part of the car is designed with aerodynamic performance in mind, including compulsory components such as the rear-view mirrors, cameras and radio/telemetry transmitting aerials.

Mirrors

In early 2010, some teams, including Red Bull Racing with the RB6, used 'outboard' sidepod-mounted mirrors to aid aerodynamics. Part of the reason for this was to move the mirrors into an area where the airflow was already turbulent, outboard of the sidepods, which allowed a cleaner airflow over the nose and cockpit areas.

From the 2010 Spanish Grand Prix onwards, outboard mirrors were outlawed after concerns about the drivers' limited rear visibility due to the position of the mirrors and the vibration they were subjected to.

Mark Webber explains: "You couldn't see a huge amount, because they weren't mounted on anything very structural. They weren't mounted to the chassis, so they used to vibrate quite a bit, and also they were a long way out of your vision, so you really had to turn your head quite a bit more to use them. You can see quite a lot in inboard mirrors."

The mirrors then returned to the traditional position on the sides of the chassis in front of the cockpit.

Because the dimensions and shape of the mirrors' reflective area is controlled by the regulations, there is little flexibility in the design of the mirrors. Even so, the mirror housings are designed to minimise drag as much as possible.

Cameras

The FIA regulations stipulate the dimensions and shape of the camera housings, and the angle at which they can be fitted relative to the airflow. For more details of the cameras and housings, refer to 'Cameras' on pages 103–104.

AERODYNAMIC ADJUSTMENTS

Aerodynamic adjustments are the most important set-up parameters for the car. More details of how aerodynamic adjustments are used to set up the car are provided in Chapter 4, 'The race engineer's view'.

⬇ For the first four races of the 2010 season, the RB6 ran with mirrors mounted on the outboard turning vanes.

SUSPENSION AND STEERING

↑ In common with most
current F1 cars, the
RB6 front suspension
comprises unequal-
length upper and lower
wishbones with inboard
torsion bars operated
by push-rods.

SUSPENSION

Compared with the suspension on a road car, an F1 car's suspension makes no concession whatsoever to driver comfort and is extremely stiff, moving only a matter of a few millimetres. The suspension is absolutely critical from a safety point of view, as any structural failure in the suspension can have extremely serious consequences.

The suspension forms one of the car's critical systems, because it is the system through which all the major forces on the car act. Mechanical forces (such as acceleration, braking and cornering forces) are fed into the suspension through the tyres, and aerodynamic forces (downforce and drag) are fed into the suspension from the chassis. These forces put a huge load on the suspension components, which must therefore be enormously strong but also, of course, as lightweight as possible. Suspension design on an F1 car is always a compromise. When deciding the suspension layout, particularly the wishbone layout, three factors have to be considered: the optimum location

from an aerodynamic point of view, stiffness requirements, and controlling the motion of the wheel (and therefore the tyre). When the designers get the compromise between these factors just right, the drivers will have smiles on their faces!

One of the key factors in suspension design is minimising the 'unsprung mass' – the mass (weight) of all the components not supported by the suspension. On an F1 car, the unsprung mass is made up from the mass of the wishbones, push/pull-rods, steering arms and driveshafts, plus the uprights and any components attached to them – wheels, tyres, brake discs/calipers and any associated components.

Any bumps or imperfections in the track act directly on the tyres and the unsprung mass, and so reducing the unsprung mass will help the tyres to follow imperfections and bumps more easily, allowing them to maintain contact with the track surface for longer and reducing the load and vibration to which the suspension components, and the chassis, are subjected.

So, all the suspension components are designed to be as light as possible, bearing in mind the aerodynamic and stiffness considerations mentioned previously.

The suspension is designed to absorb as much as possible the weight transfer that takes place on the car under the influence of these various forces. This helps to minimise the effect of weight transfer on the tyres, keeping tyre temperatures more consistent, and reducing tyre wear and the chances of wheel-locking under braking.

In other forms of racing, where aerodynamic performance is not the predominant factor in the competitiveness of the car, the suspension is the main tool used in adjusting performance and handling. With a modern F1 car, the primary roles of the suspension are two-fold. Firstly, the suspension must provide the car with a stable and consistent aerodynamic platform by minimising the disturbances caused by bumps and by braking, acceleration and cornering forces. Secondly, the suspension must ensure that the tyres work at optimum efficiency.

Although the adjustment of castor, camber and toe angles can be used to tune car set-up (primarily for wet- or dry-weather conditions and driver preference), fine adjustment of these settings is rarely used once a base set-up for the car is established. The primary suspension adjustments used in car set-up are to the anti-roll bar for mechanical balance, and to the push- and pull-rods for aerodynamic set-up.

One area where most current F1 car suspension systems differ significantly from those found in most (though not all) road cars is in the use of inboard springs and dampers, whether chassis- or gearbox-mounted. On an F1 car, the role of the springs is to provide the suspension with its stiffness by resisting the vertical movement of the wheel.

If springs were used on their own, they would tend to rebound after a bump and continue to oscillate ('bounce'). Any oscillations will reduce the grip of the tyres and affect the handling of the car, so dampers are fitted to reduce this effect. The role of the dampers (sometimes incorrectly referred to as 'shock absorbers') is to damp the oscillations of the springs, reducing suspension 'bounce'.

On the RB6, both the front and rear suspension have an unequal-length upper and lower wishbone layout, with inboard springs and dampers operated by push-rods and rockers at the front, and pull-rods and rockers at the rear. During the 2009 season, the RB5 was unique in using pull-rod rear suspension. This concept had not been seen on the rear of an F1 car for 20 years, and was carried over onto the design of the RB6. As Adrian Newey comments: "We decided to stay with pull-rod rear suspension for the RB6, but we repackaged it to suit the

← The RB6 features pull-rod rear suspension in order to optimise the packaging of the double diffuser. The pull-rod is arrowed.

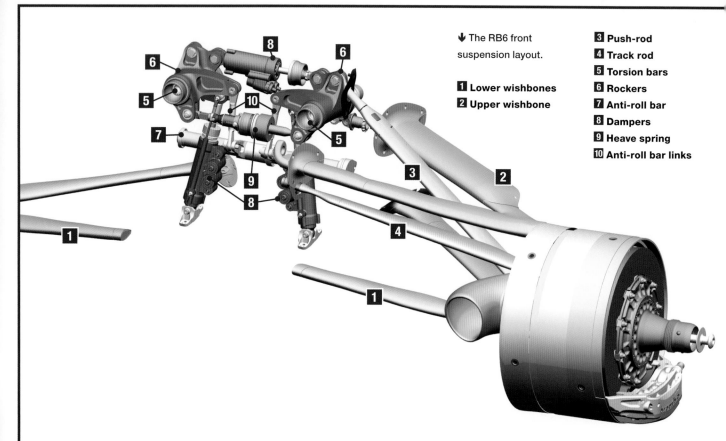

The RB6 front suspension layout.

3 Push-rod
4 Track rod
5 Torsion bars
6 Rockers
7 Anti-roll bar
8 Dampers
9 Heave spring
10 Anti-roll bar links

1 Lower wishbones
2 Upper wishbone

double-diffuser. "Without a doubt, the double diffuser makes pull-rods more difficult to package, but the inherent benefits it offers, compared to push-rods, means it's still better."

Pull-rod rear suspension was used because it enabled the springs and dampers to be fitted low down on the car, towards the bottom of the gearbox, rather than in the more usual position on top of it. This provided a cleaner airflow around the gearbox area to the diffuser and rear wing, and also helped to lower the car's C of G.

Front and rear anti-roll bars are fitted. The anti-roll bars take the form of torsion bars, resisting 'twist' as left and right rockers rotate out of phase.

↓ The RB6 rear suspension layout.

1 Upper wishbone
2 Lower wishbone
3 Pull-rod
4 Driveshaft
5 Carbon-fibre shroud
6 Brake disc
7 Axle
8 Brake caliper
9 Brake duct

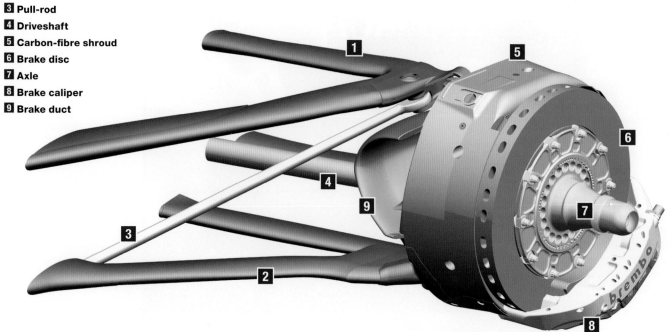

UPRIGHTS AND AXLES

The uprights carry the axle bearings, axles, brake discs and calipers, the adjustment mechanism for camber and toe settings, and upper and lower brackets to connect to the wishbones and push/pull-rods. The front uprights also incorporate brackets to connect to the steering arms.

To withstand the enormous and constantly varying acceleration, braking and cornering forces acting on them, the uprights, axle bearings and axles must be extremely strong. Additionally, the rear uprights have to withstand the forces associated with the engine power being fed through the axles to the wheels, and the front uprights must deal with the additional loads imposed by the steering. Very high brake temperatures are produced on an F1 car, and one of the design parameters for the uprights is to aid brake cooling.

Stiffness is an important factor, as any flexing of the upright will affect the suspension geometry and in turn the tyre performance, handling and aerodynamic set-up. Flexing of the front uprights can reduce accurate feedback to the driver through the steering.

Until the end of the 2009 season, to minimise weight, the uprights on the RB5 and its predecessors were manufactured from Metal Matrix Composite (MMC) – a mixture of aluminium alloy and ceramic-fibre, providing an extremely stiff, but light, material. MMC components are incredibly expensive to manufacture. So, from the 2010

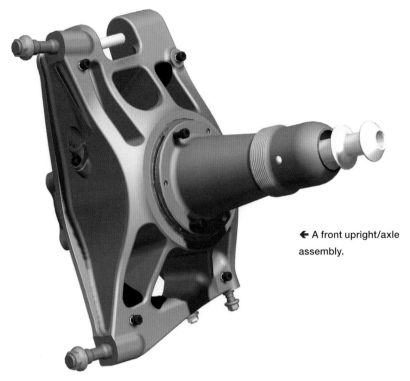

← A front upright/axle assembly.

season the use of MMCs was outlawed, and the uprights on the RB6 are manufactured from a stiff aluminium alloy.

The axles are made from steel, and incorporate locking mechanisms to secure the wheel nuts. The end of the axle is threaded to accept the single wheel nut, and two sprung, tapered lugs are recessed into the edge of the axle flange to retain the nut once screwed in place.

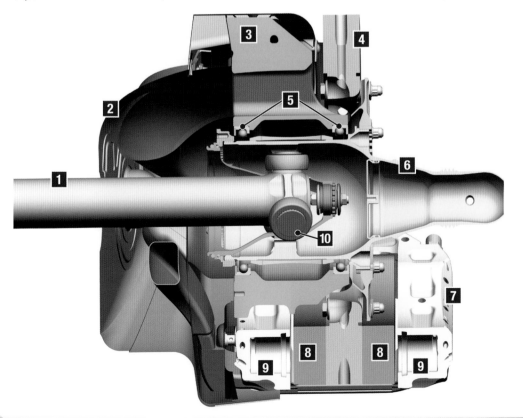

← A cross-section through a rear upright.

1 **Driveshaft**
2 **Shroud**
3 **Upright**
4 **Brake disc**
5 **Axle bearings**
6 **Axle**
7 **Brake caliper**
8 **Brake pads**
9 **Brake caliper pistons**
10 **Driveshaft tripod joint**

→ The carbon-fibre wishbones have to cope with enormous loads under braking, acceleration and cornering.

WISHBONES

The wishbones are made from carbon-fibre, with metal inserts to enable them to be mounted to the chassis/gearbox and uprights. The wishbones are designed to be as compact as possible for aerodynamic reasons (see page 46), and so they are relatively heavy.

The RB6 has unequal-length upper and lower wishbones, each with two attachment points inboard, to the chassis at the front and gearbox at the rear, and a single attachment outboard to the upright. At both front and rear, the lower wishbones are longer than the uppers, which helps to control the wheel camber angle (the angle between the vertical and a line through the vertical centre of the tyre tread when viewed from the front of the car). This means that when the suspension deflects during cornering, the longer, lower

wishbone pushes the bottom of the tyre out more than the top, increasing camber angle and lateral cornering grip.

Due to the decision to use pull-rod rear suspension, the design of the lower rear wishbone on the RB6 became a compromise. With the introduction of a double diffuser for 2010, it was necessary to move the lower wishbone as far forward, and as high, as possible, in order to allow space for the largest possible diffuser tunnels. Conversely, one of the fundamentals of achieving good suspension stiffness with a double-wishbone suspension layout is to position the upper and lower wishbones as far apart as possible. If the lower wishbone is moved up, the stiffness of the suspension drops quite rapidly. On the RB6, the rear leg of the rear wishbone was swept forward to a position that was not ideal from a structural point of view, and the wishbone also had to be quite heavy to achieve the required stiffness and structural strength. The loss of stiffness was not significant, and the weight compromise was felt worthwhile due to the aerodynamic gains from the diffuser. This is a good example of an optimum structural design solution being compromised to provide an aerodynamic gain.

Because the wishbones are critical structural components, they undergo rigorous testing and inspection procedures to ensure that they can withstand the high loads encountered on track.

No adjustment is provided for the wishbones, and all castor, camber and toe-angle adjustments are made at the uprights.

The wheel tethers and wiring looms for suspension and brake sensors run within the wishbones to avoid disruption to the airflow.

→ A lower rear wishbone-to-gearbox mounting. The wishbone bolts to a metal bracket on the carbon-fibre gearbox casing.

PUSH-RODS AND PULL-RODS

The front push-rods are so named because they activate the inboard suspension rockers (mounted on the chassis) by pushing them as the wheel and upright move upwards over bumps. The rear pull-rods activate the rockers on the gearbox by pulling them as the wheel moves upwards. Both push- and pull-rods attach to the uprights at their outer ends.

The front push-rods are shaped to minimise aerodynamic drag and manufactured from carbon-fibre, with metal inserts at each end to accommodate mountings. The rear pull-rods are made from metal.

As explained previously, aerodynamic performance predominates in F1, and a key factor in aerodynamic set-up is the car's ride height. Ride height is adjusted using shims to effectively shorten or lengthen the push-rods or pull-rods (see page 153).

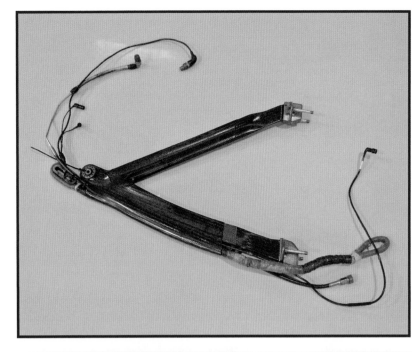

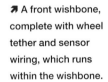

↗ A front wishbone, complete with wheel tether and sensor wiring, which runs within the wishbone.

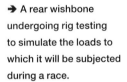

→ A rear wishbone undergoing rig testing to simulate the loads to which it will be subjected during a race.

← The RB6 features pull-rod rear suspension to benefit the packaging at the rear of the car, so that airflow to the diffuser and rear wing is optimised.

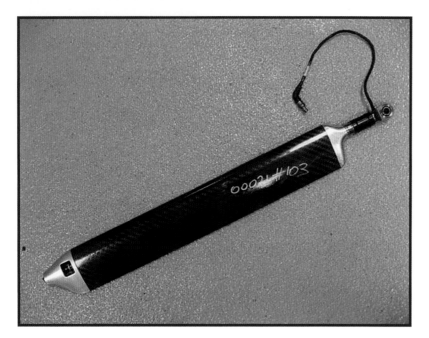

↑ A front push-rod
assembly – the left-hand
end connects to the
chassis, the right-hand
end to the upright.

↗ A front push-rod
undergoing destructive
testing on a purpose-built
test rig, which involves
putting components
through repeated load
cycles until they break.

SPRINGS

The front springs take the form of torsion bars. The
torsion bars run longitudinally along the chassis,
and are splined into brackets at the front of the
chassis. The torsion bars effectively provide the
pivots for the suspension rockers. When the car
runs over a bump, the wheel moves up, and so
does the upright, pushing the push-rod, which
in turn pushes the rocker. As the rocker pivots, it
twists the torsion bar, which provides an opposing
force. By changing the torsion bars, the effective
spring rate can be changed.

DAMPERS

Dampers are used to control the oscillations of
the suspension springs, so keeping the tyres in
contact with the track for the maximum possible
time. The dampers are tuneable, with adjustable
valving to alter damping characteristics for both
bump and rebound.

For 2010 refuelling was banned, and so the
weight change of the car during a race (around
160kg) was significantly higher than previous
years when a relatively light fuel load was
carried. As a result, one of the key parameters

→ The torsion bars are
located behind the two
round covers (arrowed) in
the chassis front bulkhead.

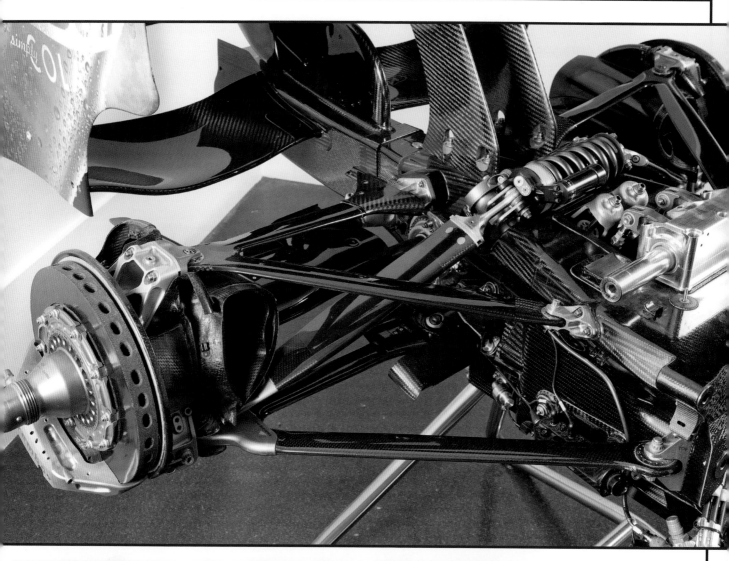

↑ A typical coil-over-damper rear suspension arrangement. This is the 2008 RB4's system, operated by push-rods.

← Spring and damper set up is extremely important for very bumpy circuits such as Monaco.

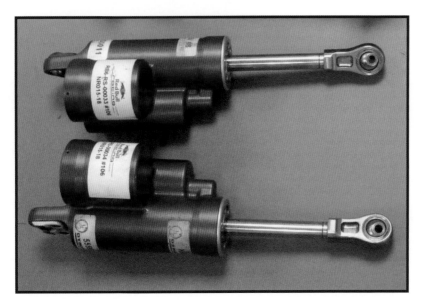

↑ A pair of Multimatic side dampers from the RB6.

0.5:1 means that the piston moves only half as far as the wheel. The motion ratio depends on the arc of movement of the rocker operating the piston, which changes according to the car's mechanical set-up (primarily ride height). This means that if the car's mechanical set-up is changed significantly, then the motion ratio will change, and so the damper valving will need to be changed to compensate. With the RB6, the team rarely changed the ride height sufficiently to warrant changing the damper valving, and once a base set-up for the car was established, there was little need to alter the dampers during the season.

Multimatic supply the dampers used on the RB6. They are fluid-filled, linear dampers, of a bespoke design to help packaging on the car. The dampers are 'four-way', with independent high- and low-speed damping valves for bump and rebound. Each of the four valves on each damper can be easily adjusted using removable valving cartridges.

In general, the centre spring/damper is used to control 'heave' (when both wheels move together) and the side springs/dampers are used to control roll (when one wheel moves independently of the other).

(car weight) for setting up a damping system is now variable.

A damper's damping action is dependent on the speed (velocity) at which the piston moves through the fluid in the damper. The piston speed depends on the 'motion ratio' of the rocker operating the piston. A motion ratio of 1:1 means that the piston exactly matches the movement of the wheel on the track, whereas a motion ratio of

➜ An exploded view of an RB6 Multimatic front damper. *(Multimatic)*

1 Piston rod
2 Piston with seals
3 Valve body
4 Valving cartridges

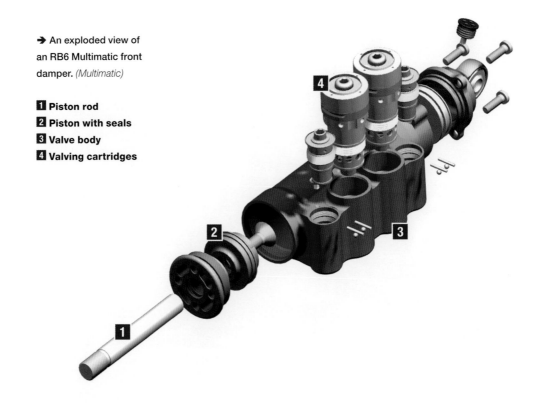

ANTI-ROLL BARS

Front and rear anti-roll bars are fitted to resist the car's tendency to roll during cornering. The anti-roll bars are the primary mechanical balance adjusters on the car. They are fitted between the push/pull-rod rockers on either side of the car, so effectively they connect one side of the car to the other.

The anti-roll bars are torsion bars, and can be easily changed. They are accessed through panels in the bodywork. Anti-roll bar changes are often made during Friday practice when fine-tuning the set-up of the car.

SUSPENSION ADJUSTMENTS

Refer to pages 150–153.

STEERING

The steering system is very similar to that found on most road cars, comprising a tubular steering column connecting the steering wheel to the rack-and-pinion steering gear. The rack is mounted across the front of the chassis, and is connected to the suspension uprights by track rods. Hydraulic power steering is fitted to reduce the very high steering loads that the driver would otherwise have to cope with, and hydraulic pressure is supplied from the main hydraulic system. The FIA regulations stipulate that no electrically powered or controlled power steering can be used.

STEERING WHEEL

Refer to pages 117–118.

↓ A schematic view of the front suspension, showing the layout of the anti-roll bar components.

1 Dampers
2 Anti-roll bar
3 Anti-roll bar links
4 Torsion bar adjusters
5 Push-rod
6 Torsion bar adjuster arms
7 Torsion bars
8 Rockers
9 Damper
10 Heave spring

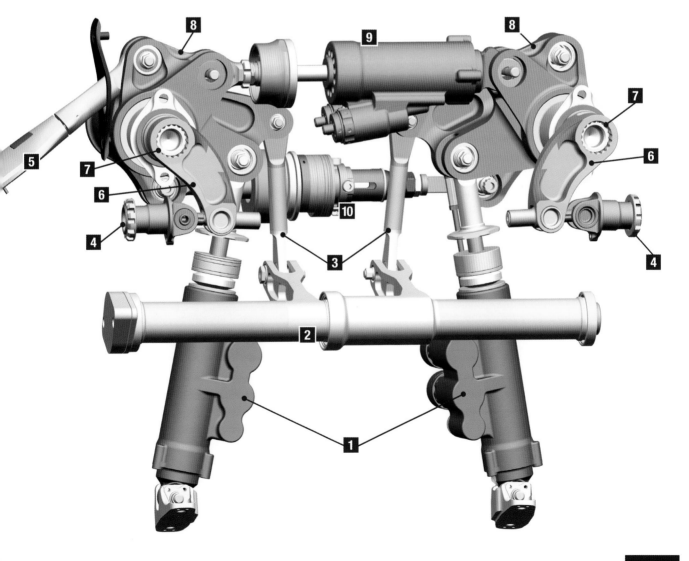

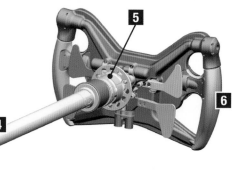

→ The steering system components.

1 Track rods
2 Power-assisted steering (PAS) unit
3 Universal joint
4 Steering column
5 Steering wheel release collar
6 Steering wheel

STEERING COLUMN

A tubular carbon-fibre steering column is fitted, with a universal joint at its lower end to allow for the angle necessary to connect to the steering gear pinion.

The column runs in bearings supported by upper and lower brackets attached to the chassis.

POWER-ASSISTED STEERING (PAS)

The steering gear is of the conventional rack-and-pinion type, and is mounted behind the bulkhead at the front of the chassis, behind the nose assembly.

A hydraulic ram is incorporated in the steering gear to provide power assistance, and hydraulic pressure is supplied via the main hydraulic system from the engine-driven pressure pump. The level of power assistance can be fine-tuned to suit driver preference.

TRACK RODS

The track rods are made from carbon-fibre, with metal inserts and brackets at each end to secure to the steering gear and uprights. Toe-angle adjustments are made using shims at the connections to the uprights.

→ An upper steering column section.

→ → The carbon-fibre track rods (arrowed) are adjustable via shims at the uprights.

→ A PAS assembly removed from the car.

→ → A track rod-to-PAS balljoint.

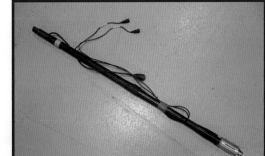
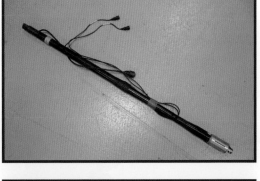

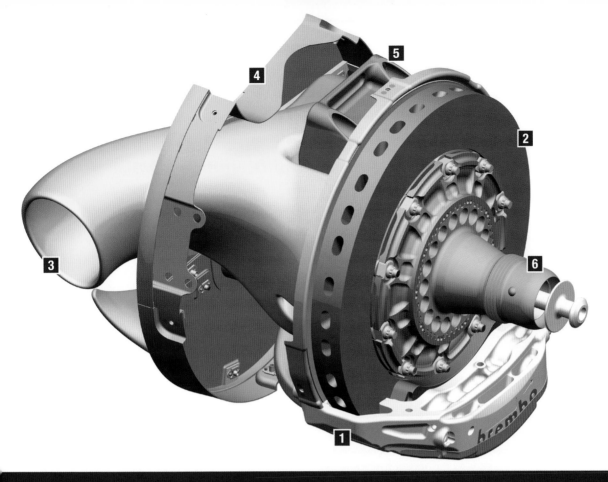

An F1 car's brakes operate in exactly the same way as those on a road car. Hydraulic fluid pressure is used to amplify the force that the driver applies to the brake pedal (typically around 75kg or more), and transmits that pressure to pistons in the brakes at all four wheels, pushing friction pads against the brake discs to slow the wheels.

Disc brakes are used on all four wheels, but anti-lock braking systems (ABS) are not permitted. The regulations state that the force exerted on the brake pads in each circuit must be the same at all times.

The big difference between an F1 car and any other racing or road car is in the sheer power of the brakes. When drivers move up from lower formulae to drive an F1 car for the first time, inevitably the experience that makes the biggest impression on them is the incredible deceleration provided by the brakes. The deceleration force under braking can reach up to 5g, whereas even a very high-performance road car will rarely exceed 1g of deceleration. To achieve this, the brakes have to dissipate a huge amount of energy, which results in extremely high brake temperatures – over 1,000°C under sustained heavy braking.

This astonishing braking performance is made possible by the use of carbon-fibre composite brake discs and pads. These are far more efficient than conventional steel brake discs, as they are able to dissipate heat more consistently, and at a higher rate. Carbon brake discs also operate consistently at far higher temperatures than steel discs, and provide a significant weight saving.

Each brake is fitted with temperature and wear sensors (see page 71).

HYDRAULIC SYSTEM

The brake hydraulic system is a closed system and is completely independent of the car's main hydraulic system. As with all modern road cars, the brake hydraulic system is split into two circuits for safety reasons, so that if one circuit fails, braking is still available on two wheels. The convention with racing cars is to split the hydraulic circuit front to rear, as this allows the bias between the front and rear brakes to be adjusted, and this arrangement is also stipulated in the FIA regulations. No powered brake assistance (including a brake vacuum servo) is permitted, so the driver has to apply very high loads to the brake

↑ A rear brake assembly.

1 Caliper
2 Disc
3 Cooling duct
4 Shroud
5 Upright
6 Axle

↑ The brake fluid reservoirs are located at the front of the chassis.

circuit bias to vary the front-to-rear brake balance according to requirements. Brake balance is fundamental to the handling of the car, particularly as the weight of the car reduces as the fuel load lightens during the race, and the driver will regularly adjust brake balance during each lap to provide the optimum handling balance for a particular corner. On the RB6, brake balance adjustment is made using a lever on the left-hand side of the cockpit (see page 156).

BRAKE FLUID

Synthetic brake fluid is used, as this is capable of consistent performance at very high temperatures. Synthetic brake fluid does not degrade significantly with use, although, like mineral fluid, it does absorb water.

Fresh hydraulic fluid is used for each race weekend.

The amount of fluid used in the system is circuit-dependent. On a circuit with a lot of heavy braking, bigger reservoirs will be used, with more fluid. For weight-saving reasons, the team will aim to minimise the quantity of fluid in the system, while leaving a safety margin. As a safety consideration in case of critical brake wear, there will always be sufficient fluid in the reservoirs to fully extend all the caliper pistons.

pedal, that can produce fluid pressures of up to 2,000psi in the hydraulic system.

Two separate hydraulic master cylinders are used (one each for the front and rear circuits), each with its own reservoir. The driver can manually adjust the front-to-rear hydraulic

↘ The braking system components.

1 Front discs
2 Front calipers
3 Rear discs
4 Rear calipers
5 Fluid reservoirs (front and rear)
6 Brake pedal
7 Brake-bias adjuster lever
8 Brake-bias adjuster linkage
9 Master cylinders

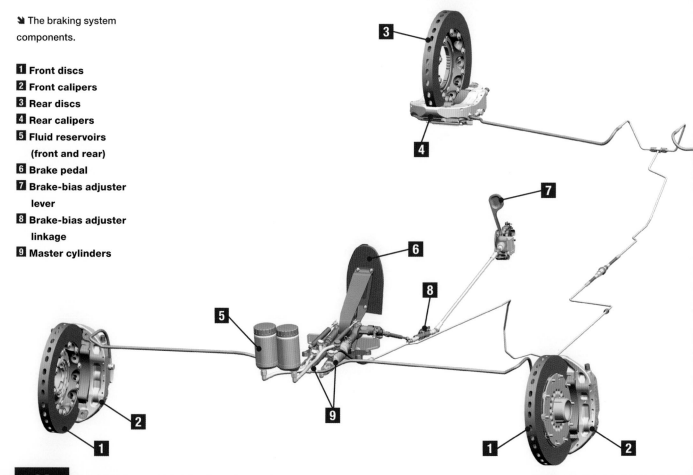

DISCS

The brake discs are made from a carbon-carbon composite material, essentially carbon-fibre suspended in a carbon matrix. The FIA regulations stipulate the maximum thickness and maximum diameter (28mm and 278mm respectively for 2010). The discs are drilled internally for ventilation by airflow from the forward motion of the car. Air is blown over the outer faces of the discs through brake cooling ducts attached to the upright assemblies, and fed to holes that pass radially through the discs. Carbon discs offer a significant weight saving – a typical new carbon disc weighs around 1kg, approximately half the weight of a steel equivalent.

The discs are 'fully floating' and slide over flanges on the axles. The axle flanges have a 'sawtooth' pattern to provide a greater surface area to support the disc and prevent it from rotating.

Brake discs are treated as consumables, and are changed at the end of Saturday practice (P3) for qualifying and the race. Although mild disc wear in itself does not cause any problem, inconsistent wear between sides can be an issue. See the 'Brake wear' panel on page 70 for further details.

In practice, the discs will always wear during a race and, for weight-saving reasons, the team's

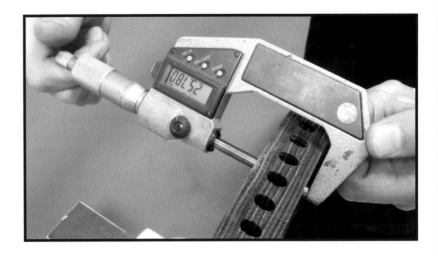

aim is to maintain the necessary safety margin while allowing the discs to wear down to the minimum practical working thickness by the end of the race.

↑ Measuring the thickness of a used carbon disc. Note the radial ventilation holes.

CALIPERS

The calipers are made from an aluminium alloy. The regulations state "No more than two attachments may be used to secure each brake caliper to the car" and "No more than one caliper, with a maximum of six pistons, is permitted on each wheel."

Each caliper fits on to studs on the upright – one at the front and one at the rear. Nuts are used to secure the caliper to the studs.

The calipers used on the RB6 are supplied by Brembo, and have three pistons acting on each pad. The calipers are designed to be as light as possible (to minimise the car's unsprung weight) while still providing the required stiffness to prevent flexing when the brakes are applied.

Each caliper is fitted with two bleed nipples to enable fluid bleeding, one for each set of pistons.

The calipers are also fitted with temperature indicator strips, which change colour to indicate the highest peak temperature reached by the caliper. This is useful data for the team, and helps to determine the service life of the calipers.

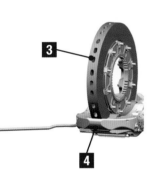

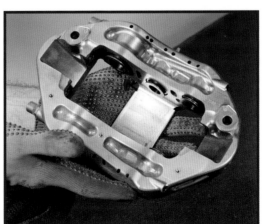

←← Removing a rear caliper securing bolt.

← The calipers are manufactured from lightweight aluminium alloy.

In terms of wear, there is a fundamental difference between carbon discs and steel discs. Carbon discs do not wear significantly in terms of loss of material due to friction: the predominant wear on a carbon disc is due to a chemical process – oxidation. As a result, the wear rate for carbon discs is non-linear – the disc does not wear in proportion to the brake pressure applied and the time for which it is applied. The wear on a carbon disc is caused by the oxidation of the disc material that is activated at a specific temperature – generally around 600°C. At this point, the carbon will break down in the presence of oxygen in the air, and the oxidised material is given off as dust, which is why a cloud of black brake dust can sometimes be seen on TV footage when a car is braking heavily.

At a certain temperature beyond the 'activation energy', the oxidation – and so brake wear – becomes exponential. This can cause a severe problem, because as the disc wears, there is less material to soak up the braking energy (heat), and so during braking the disc becomes less efficient, meaning the disc runs hotter, increasing oxidation – and so a viscious circle forms.

This is why brake overheating is such a serious issue in F1. It results not just in short-term brake fade, but can lead to catastrophic wear problems and ultimately to disintegration of the disc.

As a result, brake cooling is extremely important, and teams go to great lengths to control brake temperature during a race. By controlling the temperature (and so keeping below the 'activation energy' for oxidation of the carbon) brake wear can be reduced.

The fact that air is used to cool the brakes is a problem in itself, because directing air to the brakes effectively feeds oxygen to an oxidation process! Brake ducts are therefore very important, and are constantly developed throughout the season with the aim of optimising brake cooling at each circuit to suit circuit layout and ambient weather conditions.

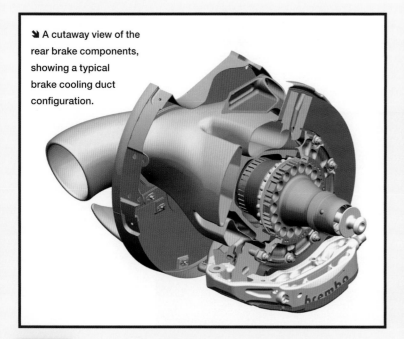

↘ A cutaway view of the rear brake components, showing a typical brake cooling duct configuration.

PADS

As with any conventional disc-brake system, each caliper is fitted with two pads, one on either side of the disc. The pads are also made from carbon-carbon, and a variety of different pad compounds are available to suit set-up requirements and driver preference. Different pad materials have different heat conductivity, and in general it is the heat conductivity of the material that is changed to give the driver a different brake 'feel'. For good initial 'bite' a high temperature is needed before the brakes will operate effectively – the brakes only operate efficiently above around 500°C. This is why it is important for the driver to ensure that the brakes are warm before the start of a race, or when running behind a safety car. Conversely, if the pad material gets too hot, the heat conductivity can drop dramatically, and this can give the impression of severe brake fade, or even of the brakes not working at all.

BRAKE-BIAS ADJUSTMENT

A brake-bias adjustment lever is provided in the cockpit, so that the driver can adjust the brake balance during a race, or indeed during a lap. More details of how brake-bias adjustment is used are given on page 156.

The system is mechanical, as the regulations prevent any automatic braking-system adjustments. A lever on the left-hand side of the cockpit is connected via bevel gears and a linkage to the brake master cylinder balance bar. By moving the lever fore and aft on a ratchet, the driver can effectively adjust the proportion of his foot force that acts on each master cylinder, which in turn alters the bias between the front and rear circuits.

↓ Brake-bias adjustment system components.

1 Bias adjuster lever
2 Ratchet assembly (transforms linear movement of lever into rotary motion)
3 Upper link rod
4 Intermediate rod, universal joints and bracket
5 Lower link rod
6 Bevel gears and adjuster spindle
7 Brake pedal
8 Master cylinders
9 Fluid reservoirs
10 Master cylinder potentiometers (to measure piston movement)

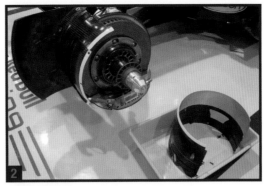

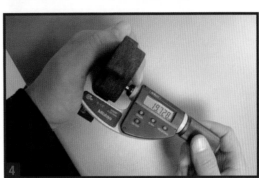

←← Before removing the brake pads, the components are cleaned to remove carbon dust.

← The carbon shroud is removed for access to the caliper.

←← The caliper is unbolted, and the pads can then be lifted out.

← The pad friction material is measured to confirm brake wear rates.

TEMPERATURE AND WEAR SENSORS

Temperature sensors

Temperature sensors are fitted to the brakes on all four wheels. Infra-red sensors are used to measure the heat radiation produced by the brake discs. The sensors are very compact and lightweight, and are mounted in the uprights. Data on brake temperatures is constantly transmitted to the engineers in the pitlane to enable them to monitor brake performance during a race.

Wear sensors

The brake wear sensors used are LVDT (Linear Variable Differential Transformer) sensors. These sensors are mounted in the calipers, and measure the movement of the caliper pistons. As brake wear increases, the stroke required for the caliper pistons to push the pads into contact with the discs will increase, and from these measurements the engineers can determine brake wear. Sensors are fitted to all four wheels.

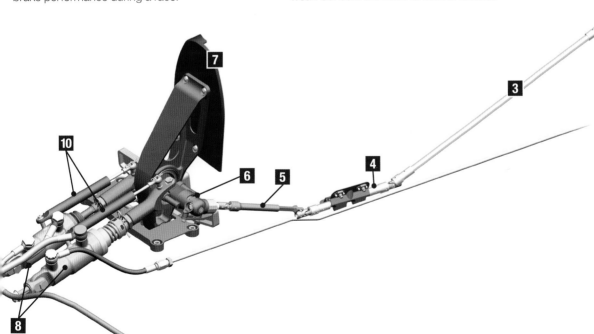

ENGINE

⬆ The Renault RS27-2010 engine that powered the RB6 to victory during the 2010 season.

The engine is the heart of the car, and a vital factor in the car's overall performance. F1 engines are the most highly developed internal-combustion engines to be found anywhere, and these 2.4-litre V8 normally aspirated engines produce incredible power bearing in mind their size and weight.

An F1 engine bears little relation to its road-car cousin, except for the fact that both operate using the four-stroke cycle, and the fundamental design principles of the cylinder block, crankshaft, pistons and valves are similar.

One basic difference between most road-car engines and an F1 engine is that an F1 car's engine is a fully stressed component. It forms an integral part of the car's structure, with the chassis bolted rigidly to its front end, and the gearbox/suspension assembly bolted rigidly to its rear. This means that the engine has to cope with the vibrations and stresses transmitted to it through the rear suspension and gearbox, in addition to the stresses produced by its own internal components. It is very important for the engine structure to be as stiff as possible, as any flexing will impact on the effectiveness of the

car's suspension and aerodynamics, and hence the handling and balance of the car.

Unlike production engines, cost of manufacture and ease of production are not major factors in the design of an F1 engine, and so the components are manufactured using whatever processes suit them best – not necessarily the same methods that would be used for equivalent components in a production engine. For example, certain components in an F1 engine, such as the crankshaft, are machined from solid metal (billet) rather than cast or forged.

ENGINE REGULATIONS

Unlike the rest of the car, there is no continuous process of development for the engine. This is due to FIA regulations introduced at the end of 2006, under which engine development was banned to reduce costs. In essence, the specification of the engines used during the 2006 Japanese Grand Prix was frozen and, other than a mandatory reduction in the rev limit from the beginning of the 2009 season, from 19,000rpm to 18,000rpm, no changes have been made to the fundamental engine specification. No performance-enhancing modifications are permitted.

In order to better understand the design of the engine, it is useful to summarise some of the details specified in the FIA engine regulations:

- Engines must be four-stroke, 2.4-litre V8s, with a vee-angle of 90°.
- Crankshaft rotational speed must not exceed 18,000rpm.
- The crankshaft centreline must not be less than 58mm above the 'reference plane'.
- Engines must be normally aspirated.
- Engines must have a minimum weight of 95kg.
- Engines must have two inlet valves and two exhaust valves per cylinder.
- Only reciprocating poppet valves are permitted.
- Cylinder bore diameter must not exceed 98.0mm.
- Spacing between cylinder-bore centres must be 106.5mm (±0.2mm).
- The centre of gravity of the engine must not lie less than 165mm above the 'reference plane' of the car.
- The longitudinal and lateral positions of the centre of gravity must lie within ±50mm of the geometric centre of the engine.
- Variable-geometry inlet systems or exhaust systems are not permitted.
- Variable valve timing and variable valve-lift systems are not permitted.
- With the exception of electric fuel pumps, engine auxiliaries must be mechanically driven direct from the engine with a fixed speed ratio to the crankshaft.
- Crankshafts and camshafts must be manufactured from an iron-based alloy.
- Each camshaft and lobes must be manufactured from a single piece of material.
- Valves must be manufactured from iron, nickel, cobalt or titanium-based alloys.

Another key factor first introduced to the regulations for the 2009 season is that each driver is allowed to use a maximum of eight different engines during the season. If any additional engine beyond the permitted eight is used, the driver will be penalised 10 places on the starting grid for the first race that engine is used. The engines can be rotated as the team chooses, and can be used for practice, qualifying sessions and races as required, but the engines are sealed for the entire season.

Because the regulations permit modifications to improve engine reliability (which must be approved by the FIA), Renault does not build the season's entire allocation of engines at the start of the year,

The sheer numbers involved when looking at the performance of a modern F1 engine, such as the Renault RS27-2010, are simply extraordinary!

Here are a few facts and figures to illustrate just what is involved in powering a modern F1 car.

- The 2.4-litre V8 engine revs to a maximum of 18,000rpm, and at this speed each piston travels up and down its cylinder bore approximately 300 times per second, with the pistons accelerating under a force of nearly 9,000g, from 0–60mph in 0.0005 seconds. This acceleration is the equivalent of a force of around 2.5 tonnes pulling on the connecting rod.

- At maximum revs, each of the engine's valves opens and closes around 150 times per second.

- During a typical race, the engine's crankshaft will complete approximately 22,000 revolutions per lap.

- The engine weighs around 95kg – 15kg less than the classic BL 'A-series' engine used in the Mini.

- The average fuel consumption of an F1 engine is around 4–6mpg.

- At full throttle the engine will consume around 450 litres of air every second.

- The engine consists of around 5,000 separate parts, of which approximately 1,500 are moving parts.

- A newly built engine produces somewhere between 700–750bhp.

- An F1 engine is incredibly noisy – the Renault engine produces approximately 100 decibels at idle, and up to 140 decibels at high revs.

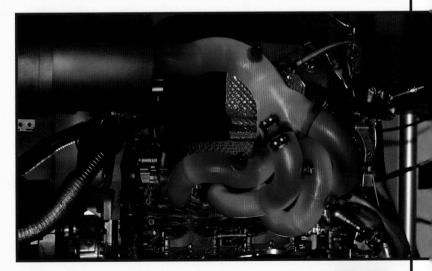

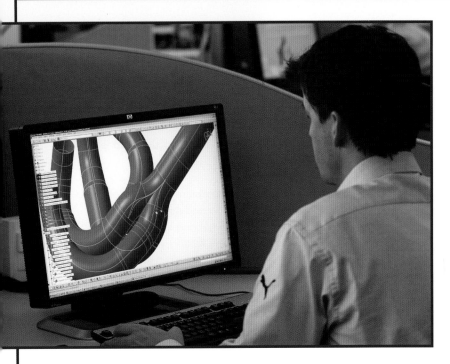

Manufacturers were free to homologate three different designs of engine inlet trumpet before the start of the 2009 season, and these three designs can be used freely during the homologation period (2009 season onwards).

So it can be seen that the specification of the engine is very tightly controlled, and this means that the only significant area of improvement left open to engineers is development of lubricants and of fuel. With the introduction of the 'eight engines per driver' rule for 2009, it became essential for all the engine manufacturers to make modifications aimed at improving reliability (previously, the regulations required each engine to last for two complete race weekends), and these modifications were monitored and approved by the FIA.

Modifications are also permitted for installation reasons – if, for example, an engine manufacturer supplies engines to a new team whose installation requirements are not compatible with the existing details of the engine.

ENGINE DESIGN
The prime aim when designing the engine is to maximise the power available, and currently F1 engines are producing over 300bhp/litre. A good high-performance road-car engine will typically produce around 100bhp/litre, often with the aid of turbocharging, which is banned in F1.

Smooth and consistent power delivery is a key requirement to enable the driver to drive the car consistently near 'the limit', maximising traction and acceleration out of corners. Additionally, there needs to be a constant production of torque (a flat torque curve) across the rev range. However, the peak torque figures produced are not significantly higher than those produced by an equivalent high-performance 2.4-litre V8 road-car engine. Throttle response is also a vital factor, both for the driver and for lap times, and to provide good throttle response, the engine's rotating components must have minimal inertia. In theory this means that the rotating components should be as light as possible, but in practice the design weight of the components is a compromise, as they must be sufficiently strong (and therefore heavy) to withstand the enormous forces and stresses imposed on them as the engine revs rise and fall.

The engine needs to be as stiff, light and compact as possible, with its mass concentrated low down to help keep the car's centre of gravity low. In order to achieve this, components mounted high up on the engine, such as the camshafts, are designed to be as light as possible.

For maximum power and torque, great attention is paid to the design of the inlet and exhaust manifolds in order to maximise gas flow.

↑ Along with computer analysis and simulation, CAD (Computer Aided Design) is used extensively as part of the engine design process. The exhaust system is designed as a cooperative effort between Renault Sport F1 and Red Bull Racing.

in order that any reliability-related modifications can be incorporated on engines built later.

Although FIA seals are fitted to the engines to prevent work on the internals, the following components may be renewed without penalty. If the work requires an FIA engine seal to be broken, this must be carried out under FIA supervision.

- Clutch and clutch basket
- Hydraulic pumps
- Engine electronic boxes (ECUs, power modules, control boxes)
- Fuel filters
- Fuel pumps
- Oil filters
- Oil tank systems
- Pneumatic bottles, regulators, pumps and pipes for valve actuation
- Exhaust systems
- Supports, brackets, screws, nuts, dowels, washers, cables, tubes, hoses, oil and air seals related to the auxiliaries mentioned above

Additionally, the following parts can be replaced with identical homologated parts:

- Throttle system
- Intake system external to the cylinder head
- Ignition coils
- Injection system
- Alternator
- Oil scavenging pumps, supply pumps and oil/air separators
- Water pump
- Electric and electronic sensors

The pressure and velocity of the air feeding the engine through the airbox above the car's roll hoop must be kept as constant as possible, regardless of the ambient weather conditions and the car's speed.

Frictional, vibrational and heat losses must be minimised.

As with other aspects of the car, computer analysis and simulation is used extensively during the engine design process, and in particular CFD (Computational Fluid Dynamics – see pages 131–132) is used to analyse gas flow in the cylinders, flame propagation during ignition, and even oil performance.

The packaging and detailing of the engine and its ancillaries is very important when designing the car itself, particularly when accommodating systems such as the exhaust and air-inlet tracts, and Renault engineers work closely with Red Bull Racing's design team during the design and development process for a new car.

ENGINE BUILDING

The RB6 uses a Renault RS27-2010 engine, designed and developed by the 250-strong Renault Sport F1 team at its Viry-Châtillon headquarters in France. Each of Red Bull Racing's Renault engines is assembled at the Mecachrome assembly facility by a pair of technicians, and will take

approximately 12 man-days to put together. This assembly process involves building the engine itself – assembling the crank, pistons and connecting rods – and then fitting pre-assembled cylinder head assemblies, pumps, manifolds and ancillaries.

Once the engine has been completed, it will be run on a test dynamometer in order to bed-in the components and check that all systems are

↑ Engines undergoing final assembly at the Viry-Châtillon facility.

↓ An engine running under load on a dynamometer, with the exhaust glowing red-hot.

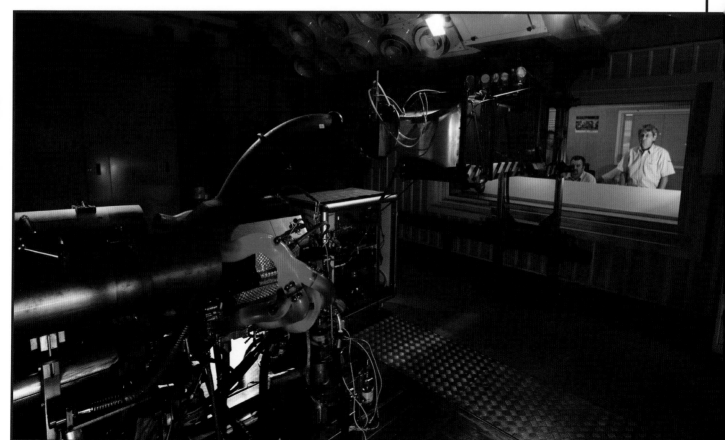

functioning correctly. The engine will be run under load on the dynamometer for three to four hours before it is supplied to the team for fitting to a car.

During testing and race weekends, Renault engineers work with the team to operate, monitor and maintain the engine.

TOLERANCES

Like all F1 engines, the Renault engine powering the RB6 is designed and built to incredibly tight tolerances compared to a production engine. As only relatively few engines are built, and they are all built by hand, there is no need to allow for the machining tolerances that must be catered for on production engines due to small inconsistencies produced by the manufacturing equipment.

The bearing and piston-to-bore clearances on an F1 engine are a matter of a few microns (one millimetre = 1,000 microns) – far smaller than a typical production engine – and all components are designed to operate within the engine's recommended operating temperature range. Because allowances must be made for expansion of the components, when the engine is cold the clearances between the moving components are too tight for the rotating parts to turn freely without damage to bearing surfaces, piston bores, etc. As a result, the engine must be brought up to operating temperature before it can be started.

CYLINDER BLOCK

The cylinder block is manufactured from aluminium alloy, and has a complex pattern of strengthening and reinforcing ribs to provide maximum rigidity. The pistons run in cylinder liners pressed into the cylinder block.

CYLINDER HEADS

The cylinder heads are manufactured from aluminium alloy, and secured to the cylinder block in the conventional way, with gaskets fitted between the mating faces. The combustion chambers are machined into the cylinder head, and give a compression ratio of around 13:1.

CRANKSHAFT

A steel crankshaft is used, and high-density balance weights are fitted. The accuracy of this balancing is vital to deal with the enormous forces passed to the crankshaft by the pistons and connecting rods.

PISTONS AND CONNECTING RODS

The pistons have very shallow crowns compared with most production engines, and the piston crowns are shaped to maximise the compression ratio. Compared with a typical road-car engine, fewer piston rings are used in order to minimise piston-to-bore friction. The connecting rods are made from titanium.

➜ Pre-assembled cylinder head assemblies, pump, manifolds and ancillaries are fitted to each engine.

CAMSHAFTS

Hollow camshafts are used to reduce weight, as it is important to avoid weight high up on the engine. The lower halves of the camshaft bearings are located in the cylinder head, and the upper halves are located in the camshaft cover, the camshaft cover effectively clamping the cams in place.

The camshafts are gear-driven via a series of gears from the front of the crankshaft.

The cam timing is fixed, as variable valve timing is not permitted within the FIA regulations. Due to the fact that the engines remain sealed, cam timing cannot be adjusted for a particular circuit, and so it must be optimised to suit all the tracks on which the car races during the season.

VALVE GEAR

Valve operation is significantly different from a road-car engine because the valves are closed pneumatically, rather than by coil springs. All F1 engines have pneumatically operated valves, but the systems used by the various manufacturers differ in detail.

On the Renault engine, when a valve opens, the camshaft cam lobe pushes down on the valve to lift it off its seat in the cylinder head in the normal way, but in place of the valve spring, a piston acting in an air chamber resists the movement of the valve. As the camshaft pushes

↑ The hollow camshafts are precision-machined to produce the required cam profiles for optimum valve timing.

← A schematic showing the principle of operation of the Renault engine's pneumatically operated valve system.

A Valve
B Piston
C Seal
D Cylinder containing air
E Valve guide
F Inlet/exhaust tract

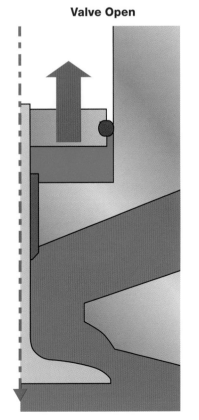

Valve Closed   Valve Open

the valve down, the air in the chamber resists the movement (air is compressible), pushing the valve closed as the cam continues to rotate.

The seals in the system are vital to avoid leaks and to prevent oil from entering the air chamber. If oil leaks into the air chamber, it can cause the piston to lock (oil is incompressible), which in turn can cause catastrophic engine failure.

The system is a low-loss system, and a reserve air supply is provided via a remote reservoir. The pressure in the reservoir is constantly monitored – a sensor transmits data back to the Renault engineers in the pitlane. The pressure is constantly monitored, and if it drops below a predetermined level, a warning will be flagged up.

The valves themselves are made from titanium for strength and low weight.

FLYWHEEL

This will come as a surprise to those familiar with most car engines, but current F1 engines have no flywheel. This is why an F1 engine can be heard to stop instantaneously as soon as the ignition is switched off.

As already mentioned, one of the prime aims in F1 engine design is to minimise the inertia of the rotating components. The main purpose of a flywheel is to smooth the power delivery to the transmission, by using a large rotating mass to damp the individual power pulses as each cylinder fires. Due to the extremely low inertia of the crankshaft, pistons and connecting rods, and the high operating revs of an F1 engine, it is possible to dispense with the flywheel.

On a road-car engine, the flywheel would normally be fitted to the end of the crankshaft, with the clutch bolted to the face of the flywheel. On the RB6, a splined shaft fitted to the end of the crankshaft takes drive directly to the clutch, which is mounted on the gearbox input shaft.

IGNITION SYSTEM

The ignition system is controlled by the FIA standard ECU, which also controls the fuel system. The engine is fitted with one spark plug per cylinder, with a coil-over-plug system – an individual coil feeding each spark plug, with the coil mounted over the top of the spark plug. The high-tension voltage at the plug is tens of thousands of volts.

FUEL SYSTEM

The fuel system comprises the fuel tank, fuel lift pump (mounted in the tank), fuel pressure pump (gear-driven from the engine), fuel rail, fuel injectors, throttles and inlet manifold, along with associated hoses, pipes and filters.

As with the ignition system, the fuel system is controlled by the FIA standard ECU. A single fuel injector per cylinder is used, and the injectors are mounted in a pressurised fuel rail, spraying fuel into the engine inlet trumpets – direct injection is not permitted under the FIA regulations. The injector spray pattern is very carefully designed in order to achieve efficient mixing of the fuel/air charge before it passes into the combustion chamber through the inlet valve.

The fuel pressure is regulated to a maximum of 100 bar, again as specified by FIA regulations. Individual butterfly throttles are used for each cylinder, and all eight butterflies operate simultaneously.

Fuel filters are fitted at the fuel lift and pressure pumps, and also at each of the eight injectors.

The regulations permit a maximum of five fuel/ignition engine maps to be stored in the ECU. For races at hot and/or high-altitude circuits, it is very important for the engineers to adjust the ignition/fuel mapping to cater for the changes in air density and temperature, which have a significant effect on engine performance.

The driver can adjust the fuel/ignition system mapping to a limited extent. For example, the fuel/air mixture can be richened or weakened in a number of steps to provide a balance between power and fuel economy (important with the ban on refuelling), and adjustments can also be made to optimise power delivery for rainy conditions, etc.

⬇ In this view of the front of the engine, the carbon-fibre oil tank (arrowed) can clearly be seen.

FUEL

Each engine manufacturer works with a fuel supplier to develop a bespoke fuel blend for their particular engine. The Red Bull Racing Renault fuel supplier is Total.

The specification of the fuel is tightly regulated by the FIA, and the constituent compounds must be those normally found in commercial fuels – power-boosting additives are not permitted.

Before any fresh batch of fuel can be used in any event, two separate 5-litre samples must be provided to the FIA for testing and approval. The FIA may also take fuel samples during an event to check the fuel specification.

LUBRICATION SYSTEM

The lubrication system is critical, and essential for the welfare of the engine. A dry-sump system is used, with a remote oil tank mounted between the engine and the chassis. This system is used for several reasons:

■ To enable the engine to be mounted lower in the car (a dry sump has no sump pan at the bottom of the engine).

■ A dry-sump system keeps oil away from the surfaces of the crankshaft that do not require essential lubrication, reducing losses due to oil splash.

■ The remote oil reservoir can be located to help weight distribution, and also allows the oil to cool and release gases absorbed due to piston blow-by and the movement of the crankshaft.

■ Dry-sump systems do not suffer from the oil starvation problems associated with wet-sump systems during high-speed cornering and extreme acceleration and braking.

The oil capacity of the engine is around 4 litres. As with the fuel, the oil is specially blended for the Renault engine by Total.

The oil tank remains attached to the engine when the engine is removed from the chassis.

The main oil pressure pump is gear-driven from the front (chassis) end of the engine. A gang of oil scavenge pumps in the cylinder block scavenges oil from the crankshaft and forces the oil through the oil cooling radiator back into the oil tank, from where

↑ The oil cooler radiator location (arrowed) in the right-hand sidepod.

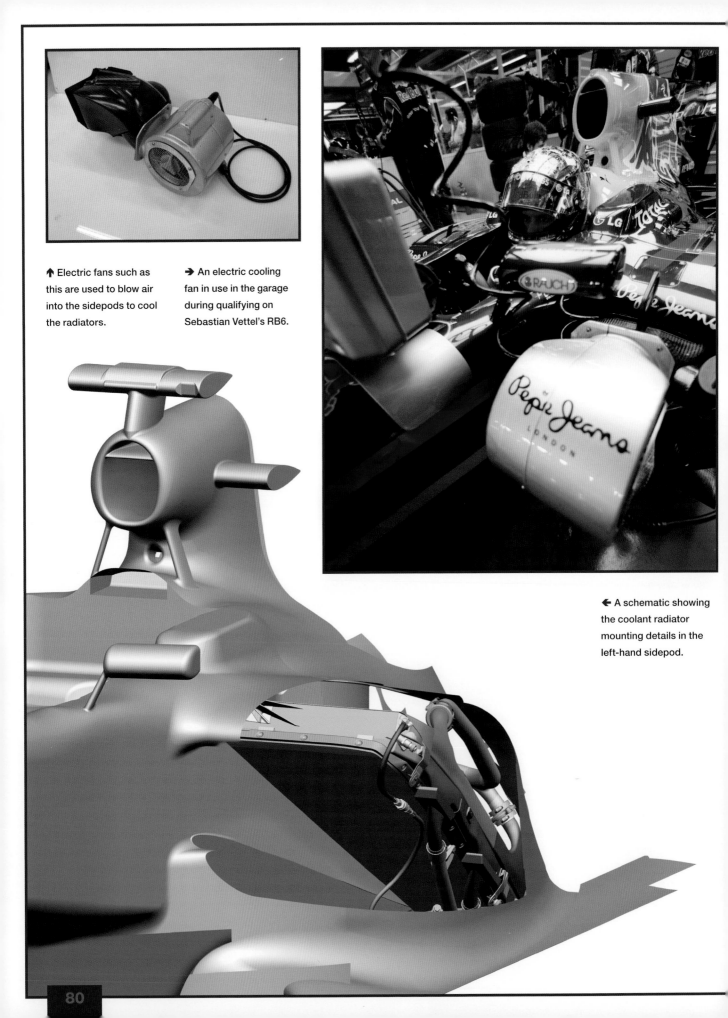

↑ Electric fans such as this are used to blow air into the sidepods to cool the radiators.

→ An electric cooling fan in use in the garage during qualifying on Sebastian Vettel's RB6.

← A schematic showing the coolant radiator mounting details in the left-hand sidepod.

it is recirculated around the engine by the main pressure pump. On the RB6, the oil cooling radiator is mounted in the right-hand sidepod.

Analysis of the oil can provide significant information about the condition and performance of the engine, and acts as a very useful diagnostic tool. Oil samples are taken regularly throughout a race weekend, for examination by the engineers. Careful analysis of the oil's condition and of the chemicals present in it can provide advance warning of impending problems. This may, for example, enable the team to carry out an engine change to avoid the possibility of a failure on-track resulting in a retirement.

COOLING SYSTEM

F1 cars have no cooling fans, and rely on the airflow over the car to cool the radiators, which are mounted in the sidepods. For weight reasons, the coolant capacity is kept to a minimum, and typically around 8 litres of coolant is used on the RB6. The quantity of coolant used remains the same for all circuits, but the level of cooling required depends on the ambient temperature and the nature of the circuit. In order to vary the degree of cooling, bodywork and cooling ducts can be modified to control the flow of air to the radiators. Australian company PWR manufactured the radiator cores for the RB6. The design of the radiators is very much a collaborative effort.

The FIA regulations specify a maximum cooling system pressure, to prevent teams from running very high pressures that could be used to improve the efficiency of the system. The system pressure is controlled by a blow-off valve on the coolant header tank, which is fitted in the sidepod below the radiator.

No thermostats are used, and the coolant circulates at full-flow all the time while the engine is running. Because the system relies on airflow to ensure sufficient cooling, when the car is stationary in the garage, or on the grid, external electric fans are used to blow air through the radiators.

The coolant pump is gear-driven from the front end of the crankshaft, and the coolant radiator is located in the left-hand sidepod.

Because it is necessary to circulate coolant remotely in order to warm up the engine (see 'Engine start-up procedure' on page 83), it is also necessary to bleed the cooling system once the remote equipment has been disconnected, to ensure that there is no air in the system. This is extremely important, as air in the system can cause hot spots inside the engine, which can reduce engine efficiency and can ultimately lead to component failure. This bleeding procedure is carried out before each session on-track.

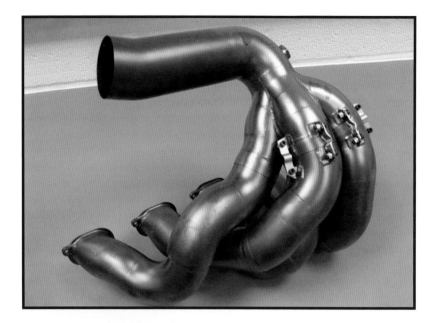

EXHAUST SYSTEM

The exhaust is critical for engine performance, and has also become an important factor in the aerodynamics of the car. The exhaust is designed as a cooperative effort between the Red Bull Racing team and Renault to suit the packaging needs of the car and the performance requirements of the engine.

The exhaust systems are manufactured from a nickel-iron alloy, and are renewed for each race. The exhaust-gas temperature at the exhaust exit is around 900°C, so the components around the exhaust must be capable of handling very high temperatures, and heat shielding is used where necessary.

↑ The exhaust systems are works of art, with precise shaping of the manifold.

HYDRAULIC SYSTEM

The hydraulic pump is gear-driven from the front of the crankshaft, and is described in more detail on pages 105–107.

THROTTLE CONTROL

Throttle control is electro-hydraulic, with an electronic throttle sensor reading from the throttle pedal, feeding signals to the FIA ECU to activate the throttle system via a hydraulic actuator.

ANTI-STALL SYSTEM

When activated, the anti-stall system disengages the clutch and blips the throttle in order to prevent the engine from stalling. The FIA regulations stipulate that the system can only operate for 10 seconds – after 10 seconds the engine stops and cannot be restarted by the driver. The 10-second maximum operating period was brought in because when the anti-stall system is in operation, the engine is outside the control of the driver.

→ Headsets are essential in the garage and pitlane due to the high level of engine noise. Here, Head of Race Engineering Ian Morgan talks to Team Principal Christian Horner. Morgan is responsible for leading the set-up of both cars at the circuit.

ENGINE NOISE

Although the awe-inspiring noise produced by an F1 engine is considered by many people to be music, it can present practical problems when working with the engine.

Due to the intensity of the sound and the associated vibration, certain pit equipment, such as laptop computers, must be insulated against the noise and vibration – for example, laptop hard-drives have been known to fail, or crash, due to the vibration levels. The team members in the garage use frequency-cancelling headsets to enable speech to be heard when an engine is running.

KERS (KINETIC ENERGY RECOVERY SYSTEM)

KERS was used during the 2009 season, but its use was suspended during the 2010 season, and it was not fitted to the RB6. However, the systems have reappeared at the beginning of the 2011 F1 season, so a brief explanation is provided here.

The KERS unit is basically a motor-generator unit, which charges a battery when the car is braking. The stored energy in the battery can be released when the car is not braking and is used to turn the KERS unit into a motor to provide an additional power boost, improving straight-line speed and acceleration. For 2011, the KERS unit can provide an extra 80hp at the press of a button on the steering wheel.

The KERS unit is gear-driven from the front of the engine crankshaft. The energy discharge is regulated by the FIA standard ECU, so that the system can only be used for a limited period of time – six seconds in 2011 – during each lap. The driver can choose whether to use all the stored energy in one 'hit' or in small 'chunks' during the lap.

The additional power boost delivered by KERS can be worth a total of up to 0.3 seconds a lap. The system can be used to aid overtaking under the right circumstances, and can provide a very useful boost during the battle to the first corner at the start of a race.

The system is a high-energy system that uses very high currents and voltages, and so precautions must be taken to avoid the risk of electric shock when working on a car fitted with KERS.

↓ Renault engineers celebrate in the team's garage with their Red Bull Racing colleagues after winning the Constructors' World Championship at the 2010 Brazilian Grand Prix.

Due to the very tight bearing and piston-to-bore clearances on an F1 engine, the engine cannot be started from 'cold' and must be brought up to the recommended start-up temperature in order to avoid damage to the moving components.

The recommended start-up temperature for the Renault engine is around 70°C. The engine is warmed using a remote electric pump to circulate hot coolant through the coolant passages prior to start-up. The pump is a purpose-built unit mounted on a trolley for ease of use in the pit garage, and connects to the engine via plug-in hose connections.

Hot coolant is used to warm the engine itself, but the engine oil also needs to be heated to operating temperature, and this is done outside the engine. The oil is warmed using a bespoke remote warming device that ensures the oil is warmed evenly to the required operating temperature. It is important that there are no 'hot spots' in the oil, as these can cause breakdown of the oil's chemical constituents, which can in turn cause engine problems. Once the oil has reached operating temperature it is pumped into the already-warm engine ready for start-up.

During the warm-up process, the temperatures of the coolant and oil are very carefully monitored at all times via sensors on both the warming devices and the engine itself.

Once the engine has reached the recommended start-up temperature, the start-up procedure itself can begin.

Before the engine can be fired up, oil must be circulated through the oil galleries to ensure that all the contact surfaces of moving components are coated with a film of oil. To circulate oil, the engine is cranked using the starter. The starter is a remote device comprising a powerful electric starter motor, with a reduction gearbox, powered by a large battery mounted on a trolley. The starter is fitted with a long shaft that is pushed through a hole in the rear diffuser to engage with the gearbox input shaft. With neutral selected on the gearbox, the starter is activated and it spins the gearbox input shaft, which in turn spins the engine crankshaft (via the clutch). The crankshaft is turned for a set period of time (usually a few seconds) to circulate oil until the appropriate start-up oil pressure is reached. The 'oil pressure cranking time' depends on how recently the engine has run – for the first start-up of the day, when there is very little oil in the engine galleries, a longer cranking time will be required than is the case when the car has recently been out on the circuit lapping, when there will still be warm oil coating the contact surfaces.

Once the recommended start-up values for the oil pressure, oil temperature, coolant temperature and the temperature of the engine itself have been reached, the engine can be started.

With the ignition and fuel systems switched on, using the ignition switches in the cockpit (see page 119), the engine is cranked using the starter until it fires up. Once the engine is running, a Renault engineer controls it via a laptop, in order to monitor the various engine parameters and to control the warm-up procedure. When the car is in the garage during warm-up, the engine is controlled entirely by the software, and the throttle can be operated via the laptop as required. The engine idles at 3,000–4,000rpm, and the engineers will follow a warm-up procedure, raising the engine revs to speed warming up and to check various parameters, particularly temperatures and pressures, at various predetermined rev check points.

Once the engine is at operating temperature and all the systems are working satisfactorily, the engine will probably be shut down again (to avoid overheating) if the car is not about to take to the track. Provided the temperatures are maintained, the engine can then be fired up again when required. If necessary a short fire-up may be carried out to warm the engine in order to maintain temperature without the need to connect the remote equipment.

Before shutting down, normally the revs will be elevated just before cutting the engine. With the Renault engine, the revs are held at 7,000rpm for around 10 seconds before stopping. This is to ensure that the engine is fully scavenged of oil, with the maximum possible quantity of oil returned to the oil tank, in order to carry out an accurate check of oil level. The oil tank is fitted with an electronic oil level sensor to read the oil level in the tank.

⬇ An RB6 connected to the remote coolant warming pump in the garage prior to start-up.

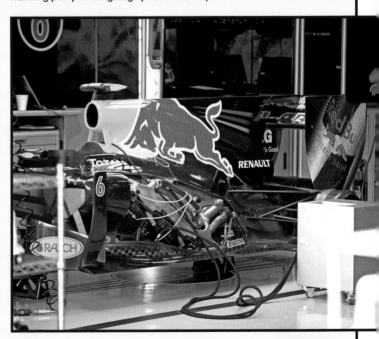

TRANSMISSION

↑ The transmission is housed in the gearbox casing, which forms a complete assembly with the rear suspension and rear wing. The example shown here is an RB4 unit.

→ A schematic showing the layout of the transmission components.

1 Clutch housing
2 Gear clusters
3 Cross-shaft, reduction gear and bevel
4 Differential
5 Driveshafts
6 Upright
7 Hydraulic manifold

The transmission comprises the clutch, gearbox, differential and driveshafts. The transmission has to cope with extremely high mechanical loads, and must be capable of reliably transferring the 700bhp+ engine power and very high torque to the rear wheels with minimal loss of power. The clutch, seven-speed gearbox and differential are all electro-hydraulically operated under electronic control to give very quick seamless sequential gearchanges.

Gearchanges typically take around 0.05sec. Clutch operation and gear actuation are controlled electronically in response to the driver-operated gearchange paddles on the steering wheel. The driver does not operate the clutch independently

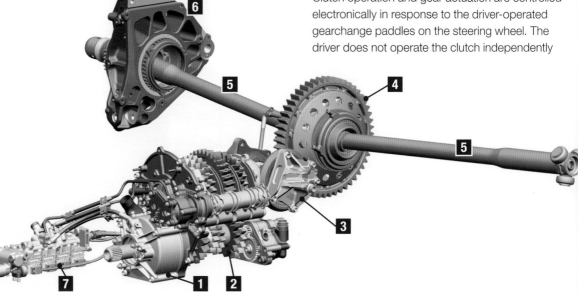

during gearchanges, and can stay at full throttle during upchanges.

The differential is integral with the gearbox casing, and is mounted at the back of the gearbox. The driveshafts take the drive from the differential to the rear wheels.

CLUTCH

Unlike most road cars, on which the clutch is mounted on the engine's flywheel, the clutch on the RB6 is mounted on the gearbox, in a housing at the end of the input shaft. A shaft connects the engine crankshaft to the clutch. This means that the gearbox and clutch can be disconnected from the engine and removed as a complete unit. The clutch is a multi-plate unit with carbon plates mounted in a titanium cage housing. Carbon plates are used because of their ability to cope with the very high temperatures produced – over 1,000°C – and multiple plates are used in order to keep the clutch compact (of small diameter) while maintaining sufficient friction material area to dissipate the heat produced. AP Racing supplies the clutch used on the RB6.

The clutch is an extremely compact unit, with a diameter of around 100mm. This helps with the packaging of the engine and gearbox, most importantly with the height of the crankshaft centreline. The minimum height of the crankshaft centreline is specified by FIA regulations (see 'Engine regulations' on pages 72–74), and teams will always aim to ensure that the figure for their car is close to the specified minimum, as this dimension determines the vertical position of the engine and gearbox in relation to the chassis. This in turn influences the position of the car's centre of gravity – the lower the engine and gearbox, the lower the centre of gravity of the car. Keeping the centre of gravity of the car as low as possible is a key factor in car performance and set-up. A small-diameter clutch also has a lower inertia, which is important as it provides better throttle response

← The clutch is located in a housing (arrowed) at the front of the transmission casing.

and reduces mechanical stresses in the engine and transmission.

The clutch is designed to be as light as possible, again to minimise inertia, and a typical clutch weighs 1–1.5kg.

Clutch operation is via hydraulic pressure from the car's main hydraulic system. Although FIA rules state that the clutch must be activated by the driver and not automatically engaged ('launch control' is now banned in F1), there is actually no mechanical connection between the driver's clutch controls and the clutch itself. To get the car moving from rest, the driver controls the clutch using clutch levers on the steering wheel rather than a pedal, and the levers act purely as electrical switches, sending signals to the transmission control system.

← ← The clutch assembly is extremely compact and features multiple carbon plates.

← The steel driven plates are sandwiched between a series of carbon friction plates, providing a high surface area of friction material to dissipate heat.

→ Either of the two lower paddles (arrowed) on the steering wheel can be used to control the clutch when moving away from standstill.

To achieve the best possible start, the clutch needs to slip when it is first engaged in order to smooth the torque delivery through the transmission and avoid excessive wheelspin. Because there is no mechanical connection between the clutch operating levers and the clutch, there is no 'feel' to the clutch as there is with a conventional clutch pedal, and so the driver cannot feel the clutch bite point. With a conventional mechanically operated clutch, a skilled driver can judge the bite point exactly from the 'feel' of the pedal, and operate the clutch accordingly to achieve the best possible start with the optimum amount of wheelspin.

The optimum amount of clutch slip for the best possible traction at the start varies according to tyre compound and other variable factors such as tyre temperature and track conditions, both of which can change significantly over a race weekend or even during a race morning. The optimum amount of clutch slip is known as the clutch 'torque setting', and the torque setting can be adjusted by the driver using a control on the steering wheel. Where possible, the driver will try to make a practice start during the reconnaissance lap(s) before the start.

Although the control software and the hydraulic system for the clutch are both very advanced, the system still relies on the driver to operate the clutch lever, and on the accuracy of the data obtained from practice starts. Invariably, the conditions under which the practice starts are carried out are not always precisely the same as those encountered at the actual race start, and so the system is not infallible. This is why, on occasions, cars can be seen to 'bog down' or, conversely, suffer too much wheelspin at the start.

Once the car is moving, the clutch action during gear upshifts and downshifts is controlled, along with gearchanges, by the gearbox control system according to the signals received from the steering wheel gear paddles.

GEARBOX

Although the general layout of the internals of a modern F1 gearbox and the basic concept of its operation are relatively conventional, the control systems and the materials and manufacturing techniques used are very advanced. The sequential gearbox operates using very similar principles to a motorcycle gearbox, allowing extremely fast gearchanging compared with a conventional fully manual gearbox. The gearbox is semi-automatic, and is operated by the driver, as fully automatic gearboxes are prohibited. Currently, all F1 gearboxes are fitted with seven forwards speeds and reverse. The gearbox changes up and down through all consecutive ratios, and cannot 'jump' ratios.

The purpose of the gearbox is essentially to ensure that the engine is always operating within its optimum power band to provide the car with maximum power and acceleration at all times, with minimal power loss through the transmission. To achieve this, friction losses in the transmission must be minimal, and a great deal of attention is paid to the design of the gearbox internals and the transmission lubrication system to minimise friction.

The power band of an F1 engine is relatively narrow, and it can accelerate to peak revs extremely quickly, even under load, so to keep the engine within its optimum operating rev band, it is necessary for the driver to change gear very frequently. The number of gearchanges made during a lap varies depending on the circuit, but as an example to illustrate how much work the gearbox has to do, at Monaco, the most gearbox-intensive race on the calendar, the driver will make over 50 gearchanges per lap, which equates to over 4,000 gearchanges during the race.

Bearing in mind the harsh environment in which it operates, the loads with which it has to deal, and the frequency with which all the moving parts of the selector mechanism must operate, the engineering and reliability of an F1 gearbox are astounding, and all the more remarkable when you take into account the fact that FIA regulations now stipulate that a gearbox must be used for a number of consecutive races (four in 2010, and five for 2011) without carrying out any work other than renewal of the lubricant and changing gear ratios. The gearboxes are fitted with FIA tamper-proof seals to ensure that this rule is observed.

Gearbox casing

The gearbox casing is a critical component. Although its primary function is to act as a housing for the gearbox components and the differential, it is also a fully stressed structural component, like the chassis and engine, to which the rear suspension, rear crash structure and rear wing are attached. Because the gearbox casing has to cope with the rear suspension loads and the aerodynamic load from the rear wing, it must be extremely strong and must have the necessary stiffness to resist flexing under these substantial loads.

Over the past decade, the trend has been to move away from cast aluminium alloy, titanium or magnesium material for gearbox casings in favour of carbon-fibre, which offers improved rigidity and a significant weight-saving benefit – and therefore a weight-distribution benefit – compared with metals. A carbon-fibre casing is used on the RB6, but not all current F1 teams use carbon-fibre casings. In the early days of carbon-fibre casings there were numerous problems, mainly related to dealing with the high temperatures encountered, providing the necessary rigidity for bearing mountings, and preventing lubricant leakage. In recent years, these problems have been largely overcome with developments in design and manufacturing techniques. With the recent changes to regulations

meaning that gearboxes must be sealed for a number of races, carbon-fibre is considered by many teams to offer improved longevity and robustness over metallic casings.

As mentioned previously, aerodynamic performance is the driving factor in the design of almost every aspect of the car, and the gearbox casing is no exception. Because of its location, the gearbox has a significant effect on the airflow at the rear of the car, and so it needs to be as compact as possible to allow the aerodynamics to be optimised. On the 2009 RB5, the top surface of the gearbox casing was designed to act as an aerodynamic surface in its own right, and for the RB6 a new gearbox casing was designed specifically to allow the double diffuser to work to maximum effect. This resulted in a casing that was much lower and more tightly packaged than those on rival cars.

The front end of the gearbox casing is bolted to the engine. The main gearbox casing carries the forward suspension (wishbone) pick-up points, rockers, springs, dampers and anti-roll bars, while the rear crash structure carries the rear wishbone pick-up points, the main support for the rear wing, and the jacking 'hook' used to jack the rear of the car during pit stops. Under some circumstances, the gearbox casing can also be used as a mounting for ballast, to adjust the car's weight distribution.

↑ The gearbox is housed in a carbon casing, which carries the rear suspension, rear wing and rear crash structure. An RB4 unit is shown.

→ The gearbox casing houses the gear clusters and differential. The RB6 casing is extremely low and compact to optimise the airflow at the rear of the car.

1 Gearbox casing
2 Gear selector barrel
3 Clutch housing
4 Hydraulic manifold
5 Gear clusters
6 Driveshaft
7 Differential
8 Suspension pick-up bracket

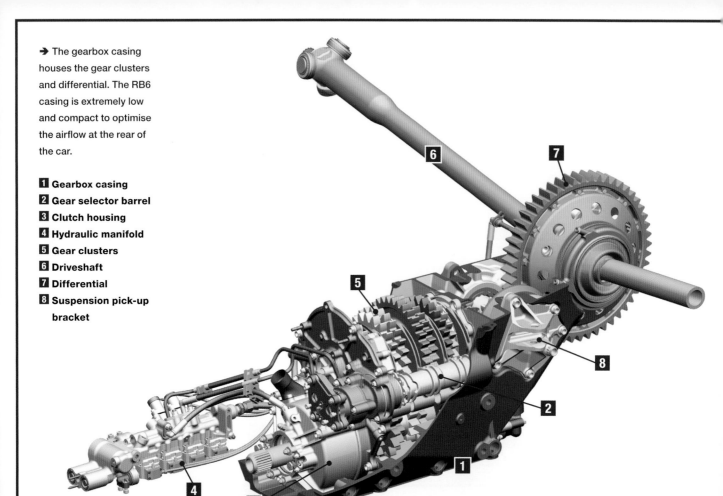

→ The suspension pick-up points on the gearbox casing are fitted with metal brackets to provide mountings for the wishbones. An RB4 unit is shown here.

← The gear clusters are mounted in a removable cassette.

Gear clusters

The layout of the gear clusters is conventional, with two shafts – an input shaft and output shaft – located longitudinally inside the gearbox casing. The clutch is attached to the end of the input shaft, at the front of the gearbox. A bevel gear (pinion) on the rear end of the output shaft takes drive to the differential, via an intermediate bevel and a reduction gear on the cross-shaft. All the gears are straight-cut to minimise power losses and to provide the maximum possible strength and durability; the gears of most road-car gearboxes are helical, to reduce noise.

For many years it was the convention on F1 cars to locate the gear clusters behind the differential, for ease of access in order to change gear ratios, although this compromised weight distribution and aerodynamic performance. The current trend, with the gear clusters at the front (engine) end of the gearbox, means that the gearbox must be removed to change the gear ratios. The gear cluster (input shaft and output shaft) is mounted in a removable cassette, which can be removed once the gearbox/rear suspension/wing assembly has been removed from the rear of the car.

The input shaft and output shaft each carry seven gears, and each pair of gears (one on the input shaft and one on the output shaft) is carefully selected to give the required gear ratio. The FIA regulations stipulate that each car is allowed 30 pairs of gear ratios from which to choose during the entire season, and these 30 ratios must be declared to the FIA before the first race of the season. The 2010 FIA regulations stipulated that all gears must be manufactured from steel, with a minimum weight (0.6kg) for gear pairs, and a minimum thickness (12mm) for each gear.

All cars must be fitted with a reverse gear to comply with the FIA regulations, and reverse is operated using a button on the steering wheel which engages an intermediate gear between the gearbox input and output shafts to reverse the direction of rotation of the output shaft.

Details of the gearing are provided on page 155.

↑ When reverse is selected, a solenoid-operated intermediate gear (arrowed) is engaged between the input and output shafts.

Selector mechanism

The gear selector mechanism is hydraulically controlled, and the hydraulic actuators themselves are controlled electronically by the gearbox control system.

The selector mechanism itself is very similar in operation to that used in a motorcycle gearbox, with selector forks acting on each of the gears on the output shaft, to lock the appropriate gear to the shaft to engage the required gear. All the gears on the output shaft are in constant mesh with the gears on the input shaft, and any gear that is not engaged simply rotates freely (idles) on the shaft.

The mechanical components of the selector mechanism comprise the selector barrel, selector forks and selector collars. Pegs on the selector forks run in curved grooves in the selector barrel. If the selector barrel is rotated, the selector forks move slightly along the selector barrel. The shapes of the grooves in the barrel, and the rotation of the barrel, determine the movement of the forks. The forks operate collars that are locked to the output shaft (and rotate with the shaft, inside the arms of the forks), but are free to slide along it according to the position of the forks.

When the driver operates the gearchange paddle on the steering wheel to select a gear, the gearbox control system operates the clutch, sends a signal to the engine control software to cut the ignition or blip the throttle (as applicable) to synchronise the speeds of the input shaft and output shaft, and operates the selector barrel as required to engage the correct gear. A hydraulic actuator rotates the selector barrel, moving the selector forks to lock the required gear to the output shaft. The selector fork moves the collar so that the holes in the collar engage with the dogs on the gear, locking the gear to the output shaft and engaging the gear. This whole process takes around 0.05 seconds.

The quality and smoothness of the gearchanges has improved significantly in recent years, as Mark Webber explains: "That's an element that the drivers get quite fussy with, and over the years we've been very advanced in the quality control. Whereas in the past the driver would have been able to 'heel and toe' to match the gearbox and engine speed together, now we just pull the downshift lever. We can stack the downshifts very close to each other,

⬇ The gear selector barrel (1) rotates to move the selector forks (2) in order to lock the required gear to the output shaft.

and the software and the mapping will do all that for you, so it's not very violent, and the downshifts and upshifts are quite smooth. One of the most beautiful feelings someone would appreciate if they drove an F1 car is how nice the gearboxes are."

Because the selector barrel controls gear selection, it is not possible to 'skip' gears, which is why the gearbox operates sequentially, always moving through all gears sequentially under braking or acceleration conditions. This is not an issue because of the high speed of each gearchange.

In order to allow the car to be moved in the pitlane, a 'neutral' position is required. When the neutral button is operated, the gearbox control system moves the selector barrel to a position to operate the forks to disengage all gears.

Gearbox lubrication

The gearbox has a forced-lubrication system, with a high-pressure oil pump driven mechanically from the gearbox. A dry-sump system is used, and oil is scavenged from the gearbox casing and pumped through a sidepod-mounted oil cooler, from where it flows back to the gearbox oil passages. The gearbox lubrication system contains approximately 3.5 litres of oil.

When designing the gearbox and its lubrication system, a great deal of attention is paid to reducing friction in every area, in order minimise power loss and component wear.

Gearbox control system

The gearbox control system is a critical system, as any failure or fault in the system can wreck the gearbox, and stop the car, in a fraction of a second. The control system is activated by the gearchange paddles on the steering wheel, and the neutral button, and controls the clutch and gearchange barrel. It also sends signals to the engine control system to cut/adjust the ignition timing and/or throttle to ensure reliable gearchanges by matching the speeds of the gearbox input and output shafts. Various sensors, including input shaft and output shaft speed sensors, are fitted to enable the control system to achieve this.

An external switch is provided, recessed into the top of the left-hand side of the chassis, in front of the cockpit, to allow the marshals to disengage the clutch, so that if the car stops on the circuit the car can be pushed without having to turn the engine over. This system can be operated even if the car's hydraulic or electrical system has failed.

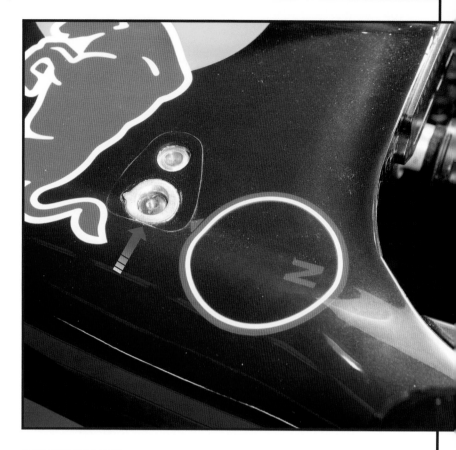

DIFFERENTIAL

An F1 car needs a differential to allow for the fact that the driven (rear) wheels rotate at different speeds when the car is cornering – the wheel on the outside of the corner needs to rotate faster than the wheel on the inside of the corner. If no differential were fitted, both rear wheels would rotate at the same speed, seriously compromising the car's handling, and resulting in severe tyre wear problems.

A normal (non-limited-slip or 'open') differential will transmit equal torque to both driven wheels under all conditions, whereas a limited-slip differential (LSD) can deliver differing torque to each driven wheel to optimise traction through a corner. On an F1 car, the differential is very sophisticated, and comprises an epicyclic differential that can be locked or slipped by a hydraulically operated clutch that links the left-hand and right-hand driveshafts. This enables the torque acting on each rear wheel to be varied through the various phases of cornering. Because the differential can be used to affect how the car behaves at different phases around a corner, it can be a significant tuning aid.

The torque relationship between the rear wheels can be altered to help to 'steer' the car through corners, and to maintain optimum traction under hard acceleration. Using the hydraulic control system, it is possible to emulate

↑ A neutral button (arrowed) for use by the marshals is located on the top of the chassis, in front of the cockpit.

any type of mechanical differential. Mechanical differentials are available with either a torque-related locking action or a locking action relating to the speed differential between the driven wheels, and both these types can be replicated using a hydraulic differential.

Relatively large adjustments need to be made to the differential to have a significant effect on the car. This is because the differential only acts on the rear axle, so, in effect, altering the action of the differential affects the car by trying to rotate it about the centreline of the rear axle.

The driver can adjust the differential via controls on the steering wheel. These controls send signals to the differential control software that operate the hydraulic actuators via Moog-manufactured servo valves (see 'Moog valve' section on page 108) to adjust the differential locking action. The driver can adjust the differential during a race to adjust the balance of the car as the fuel load lightens, or to address tyre wear issues. The differential can be adjusted to alter the car's balance for a specific section of a lap.

DRIVESHAFTS

The driveshafts must be extremely strong to cope with the very high torque loads that they are subjected to at the start, and throughout the race. Driveshaft failures have accounted for a significant number of F1 retirements over the years, although such cases are now rare.

Hollow steel driveshafts are used on the RB6, fitted with tripod joints at their inner and outer ends to connect to the differential and rear axles.

⬆ A typical differential unit. The epicyclic planet gears can just be seen through the casing holes. The pipe to the rear supplies hydraulic pressure.

⬇ A complete driveshaft assembly, with tripod joints at each end.

◥ The tripod joints are identical in operation to similar joints used on road cars, but must cope with extremely high loads.

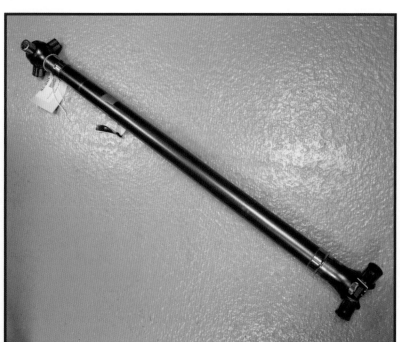

WHEELS

The wheels, needless to say, have an important role to play, and a number of parameters need to be considered in their design:

■ The provision of suitable sealing surfaces to mount the tyres.
■ The importance of lightness, to minimise the unsprung weight of the car.
■ The requirement to dissipate the high levels of heat generated by the brakes, and allow good cooling airflow to the brakes.
■ Wheel shape must minimise aerodynamic drag and interrupt the airflow over the car as little as possible.

The dimensions of the wheels are limited by FIA regulations, but the design is free, and the number of spokes, spacing between the spokes, etc, can be set to suit the design requirements of the car.

Each wheel weighs less than 2kg, and the tyre fitted to each rim is heavier than the rim itself.

TYRE FITTING

During a race weekend the team provides a set of wheel rims to the tyre supplier, who will fit tyres to the rims.

A special paste is used to ensure an airtight seal between the tyre and rim, and once the tyre has been fitted, each wheel/tyre assembly is finely balanced, in exactly the same way as a road-car wheel. Small balance weights are secured to the wheel rims in the required positions to make any adjustments.

The supplier delivers the rims, with tyres fitted and inflated, back to the team.

WHEEL-SECURING MECHANISM

Pegs on the rear of each wheel locate in corresponding holes in the axle to prevent the wheel from rotating, and a single threaded nut secures each wheel.

The wheel nuts have right- or left-hand threads, according to which side of the car they are fitted, in order to resist the rotational forces trying to loosen them. The wheel nuts are tightened to a specific torque, which is pre-set on the wheel-nut

↑ The wheels used on the RB6 are supplied by OZ Racing.

➔ Pegs on the rear of the wheel locate in holes in the axle to prevent the wheel from rotating.

guns. If the nuts are too tight, they will be difficult to remove during pit stops; if they are too loose, there is a danger of the wheels coming off the car.

Each nut screws on to a threaded boss on the axle. As the nut is screwed on, it slides over two spring-loaded lugs recessed into the axle and these pop up once the nut is fully in place and the wheel gun is removed. The lugs are designed to retain the nut on the axle if it works loose. When the wheel gun is used to remove the wheel, the socket pushes the spring-loaded lugs down to enable the nut to be removed from the end of the axle threads.

➔ The wheel nuts screw on to threads on the axle and are tightened to an accurate pre-set torque.

➔➔ Lugs on the wheel-gun socket engage with recesses in the axle nut.

TYRES

An F1 tyre has to cope with all the aerodynamic and mechanical loads acting on the car. With an F1 car able to produce up to 5g longitudinally under braking, 4g laterally under cornering, and with over a tonne of vertical downforce acting on it at maximum speed, the loading on the tyres is huge.

Until the 2009 season, 'grooved' dry-weather tyres – with four grooves around their tread – were used in an attempt to lower cornering speeds and improve overtaking and safety. The 2009 season saw a return to slicks, offering improved grip.

Compared with their road-car counterparts, F1 tyres have to last a very short length of time. A full race distance is only around 190 miles (300km), and the FIA regulations state that each car must have at least one tyre change during a race, so in reality it would be rare for a set of tyres to be used for more than 125 miles (200km). As the tyres wear, tiny beads of rubber are shed, and this can be seen as the often-mentioned rubber 'marbles' that gather just off the racing line, making the track surface relatively slippery off-line during a race.

Control tyres are used in F1, which means that a single manufacturer supplies tyres to all the teams, with a single specification of tread pattern and compound for each specific type of tyre. During the 2010 season Bridgestone supplied the tyres, but in 2011 Pirelli became the official F1 tyre supplier.

The tyres must be designed to cope with the very high forces that they are subjected to, providing maximum possible grip, and must be as light as possible.

Tyre behaviour is critical – the car's performance is dependent on making sure that the tyres are working effectively. Optimum grip is produced when the maximum possible area of the tyre's contact patch is at the optimum working temperature and orientation to the road surface. Tyre temperature is one of the most important parameters affecting the performance of the car, and engineers will go to great lengths to adjust the car set-up to ensure that the tyres are working as effectively as possible, although ultimate performance must be balanced against wear rate. A relatively small change in tyre temperature can have a significant effect on tyre performance and wear rate.

↑ Tyres are a vital part of the performance equation, and the car must be set up to ensure that the tyres are working effectively.

For the 2010 season, the FIA regulations stipulated that each driver could use no more than 11 sets of dry-weather tyres during a race weekend, six of 'prime' specification and five of 'option' specification, prime being the harder compound and option being the softer compound, to be used as follows:

- Three sets of dry-weather tyres for use during P1 and P2 practice sessions on Friday (two sets of prime and one option). One set of prime tyres to be returned to the supplier before the start of P2 and one further set of prime and one set of option to be returned before the start of P3.
- Eight further sets of dry-weather tyres, four each of prime and option, to be used for the remainder of the event. One set of each specification (prime and option) must be returned before the start of the first qualifying session (Q1) and may not be used during the remainder of the event.
- Prior to the start of Q1, intermediate and extreme-wet tyres may only be used if the track has been declared wet by the Race Director, following which intermediate, wet or dry-weather tyres may be used for the remainder of qualifying.
- At the start of the race, each car that took part in the final qualifying session (Q3) must be fitted with the same tyres with which the driver set his grid time. This is only necessary if dry-weather tyres were used to set the grid time and if dry-weather tyres are used at the start of the race.
- Unless he has used intermediate or wet-weather tyres during the race, each driver must use at least one set of each specification (prime and option) of dry-weather tyre during the race.

CONSTRUCTION

The tyres are of radial construction, but precise details are kept a closely guarded secret by the tyre manufacturers. The tyres are designed with minimum weight and maximum strength in mind.

Rather than a road car's steel-belted-carcass tyres, which are designed with durability and resistance to road imperfections in mind, F1 tyres use a lightweight nylon and polyester carcass, made up from a complex weave pattern designed to cope with the high vertical, lateral and longitudinal loads acting on the tyre. Although the surface of most F1 tracks is relatively smooth, the tyres must still be able to cope with the punishment inflicted on them when the car runs over the kerbs (or 'rumble strips') around the track. On some street circuits, such as Monaco, the tyres also have to cope with the car running over drain covers, etc.

A tyre produces grip in two main ways – through adhesion and by deformation.

Adhesion is effectively the chemical interaction between the tyre and the track surface that enables the tyre to 'stick' to the track. An important factor affecting adhesion is the layer of rubber that is deposited on the track surface during a race weekend. This generally improves the grip available as the weekend progresses, and this is why a driver will spin the rear wheels to lay down a strip of rubber when he moves away from his grid slot at the start of the parade lap. When taking up his grid position for the start, the driver will aim to ensure that the rear wheels are positioned on the previously laid-down rubber, to improve adhesion and acceleration at the start.

In F1 tyre-technology terms, deformation refers primarily to the actual tyre tread compound layer rather than the tyre itself. The tyre construction, pressure and compound all influence the time taken for the whole tyre to deform and regain its intended shape when passing over imperfections in the track.

The tyre compound is designed to allow the tread to deform as it runs over imperfections, to maximise the area of rubber in contact with the track surface. More rubber in contact with the track results in greater adhesion. But increased deformation also results in energy loss and increased friction, so a delicate balance has to be maintained. The 'hardness' of the tyre compound has a direct effect on its deformation, and one of the aims when engineering a tyre compound is to produce compounds that allow the tread to deform quickly and regain its shape relatively slowly. This helps to maintain grip by keeping more rubber in contact with the track surface for longer.

The tyre tread has bracing plies embedded in it to provide rigidity and to hold the rubber tread together. The tread compound itself is the subject of a great deal of research and development. The main chemical constituents are carbon, oil and sulphur. By changing the percentages of these main constituents, and by altering the recipe of other constituents, different tyre compounds can be created. In general, the higher the percentage of oil used, the softer the compound.

Because of the way the tyre plies are laid up during manufacture, the tyres exhibit a condition known as 'ply-steer'. The effect is to cause the tyre to generate a lateral (sideways) force as it rolls. The force generated may tend to push the tyre towards the car, or away from it, depending on the tyre, and for this reason even slick tyres are 'handed' for use on a specific side of the car, and marked accordingly.

TREAD PATTERNS AND COMPOUNDS

During 2010 four different tyre compounds were available – super-soft, soft, medium and hard. Each compound varied in grip level, heat and wear-resistance, and each had a different optimum working temperature window. The two softer-compound options had a lower working temperature range than the two harder compounds.

To suit varying weather conditions, three tyre tread patterns were available – slicks (dry conditions), intermediates (damp track and light rain) and extreme-wets (heavy rain and standing water). Slick tyres have no tread and are intended for use in dry conditions. Intermediate tyres have a shallow tread all the way across the width of the tyre. Extreme-wet tyres have a deep tread designed to move standing water away from the track surface, therefore preventing a film of water building up between the tyre and the track surface.

For each race weekend, the tyre manufacturer selected two tyre compounds (from super-soft, soft, medium and hard) to be made available to all teams. For circuits with a warm climate, medium- and hard-compound tyres were usually selected, while for low ambient temperatures, soft or super-soft compounds were used. The FIA regulations stipulated that each car must use both of the selected compounds at some point during the race, meaning that at least one tyre-change pit stop was compulsory.

TEMPERATURES AND PRESSURES

The operating temperature and pressure of the tyres is critical to their performance. The tyres operate at maximum efficiency within only a narrow temperature range, and at the start of the race, after a pit stop to fit new tyres, or after running behind a safety car, the tyres will often cool to a temperature outside that optimum range. This affects the handling of the car, as lower grip will be available. The driver must then drive accordingly until the tyre temperature is back within the optimum working range, as Mark Webber explains: "The pace of the safety car is quite slow. The cars don't like driving behind the safety car – the engines get hot, but everything else gets cold, brakes and tyres mainly – which is a big performance thing for the drivers. The tyres also lose pressure, and then the car will start touching the ground a little harder as well, so lots of things come into play when the car is driven slowly. The aero won't change a huge amount, but the car will become quite unpredictable on cold tyres."

When the car is in the garage or pitlane, electric tyre blankets are fitted to the tyres to heat them to optimum working temperature. These blankets are left in place for as long as possible, and removed just before the car takes to the track. On the parade lap prior to the start of the race, and prior to the restart when running behind a safety car, drivers can often be seen weaving their cars

⬇ Intermediate tyres are used on a damp track or in light rain.

furiously from side to side in an attempt to build up tyre temperature. If tyre temperature drops, pressure will also drop as a consequence.

The density of air changes with temperature, so temperature changes can lead to a significant change in tyre pressure. To minimise variations in tyre pressure, in 2010 Bridgestone supplied tyres filled with dry air.

A very small variation in tyre pressure (just 0.2bar or 2–3psi) can have a significant effect on handling. The typical pressure for an F1 car is around 1.1bar (16psi), around half that of an average road car.

By analysing data collected during testing, races and simulation, the team can make crude predictions of tyre wear and performance at a particular track before the car turns a wheel. Supplemented by the tyre manufacturer's data and predictions, this data can be used to arrive at a base set-up for the car at the start of the race weekend.

To enable the team to monitor the condition of the tyres when the car is on-track, tyre pressure and temperature sensors are fitted. A wireless tyre pressure sensor is fitted inside each wheel rim behind the tyre valve. The tyre temperature sensors monitor the external surface temperature of the tyres – the front sensors are mounted in the mirror housings and the rear sensors are mounted on the upper surface of the floor. The sensors transmit data back to the engineers, enabling them to monitor tyre performance and to warn the driver of any developing problems. The temperature sensors are infra-red, similar to the brake temperature sensor described on page 71.

Details of how the car is set up to optimise tyre performance are given on pages 148–157.

↑ To reduce the time taken to reach optimum operating temperature, the tyres are heated in electric blankets before fitting to the car.

→ A tyre showing signs of lateral graining. The surface of the rubber has failed under high lateral (cornering) loads and rolled up into ridges on the surface of the tyre.

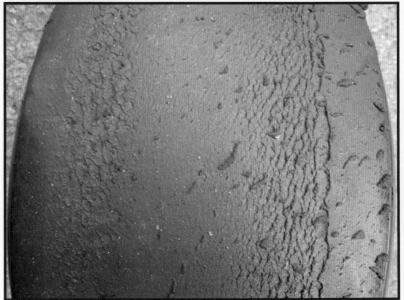

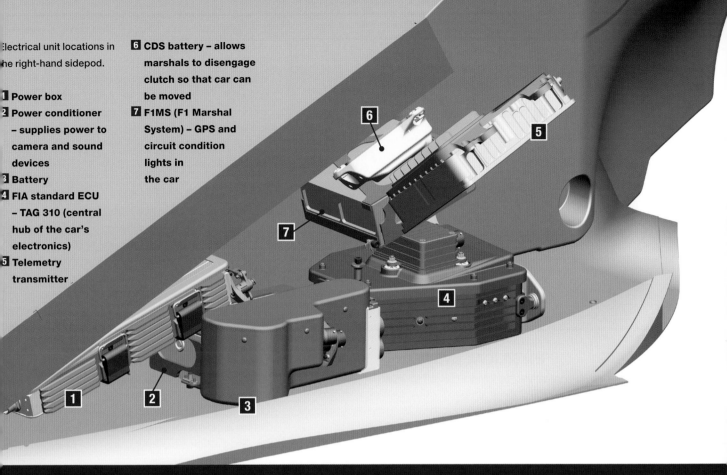

Electrical unit locations in the right-hand sidepod.

1 Power box

2 Power conditioner – supplies power to camera and sound devices

3 Battery

4 FIA standard ECU – TAG 310 (central hub of the car's electronics)

5 Telemetry transmitter

6 CDS battery – allows marshals to disengage clutch so that car can be moved

7 F1MS (F1 Marshal System) – GPS and circuit condition lights in the car

ELECTRONICS

lectronics are the life-blood of the modern F1 car, and without electronic control systems the cars simply could not function in their current form. Electronics are used in some form in almost every system on the car.

One-way telemetry is permitted – from the car to the pits. No pit-to-car telemetry is permitted, which means that no adjustments to the car's systems or set-up can be carried out remotely.

There are strict limits imposed by the FIA on the use of electronic systems, particularly in relation to driver aids, and the use of systems such as anti-lock braking (ABS) and traction control is banned. In order to police the regulations, the FIA has access to the components and software used in all the electronic control systems on the car, and FIA engineers are able to check that there are no 'hidden' systems that would break the intent or spirit of the regulations. In effect, the regulations state that anything that fits on the end of a wire – ECUs, sensors, actuators, etc – must be checked and approved by the FIA before it can be used during a race weekend. This enables

the FIA to determine exactly what each device and system is being used for.

A 12-volt electrical system is fitted, and on the RB6 the working current is around 30–40 amps, similar to that used in a well-equipped family car.

⬇ The umbilical can be seen on the left of this picture connected to the 'flying saucer' gantry above the car.

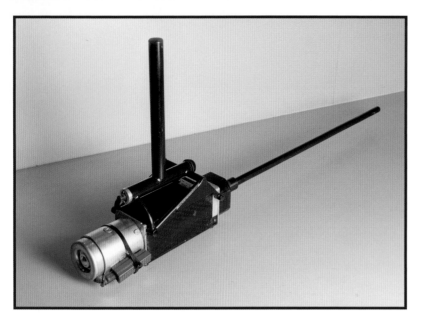

↑ Various types of electric starter are used, but they all consist of an electric motor, a long driveshaft and a handle (single vertical grip in this case).

STARTING SYSTEM

One notable feature missing from F1 cars is an on-board starter system. The engine must be started using an external, remotely powered and operated starter motor. The starter is not part of the car's electrical system, but it is worth explaining here how it works.

The starter takes the form of a high-torque motor, a reduction gearbox and a long driveshaft that passes through the diffuser to engage with a shaft at the rear of the transmission. Heavy-duty cabling connects the starter to a large – and very heavy! – 24-volt battery mounted on a trolley for portability.

The starter and the battery used to power it need to be heavy-duty due to the very high torque, and revs, required to start the 2.4-litre V8 engine. Unlike an 'ordinary' car engine, which will typically start at around 1,000rpm, most F1 engines idle at around 2,500rpm minimum, and so must be turned a lot faster to get them started. Starting the engine is not the most pleasurable job in the pitlane, as it involves holding the starter still as it tries to twist away from the operator's grip, while keeping it engaged with the transmission, and then moving rapidly out of the way once the engine fires to avoid the hot (around 900ºC) exhaust gases blowing through the diffuser at the back of the car!

UMBILICAL SYSTEM

When the car is in the pit garage, pitlane or on the grid, an 'umbilical' cable is plugged in. This cable attaches to a connector in the right-hand sidepod, and provides remote power for all the car's systems (to avoid battery drain), and a means of downloading data and monitoring the car's systems. If the car is in the garage, the umbilical will be plugged in to the overhead 'flying saucer' gantry suspended from the garage roof above the car.

BATTERY AND ALTERNATOR

The power supply system for the car works in exactly the same way as any car, with a 12-volt battery charged by an alternator.

The big difference between the system fitted on an F1 car and that on a road car is the size and weight of the components. Whereas a 'normal' car battery is often a challenge to lift and of substantial size, the lithium battery used on the RB6 is around the size of a typical camcorder battery, and can easily be held in the palm of the hand. The battery is located in the right-hand sidepod.

The alternator is gear-driven from the front of the engine crankshaft at around half engine speed, and it too is extremely compact and light, both to save weight and to help with packaging around the engine.

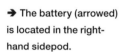

→ The battery (arrowed) is located in the right-hand sidepod.

→ The extremely compact lithium battery, little bigger than a camcorder battery.

→ → The car's main electrical units.

1 Power box
2 FIA standard ECU
3 Telemetry transmitter

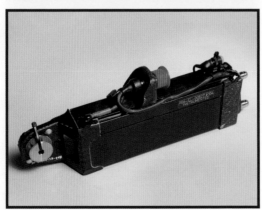

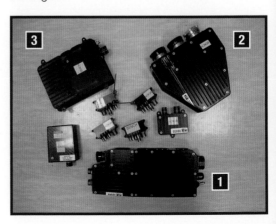

FIA STANDARD ECU

The FIA regulations specify: "All components of the engine, gearbox, clutch, differential and KERS (not used during 2010) in addition to all associated actuators must be controlled by an Electronic Control Unit (ECU) which has been manufactured by an FIA-designated supplier to a specification determined by the FIA." The current designated supplier is McLaren Electronic Systems, who supply the 'standard' ECU to all the teams on the grid.

All the teams must use exactly the same ECU and the supplied software to run the car's systems, but they are free to tune the software using data as they choose. The software has built-in protection to prevent the teams' software engineers from using hidden codes to run illegal systems such as traction control. All a team's data logging information for the car is stored in the ECU in a standard format, and is accessible to the FIA at any time.

The ECU is powered by a regulated power box, which takes an electrical feed from the alternator and battery, and feeds all the electrical systems on the car. The power box and ECU can be located on the car wherever the team chooses, and on the RB6 both units are in the right-hand sidepod. Both are shielded against electrical interference and are fixed on flexible mountings to reduce the effects of vibration. The ECU has three substantial multi-plug wiring connectors, with over 100 pins in each connector.

RADIO COMMUNICATIONS

The car's radio communications system allows the driver to communicate with his engineers when on-track. Two-way verbal communications are allowed under the regulations, but all other communications between the car and pits must be one-way.

The driver's radio system has a push-to-talk button on the steering wheel, and the voice data is transmitted over a secure, encrypted channel to prevent other teams from listening in to the conversation. The team must provide the decryption code to the FIA to enable monitoring of radio traffic. The FIA can listen in to the voice data on a small time delay, but they can hear all the conversation, so they are aware of exactly what is happening between the driver and engineers. The FIA also shares this time-delayed voice data with FOM (Formula One Management) so that it can be broadcast as part of the TV and radio coverage.

Even though the radio is an important tool during a race, it does not replace the pit-board signals, which remain an essential source of information for the driver, as Sebastian Vettel explains: "You have to check every single time because your radio could fail. You tend to rely on the radio, but

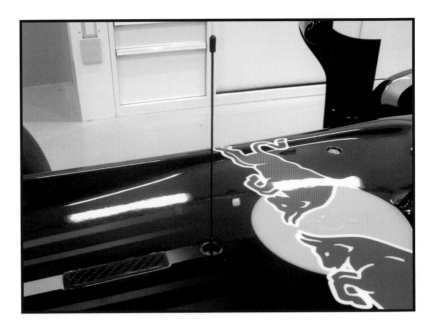

you should never forget the pit board and you do get some information shown on the pit board, like position and laps. It is unnecessary to talk too much over the radio, as you can do it simply via the pit board, but you have to watch it every single lap. There are some laps where you struggle to see it, in particular when you are racing many cars, because everybody is showing their pit boards to their drivers, but you get used to it."

The driver listens to the radio using earpieces taped directly into his ears to try to reduce the effects of ambient engine and airstream noise, and a microphone is fitted inside the driver's helmet. The microphone uses a noise-cancelling system, similar to that used in some light aircraft, to reduce the unavoidable effects of engine noise.

During practice and the race, there's often a lot of radio 'chatter' between driver and team, but during a qualifying session, when the driver is on a 'hot' lap, the radio is an unnecessary distraction, as Sebastian Vettel confirms: "Usually I don't talk on a 'quali' lap. You are all by yourself, alone with your car."

The aerial for the radio system is located on the top of the chassis, ahead of the driver.

COCKPIT DISPLAY

See pages 116–117 for details.

DRIVER'S DRINK SYSTEM

For races at particularly hot or physical venues, a drinking system is fitted to enable the driver to take on fluids during the race. The drink itself is usually a bespoke sports drink blended for the driver, and is contained in a flexible bladder cell. The bladder is housed in a casing on the left-hand side of the cockpit, with an electric pump mounted on the floor under the driver's seat. The driver uses a button on

↑ The aerial for the pit-to-car radio is located on the chassis ahead of the driver.

the steering wheel to activate the pump when he wants to drink. The liquid is pumped from the bladder through a tube that passes into the driver's helmet.

Before the race, the filled bladder is placed in a container that exactly replicates the casing in the car, and this container is put in a freezer. Once frozen, the bladder is fitted into the housing in the car. In this way the drink is made more palatable, at least for the early stages of the race.

Although the drink isn't the last word in refreshments, it does its job, as Mark Webber explains: "We won't be drinking in a braking area, but every driver will have a drink on some of the straights when they get a chance, just to wet their mouths and try to get some fluids in. We're working pretty hard in there and it gets pretty hot with all our gear on, so it's nice to be able to have a drink. It's not, obviously, fresh out of the fridge, it's pretty warm, it's not extremely palatable, but it's important just to get the fluids back in the body."

DATA-LOGGING EQUIPMENT AND TIMING SENSORS
FIA data logging and medical warning light
The FIA specify the fitment of an Accident Data Recorder (ADR) unit, which is located under the driver's seat. This unit must be connected to two accelerometers mounted on the centreline of the survival cell, and contains a 'rolling' data logger, which holds two minutes' worth of data. If the car is involved in an accident, the logger stops, and data from the two minutes preceding the accident is stored and can be analysed. This can be very useful in determining the cause of an accident, and is important from a safety point of view.

The ADR is connected to a medical warning light, which is located in front of the car's cockpit opening. The medical warning light is a blue LED that flashes when set parameters are met to give the marshals

an instant indication of the severity of an accident.

The team do not have direct access to the data stored in the ADR, and the data must be downloaded by the FIA and passed on to the team.

Team data logging
The team is free to fit any sensors it chooses for data-logging purposes, and they can be located anywhere on the car, but all sensors must be checked and approved by the FIA before they can be used during a race weekend.

Numerous different types of sensors are used on the car to measure a vast number of parameters, and typical examples include:

- Tyre pressure and temperature sensors
- Ride-height sensors (laser sensors are used to measure front and rear ride-height)
- Air speed (pitot tube)
- Engine oil and coolant temperature and pressure sensors
- Transmission oil temperature and pressure sensors
- Strain gauges fitted to the suspension push-rods and pull-rods
- Steering torque sensor
- Numerous engine sensors
- Gearbox input and output shaft speed sensors
- Brake temperature and wear sensors

Numerous other sensors are used around the car, and when the car is on-track all these sensors

➜➜ A pitot tube on the front of the chassis measures the air speed over the front of the car.

➜ A medical warning light (arrowed) warns the marshals of the severity of an accident.

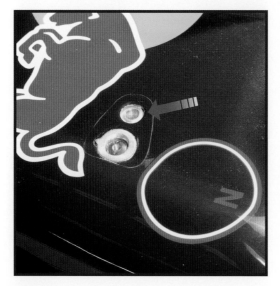

transmit information continuously back to the team in the pits. A limited bandwidth is available to transmit 'real-time' data during a race weekend, and this effectively limits the amount of data that the team can monitor accurately.

Compared with some other sensors, for example, a suspension transducer needs quite a significant bandwidth to be able to transmit a useful level of data – if it transmits at a low frequency to leave bandwidth available for other sensors, the data trace produced in the pits is likely to be more of a 'sawtooth' trace than a smooth curve, which limits its usefulness. The choice is really between a lot of sensors transmitting information at a low frequency, which is only of limited use, and a few selected sensors transmitting at a high frequency, which is far more useful.

The team can also record data in the FIA ECU, for later download in the pits. This data is accessible to the FIA at any time.

TIMING TRANSPONDERS

The car is fitted with timing transponders to activate the FIA timing equipment at each circuit. The timing transponder for each car carries a unique identifying code. The timing equipment is activated when the car passes over transponder loops buried under the surface of the track. The loops are located at various points around the track, enabling track 'sector' timing comparisons.

The transponders can also receive data from the timing loops to activate the on-board cameras, and also to activate the red, yellow and blue 'track-condition' lights in the cockpit.

The primary transponder is fitted in line with the front-wheel axis. A back-up sensor is fitted at the rear of the car, on the crash structure under the rain light, in case the primary transponder fails.

A set of RB6 chassis wiring looms.

WIRING AND CONNECTORS

The wiring and wiring connectors used on an F1 car have to survive in an extremely hostile environment, and must withstand high vibration levels and, in some areas of the car, very high heat levels. The wiring harnesses are designed to be as light as possible, and must be screened to guard against electrical interference.

Bespoke wiring looms are made for the car, and each loom must be manufactured with high accuracy and to tight tolerances to ensure that it fits in the car as intended by the design team. Aerospace-quality wiring and connectors are used throughout.

CAMERAS

All F1 cars carry cameras to provide on-board footage for TV coverage. The cameras provide a feed to FOM (Formula One Management), the organisation that provides on-board TV footage to broadcasters around the world.

The FIA regulations specify that the car must be able to carry cameras in eight locations – one on top of the roll hoop, one either side of the airbox, one either side of the nose, one on the chassis ahead of the cockpit opening, and one in each rear-view mirror. For all locations except the mirrors, special camera housings must be fitted on the bodywork to accommodate the cameras. The housings must be fitted in all required locations even if cameras are not mounted in them for a particular race. The camera housings are designed to be aerodynamically neutral, so that no aerodynamic advantage can be gained from them.

FIA regulations stipulate the dimensions and shape of the camera housings, and the angle at which they can be fitted relative to the airflow. The angle between the main horizontal axis of a camera and the 'reference plane' (the flat plane running through the lowest point of the car's floor) can be no more than 5°.

The aerial for the FIA GPS system is located on the right-hand sidepod. The GPS system transmits track-position data to Race Control, enabling the monitoring of each car's position on the track.

→ This T-shaped housing accommodates two cameras, one facing forwards, the other rearwards. A lower housing provides an alternative location.

→ → Each mirror can house a camera in the arrowed location, which is empty in this photo.

→ In the early part of the season, the RB6 carried camera housings on either side of the nose.

→ → From the British Grand Prix, the nose camera housings were moved to a position under the nose, just above the front-wing mainplane.

↓ The rear rain light is mounted on the rear crash structure.

↘ The rain light is designed to improve the car's visibility to following drivers in heavy spray.

Cameras are not always fitted in all the locations provided. If no camera is fitted, the housings are ballasted to the same weight as a housing with a camera fitted. At each race, the officials will suggest to the teams where they would like to have cameras fitted on each car, although two cameras – one facing forwards, the other rearwards – are always fitted in the T-shaped housing on top of the roll hoop.

The transmitter and aerial that send the camera signals from the car to FOM's receiving equipment is located in the 'T'-shaped camera housing on top of the roll hoop.

All camera equipment is provided to the teams by FOM.

REAR RAIN LIGHT

All cars must carry a red LED light on the rear crash structure to make the car more visible from the rear in heavy rain or spray. The lights are supplied by an FIA-approved supplier – McLaren Electronic Systems during 2010.

The light contains 15 high-intensity red LEDs and the associated control circuit. When activated, the light flashes at a frequency of 4Hz (four times per second). The driver can switch on the light using a switch on the steering wheel.

Sebastian Vettel provides these observations about the visibility of the rain light on the car in front during a race: "It depends on how much spray there is, how much water. Because of the aerodynamics the cars suck out a lot of water on the track, so you don't necessarily see the rain light, you see the spray more – the closer you get the better you can see the rain light in general. It's a good tool for us to work out how far the other car is ahead and to see the other car."

HYDRAULIC SYSTEM

The hydraulic system is a vital part of any modern F1 car, and is used to actuate many of the car's major systems. The hydraulic system can be likened to the electrical system in a road car, in that it provides a reservoir of energy that can be switched and routed to operate a number of systems. Whereas on a road car the electrical system typically operates the lighting system, heater, windscreen wipers, electric windows, central locking, etc, on the RB6 the hydraulic system operates the following systems:

- Throttle
- Clutch
- Gearchange
- Differential
- Power steering
- Front-wing adjuster mechanism

Although the brakes are hydraulically operated, the brake hydraulic circuit is completely isolated from the car's main hydraulic system.

Hydraulic actuators are used in preference to electrical or pneumatic actuators because a hydraulic (fluid) system has a relatively large 'power density' compared with an electrical or pneumatic (air) system – a very small hydraulic actuator can do a lot of work, and therefore offers a significant weight-saving and packaging advantage over an equivalent electrical or pneumatic actuator. Similarly, once a pump has generated hydraulic fluid pressure, a relatively small high-pressure accumulator can store a large amount of energy in a small space – the high-pressure hydraulic accumulator typically holds less than 300cc of fluid. Although a pneumatic system works in a similar way to a hydraulic system, a pneumatic system requires significantly larger actuators and works at a lower pressure, so is not capable of providing the power required to operate all the systems on an F1 car. Put simply, hydraulics offer a lot of bang for your buck in terms of weight and size!

On the RB6 an engine-driven hydraulic pump supplies fluid to a high-pressure accumulator, from where the fluid is fed to a hydraulic manifold supplying the throttle, clutch, gearbox, differential, power steering and front-wing adjuster mechanism hydraulic circuits. After passing through the relevant

⬆ The hydraulic manifold is designed to be removed with the gearbox to avoid the need to break into the hydraulic circuit. An RB4 manifold is shown here.

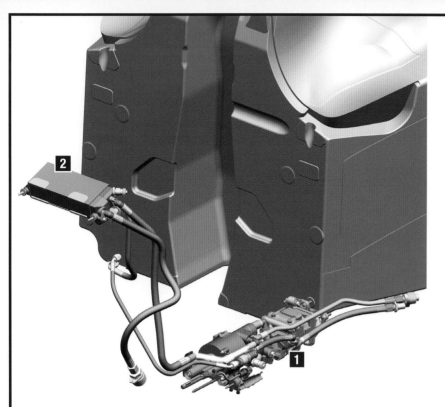

is absolutely critical, and failures in the hydraulic system are one of the most common causes of retirements during races. This was particularly evident during 2010, when several of the newer teams experienced problems with hydraulic system reliability. The hydraulic system components have to operate in a very harsh environment, and are subjected to high vibration levels and high temperatures, with the hydraulic fluid typically operating at a temperature of over 100°C. Due to weight considerations, an F1 car has no back-up systems – probably its greatest vulnerability. Tolerances, fits, component surface treatments, seals and filtration are all critical and, over time, a team builds up a significant database of experience to help them reduce the chances of problems. Many of the parts used in the hydraulic system are long-lead-time components in terms of manufacturing, and so any fundamental problems requiring parts to be re-engineered can take several days at best.

⬆ A schematic view of the engine/gearbox-mounted hydraulic system components.

1 Hydraulic pump
2 Fluid cooler

actuator, the fluid returns through low-pressure lines to a low-pressure accumulator that feeds the inlet to the hydraulic pump.

　　Reliability of the hydraulic system on an F1 car

PRESSURE PUMP

The hydraulic pump is driven via a shaft from the engine, and pressurises the hydraulic fluid to around 200bar (2,900psi). The pump is a variable-displacement swash-plate pump, which,

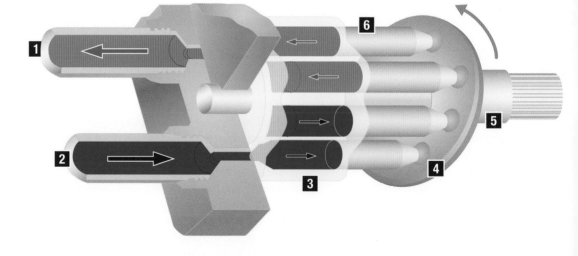

➡⬎ A schematic view showing the operating principle of a typical swash-plate pump.

1 Outlet port
2 Inlet port
3 Cylinder block
4 Swash-plate
5 Driveshaft
6 Piston

▮ System pressure
　(high)
▮ Return line pressure
　(low)

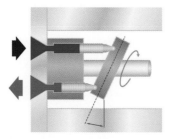

Maximum swash-plate angle
(maximum displacement)

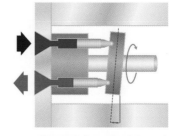

Decreased swash-plate angle
(partial displacement)

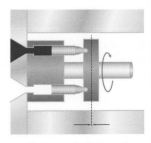

Zero swash-plate angle
(zero displacement)

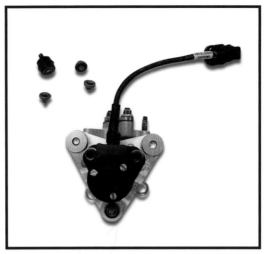

by varying the swash-plate angle, is able to deliver pressure and volume of fluid based on demand, regardless of engine speed. A swash-plate pump is very efficient, and is controlled by an internal hydraulic control valve to ensure that the required pressure and flow of fluid is always available.

ACCUMULATOR

A diaphragm-type high-pressure accumulator is used and typically holds around 300cc of fluid. The accumulator is cylindrical, and contains a rubber diaphragm, one side of which is charged with a high-pressure inert gas (usually nitrogen) and the other side of which is directly in contact with the hydraulic fluid. The accumulator is fitted to ensure that constant pressure is always maintained in the system, and that a sufficient reserve of fluid is available for situations where high demand is made on the system.

MANIFOLD

The main hydraulic manifold is mounted on the gearbox. When the gearbox is removed, the manifold stays with it to avoid the need to break into the hydraulic circuit. Where any hydraulic lines need to be disconnected to remove the gearbox, dry-break couplings are used.

VALVES

The key to the operation of the hydraulic system, and the reason why it can do its job so effectively, is the Moog valve (see panel on page 108) – a highly efficient electrically operated servo valve that controls an hydraulic actuator. A typical Moog valve can control the equivalent of 5bhp hydraulic power using just a tiny electrical current of around 10mA, and is able to control the flow of hydraulic fluid extremely precisely. Not only is a Moog

valve very efficient but, critically, it is extremely accurate and incredibly quick to respond to control inputs. A Moog valve has a response time of less than one millisecond, and the ability to move a valve from its fully closed to fully open position in less than three milliseconds.

To provide accurate control of a particular system or component, the circuit operating a Moog valve needs to receive information on the state, or position, of the component being controlled, usually via feedback from a position or pressure sensor, depending on the system. For example, the valve controlling the position of the gear selector barrel responds according to signals received from a sensor reading the position of the selector barrel.

FILTRATION

Two things can destroy a hydraulic system very quickly – air and dirt. To avoid any possibility of air entering the system, the components are all manufactured to very high tolerances, and very effective seals are used throughout.

To reduce the risk of dirt or contamination entering the critical components, a very high level of filtration is used throughout the system. Renewable cartridge filters are used, and these are changed as a matter of course when the system is bled.

MAINTENANCE

Due to its sensitivity to dirt and contamination, and the fact that the hydraulic components are very reliable, the hydraulic system is rarely broken into. Any hydraulic lines that need to be disconnected to carry out work on the car, such as the front-wing hydraulic actuator connections on the nose, or the pump connections to the engine, are fitted with dry-break couplings to avoid the need for routine bleeding.

Moog valves appeared in the 1950s and have been developed constantly ever since. The design is very clever: a Moog valve uses the pressure of the fluid flow that it is controlling to power the valve, and therefore can control such a relatively large amount of power using such tiny electrical consumption.

The basic principle of operation of a Moog valve is as follows:

■ The valve allows a small amount of fluid to flow continuously through two small jets located opposite each other. A small flap valve is located between the two jets, connected to the armature in a torque motor. This is similar to an electric motor, but instead of the armature rotating, it twists a very small amount – around two degrees at most – under the influence of the electromagnetic field generated in the coils wound around it.

■ When the armature moves (twists), it moves the flap valve, which then partially obstructs the flow through one of the two jets, increasing the pressure in that jet compared with the other, which is unobstructed.

■ Both jets are connected, via fluid galleries in the valve body, to either end of a sliding valve, known as a spool valve, which runs in a cylinder containing several valve ports.

The difference in pressure between the two pressure feeds from the jets causes the spool valve to slide along the cylinder in the direction required, so partially, and eventually fully, uncovering one of the main pressure feed ports. The fluid from the uncovered main pressure feed port acts directly on the spool valve, and also vents from the cylinder via an outlet port, which provides the control pressure to the actuator to which the Moog valve is connected.

■ A cleverly designed feedback spring fixed to the end of the armature-mounted flap valve is the key to the Moog valve's accuracy and level of control. The feedback spring comprises a flexible 'arm' with a ball-shaped end that locates in a groove in the spool valve. As the spool valve moves in the cylinder, the feedback spring opposes the movement of the flap valve and armature, and at a certain point the two opposing forces reach equilibrium, stabilising the position of the spool valve, which in turn stabilises the degree of restriction to the fluid flow through the main pressure feed port. This enables very small changes in the control current at the armature to produce precise changes in the fluid flow, and so the movement of the actuator.

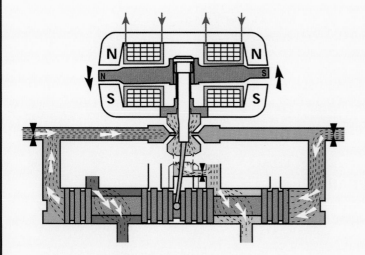

Valve responding to change
in electrical input

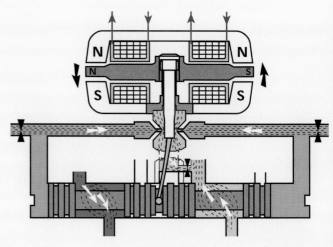

Valve condition
following change

SAFETY EQUIPMENT

Safety is paramount in F1, and the level of safety has improved dramatically in recent years. After the tragic death of Ayrton Senna in 1994, a raft of improvements to track and car safety were implemented, and safety improvements are now constantly on the agenda. Driving an F1 car will never be risk-free, but the safety measures in place today mean that, thankfully, serious injuries are extremely rare. Mark Webber's frightening accident during the 2010 European Grand Prix at Valencia, when he hit the rear of Heikki Kovalainen's Lotus, is a good example of F1 safety measures in action, and is testament to the strength of the RB6. In spite of the car being launched into the air and landing inverted, before righting itself and impacting the tyre wall at high speed, Mark unfastened his harness and walked away unscathed.

SURVIVAL CELL

One of the most important safety features of the car is the survival cell, which is integral with the chassis and designed to protect the driver from serious injury in the event of an accident.

The FIA regulations stipulate that the survival cell must form a continuous closed structure containing the fuel tank and the cockpit, with a bulkhead between the two. The regulations also specify certain minimum dimensions, and the location and dimensions of side-impact protection that must be fitted to the survival cell.

As part of the chassis homologation procedure, the survival cell is subjected to various impact tests and static 'squeeze' tests prior to the start of the season. All the tests must be passed, without damage to the main structure, before the chassis is homologated and the completed car is allowed to race. See 'FIA crash tests' on pages 176–177 for more details of the various requirements. Further details of the design and construction of the chassis and survival cell are given on pages 26–32, in the 'Chassis ('tub')' section.

ROLL STRUCTURES

In order to protect the driver from the risk of injury if the car becomes inverted during an accident, the FIA regulations state that two roll structures must be incorporated into the structure of the chassis – one behind the driver's head and one on the top of the chassis in front of the driver. Details of the roll structures are provided on page 31.

⬆ The most obvious items of safety equipment are the drivers' helmets.

↘ A schematic showing the RB6 crash structures (red). The side-impact structures are located in the sidepods.

CRASH STRUCTURES

To protect the driver in the event of an impact, the FIA regulations stipulate that impact-absorbing crash structures must be fitted to the front, rear and sides of the car, as follows:

- The front crash structure need not be an integral part of the survival cell, but must be solidly attached to it, and on the RB6, as with all other F1 cars, the crash structure is incorporated in the nose design.
- The rear crash structure must be fitted behind the gearbox.
- The side crash structures must be fitted "between the front and rear roll structures, on each side of the survival cell, and must be solidly attached to it".

The crash structures are designed to absorb energy in the event of an impact. Whereas a road-car crash structure absorbs energy by deforming (crumpling), the carbon-fibre crash structures on F1 cars absorb energy by disintegrating, which is why it is sometimes possible to see a cloud of carbon dust and debris if an F1 car suffers a heavy impact.

HEAD PROTECTION

To provide extra protection for the driver's head, removable foam headrest padding is provided around the cockpit opening. This headrest padding takes the form of a one-piece foam structure, covered with kevlar plies. The headrest padding locates on two horizontal pegs behind the driver's head, and is fastened by two turnbuckle fasteners, one at each front corner of the structure, which can easily be released by the driver.

The headrest padding is designed to compress if the driver's helmet hits it, to prevent his head from coming into contact with any structural part of the car.

The headrest padding has to be removed for the driver to get in and out of the car, as it fits over the tops of his shoulders in order to allow the padding to be close to his helmet when he is sitting in the car. Once the driver is strapped into the cockpit, the pit crew will fit the headrest padding before the car is allowed out on to the track.

LEG PROTECTION

Foam padding is fitted inside the front of the chassis, around the driver's legs, to reduce the chances of injury in the event of an accident.

⬇ The driver's head is extremely well protected in the cockpit, with side and rear protection to reduce the risk of injury.

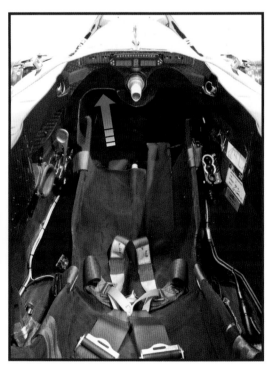

↖↖ Two turnbuckles (arrowed) secure the headrest padding.

← Padding (arrowed) in the footwell protects the driver's legs.

↖ The cockpit headrest padding removed from the car.

↓ The footwell foam padding removed from the car.

↑ A view of the rear of the cockpit with the headrest padding removed, showing how the top of the chassis is sculpted to provide support for the padding.

WHEEL TETHERS

Wheel tethers are fitted to prevent the wheels from flying off in the event of an accident. If a wheel does become detached, its tether will also reduce the chances of the wheel making contact with the driver's head.

The wheel tethers connect the front suspension uprights to the chassis, and the rear suspension uprights to the gearbox. The tethers take the form of ropes made from a synthetic polymer compound that has similar strength characteristics to carbon-fibre but can be woven into long strands. On the RB6 the tethers run through the suspension wishbones, protecting them in an accident and avoiding interference with the car's aerodynamics.

← The wheel tethers are made from synthetic polymer rope.

FUEL TANK AND FUEL LINES

The fuel tank is located inside the survival cell, with a bulkhead between the fuel tank compartment and the driver. The tank is designed to be resistant to impacts and tearing. Further details of the fuel tank are provided on page 32.

The fuel lines are fitted with dry-break connectors, which prevent fuel spillage if the connectors are separated during an accident. The fuel lines connect the fuel tank directly to the fuel pump and engine. A wire lanyard secures the fuel line connectors to the engine, so that in the event of an accident in which the engine comes away from the chassis, the fuel line connectors separate, effectively sealing the fuel lines to reduce the risk of fuel spillage and fire.

FIRE EXTINGUISHER

To comply with the FIA regulations, the car "must be fitted with a fire extinguishing system which will discharge into the cockpit and into the engine compartment."

A single extinguishant reservoir is fitted on the floor of the cockpit, between the driver's legs. This reservoir feeds discharge nozzles in the cockpit, and on the rear face of the rear chassis bulkhead, aimed into the 'engine compartment', towards the fuel line connections and the fuel rail on the engine. The reservoir can be tested and charged remotely to avoid having to remove it from the car. A fluid extinguishant is used, and a gas-discharge cylinder fitted to the top of the reservoir provides the pressure to discharge the system.

The regulations state that all parts of the extinguishing system must be located within the survival cell, and the fire extinguishing system must discharge 95 per cent of its contents at a constant pressure in no less than 10 seconds and no more than 30 seconds.

Three switches are fitted to operate the system – one can be operated by the driver, and is located in a panel on the right-hand side of the cockpit, and the other two are located externally, on either side of the bodywork, at the base of the rear roll hoop, above the sidepods. These external switches can be operated by marshals in the event of an accident or trackside fire, and have a loop that can be operated from a distance using a hook, in case a marshal cannot reach the switches by hand.

ELECTRICAL CUT-OFF

Three master electrical cut-off switches are fitted to the car, to cut the electrical supply to the ignition, fuel pumps and rear rain light, by means of a circuit-breaker switch. These switches are integral with the three fire extinguisher switches described previously.

FIA ACCIDENT DATA RECORDER (ADR) AND MEDICAL WARNING LIGHT

Details are provided on page 102.

→ The fire extinguisher reservoir is located on the cockpit floor, between the driver's legs. The gas discharge cylinder is arrowed.

→→ Two fire extinguisher nozzles (red) on the rear chassis bulkhead (viewed with engine removed).

→ External fire extinguisher switches (arrowed) are located on each side of the car (right-hand side shown).

DRIVER'S HARNESS

A six-point quick-release harness is fitted for the driver, with two shoulder straps, one pelvic strap and two crutch straps, all of which are secured by a central quick-release buckle. The harness needs to be very tight, and so must be fitted and tightened by one of the pit crew once the driver is sitting in the car. The harness fitted to the RB6 is supplied by Sabelt, and has a turnbuckle release mechanism – the driver has to turn the lever on the centre of the buckle in either direction to release the harness. When the turnbuckle is in the central position, with the lever pointing down, the buckle plates on the ends of the straps can be pushed into the buckle to lock them in place.

The harness mounting points are bonded and bolted into the chassis to ensure that they are secure and cannot separate from the chassis in a severe impact.

The harness components (including the webbing) are homologated by the FIA, and subjected to rigorous testing and inspection.

DRIVER'S SEAT

The driver has a bespoke seat that is moulded to fit the contours of his body exactly. To make the seat, a carbon-fibre shell is filled with quick-setting foam and covered with plastic sheeting. The driver then sits in the foam, wearing his overalls, and the foam moulds to the shape of his body, setting in exactly the correct shape.

All F1 cars have 'extractable' seats, so that the driver can be removed from his car in his seat, under medical supervision, in the event of an accident. The seat has a slot in the back to allow the fitment of an FIA-approved head-stabilisation device, which is carried by all extraction teams at F1 races in a standard 'FIA Extrication Bag'.

The seat locates on two pegs in the floor of the car, and is designed so that once the driver's harness has been released, the pelvic straps fall away over the edge of the seat as it is removed, and the crutch straps slide away through slots in the seat (the seat buckle is attached to one of the shoulder straps).

The seat is fitted with FIA-specified straps that can be used in conjunction with straps supplied in the FIA Bag to immobilise the driver in his seat prior to extraction. The driver can then be lifted from the car in his seat, using lifting straps that fit on to the straps on the seat using snap hooks.

← The driver's six-point harness and seat in position in the cockpit.

↓ Sebastian Vettel's seat removed from the car to show the attachment points for the FIA lifting straps (arrowed).

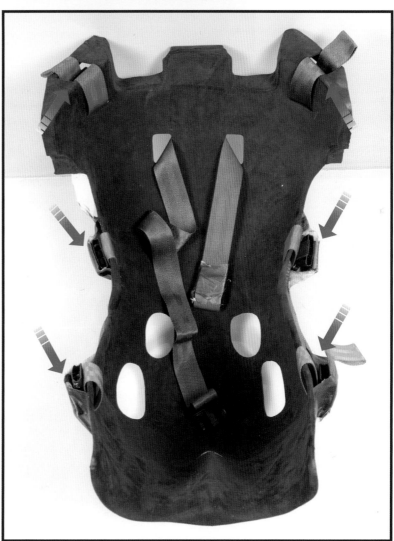

↑ The HANS device fits over the driver's shoulders, and the car's harness straps hold the shoulder yoke in position.

↓ This rear view of Mark Webber's HANS device shows the restraint strap which connects to the sides of his helmet.

HANS DEVICE

All drivers must use a HANS (Head And Neck Support) device to protect the head and neck in the event of an accident. The purpose of the HANS device is to prevent potentially fatal injuries that can occur in a heavy accident if the driver's head 'whips' forward, by maintaining the position of the driver's head in relation to his body.

The device consists of a yoke that fits over the driver's shoulders, with two tethers, one on either side, which attach to buckles on his helmet. The device is supported by the driver's shoulders, and fits under the harness shoulder straps, so that the device is secured to the driver, rather than to his seat or the car.

The HANS device is made from carbon-fibre, and must be homologated by the FIA.

DRIVER'S CLOTHING

The driver always wears protective clothing to provide protection in the event of a fire. The following items of clothing are worn, made predominantly from a special aramid plastic fabric called Nomex:

- Boots
- Gloves (gauntlet type)
- Balaclava
- Underwear (long-johns and a long-sleeved vest)
- Three-layer race suit

The race suit is designed to be as light as possible, and 'breathable' to cope with the perspiration produced by the driver during a race. All the sponsor's logos on the race suit are made from the same fire-resistant material, and even the thread used to sew the suit together is fire-resistant. The zip must be designed so that it does not melt in the high temperatures experienced in a fire, and does not transfer heat through the suit to the driver. The suit must have two epaulettes ('handles') incorporated on the tops of the shoulders to enable the driver to be pulled from the car if necessary.

The special Nomex material from which the race suit is manufactured is tested by exposure to an open flame with a temperature of around 300–400°C from a distance of 30mm. The material must not ignite for at least 10 seconds.

Race boots have very thin soles compared with normal shoes, to enable the driver to feel exactly what is happening when he operates the pedals, and to provide good grip. Similarly, the gloves are thin and supple to provide maximum feedback from the steering wheel and maximum 'feel' for the driver when operating the various controls on the steering wheel and in the cockpit.

DRIVER'S HELMET

The driver's helmet is a very personal item, but must conform to strict FIA safety regulations. The helmet is aerodynamically designed to minimise drag and disruption to the airflow over the car, and incorporates a microphone for the radio system and a hole for the tube of the on-board drink system.

Sample helmets undergo rigorous tests before they are homologated for use in F1, including impact tests, penetration tests and crush tests, plus a test of the HANS device buckles.

Helmets are designed to be as light as possible, both for comfort and safety reasons. A lighter helmet reduces the effect of high g-forces on the driver's head, and also reduces the loading on the driver's neck. An average F1 helmet weighs around 1.2kg.

The inside of the helmet contains foam padding to provide a comfortable fit and protection for the driver, and the padding has a Nomex fire-resistant covering. The outer shell of the helmet is usually formed from two layers, with an outer layer of carbon-fibre, covered with a reinforced resin to provide a smooth finish, and an inner Kevlar layer to provide added strength and impact resistance.

Helmets are fitted with air vents to allow a flow of air through the helmet, and these contain filters to keep out the worst of the debris from the track (such as fine rubber particles).

The visor is manufactured from polycarbonate, which provides a very high level of impact protection, and good visibility. Visors can be fitted with a series of 'tear-off' covers that can be pulled off by the driver once they pick up dirt, to clear his field of vision during a race.

⬆ The driver's underwear and balaclava provide extra protection in the event of a fire.

COCKPIT CONTROLS

↑ The cockpit is functional, with all controls easily accessible.

↓ A multi-function LED display is mounted at the top of the cockpit.

A modern F1 car is extremely complex to operate, and as well as 'simply' driving the car – steering, accelerating, changing gear, braking, and keeping an eye on the position of other cars on the track – the driver constantly has to monitor and adjust a number of systems designed to optimise the performance of the car. This level of multi-tasking is probably on a par with that required by a military jet pilot, and so to ease the driver's workload, the controls in the cockpit must be designed to be as intuitive to operate and as accessible as possible.

Most of the important controls that require frequent use during a race are mounted on the steering wheel. Although the control layout can be tailored to suit each driver's preferences, the team aims to keep the controls common to both cars wherever possible in order to avoid confusion for the engineers and mechanics working on both cars.

COCKPIT DISPLAY

Cockpit instrumentation is minimal, and on the RB6 a multi-function LED display is used, mounted at the top of the cockpit, above the steering wheel. This is relatively unusual, as many teams now incorporate the display in the steering wheel.

The driver can select the data displayed on the screen, and he can toggle between data such as engine revs, engine temperatures and pressures, gear selected and lap and sector times, as Sebastian Vettel explains: "It's the driver's choice

because the software allows different options of what can be displayed. Typically I have a display showing current gear, speed, lap time and delta time [his time compared to the fastest sector time]."

A series of gearchange indicators lights is fitted above the main display to inform the driver of the optimum point to change into a higher gear. The lights are important to ensure that the driver gets the best from the engine, as Mark Webber explains: "The lights are in our peripheral vision. You can change up quite well acoustically, but you definitely need the lights to be really, really accurate, to get the best from the engine's performance."

In addition, the main cockpit display incorporates red, yellow and blue lights, which display data transmitted from an FIA-controlled data system to mirror the trackside 'track condition' lights and marshals' flags. As with the flags, red means that the race has been stopped, yellow means 'caution' and blue means that a faster car is trying to overtake.

STEERING WHEEL

The steering wheel is one of the most important components on the car. As well as performing its obvious function as the interface between the driver and his car, providing him with feedback from the steering and front suspension, the steering wheel also acts as the platform for many of the car's main controls.

The steering wheel is made from carbon-fibre, and contains a built-in electronic control unit (ECU) to provide electrical feeds to the various systems controlled by the switchgear mounted on it. A multi-pin electrical connector provides the connection to the car, and pins in the back of the steering wheel engage with a connector in the centre of the steering column when the wheel is pushed into place.

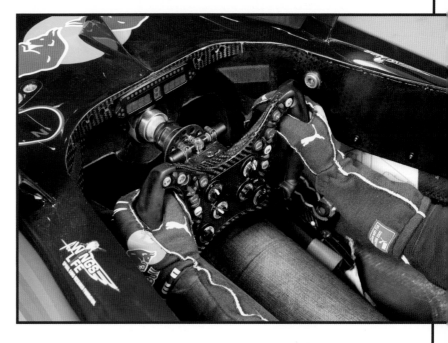

The wheel is fitted with a quick-release mechanism to allow the driver to remove and refit it easily. This is necessary because the steering wheel must be removed to allow the driver to get in and out of the car. The wheel locks into place on the end of the steering column, and the quick-release mechanism is operated by a collar, located behind the centre hub of the wheel, which the driver pulls towards him to release the wheel. To refit the wheel, the driver simply pushes the wheel into position on the mounting hub until the locking mechanism locks it in position.

Because the steering on an F1 car is extremely sensitive, and the lock-to-lock range is only around three-quarters of a turn at most circuits, there is no need for the steering wheel to be circular, and so the wheel is shaped more like an aircraft control wheel, with two grips and cutaway upper and lower sections.

The layout of the controls on the steering

↑ The steering wheel is one of the most important components on the car, incorporating the clutch and gearchange paddles and many of the main controls that the driver needs to operate the car.

←← To remove the steering wheel, the driver pulls the collar behind the wheel towards him.

← The wheel then slides from the boss on the end of the steering column.

wheel is generally kept as similar as possible for each driver, to ease manufacture and to reduce the scope for confusion among the mechanics and engineering staff, but the various buttons and controls are tailored for each driver's preferences. The systems that require frequent adjustment have controls that are easily accessible on the wheel, with buttons that can be accessed without the need for the driver to change the position of his hands on the wheel.

Mark Webber gives the driver's view on the steering wheel controls: "Ergonomics are probably 70% of what the team require for us to have – they know what the priorities are for the driver – and the remaining percentage is definitely tuning for where we would like to have things in terms of priority. For example, a drink button

is quite low-priority – it's important, but it's low down on the list in terms of where it might be. But a pit-stop button, or a neutral button or radio, are high-priority, so you want them within striking distance to get to them pretty quick, because you need to use them quite a bit, and they're quite important. The template for the wheel changes a little bit each year, but it doesn't change a huge amount because there's an element of carry-over. The wheel won't have anything on it that doesn't really need to be there."

On the RB6 there are four paddles at the back of the steering wheel. The upper paddle on the left is used to upshift, by pulling towards the driver, and the upper paddle on the right-hand side is used to downshift. Either of the two lower levers may be used to operate the clutch.

⬇ The steering wheel controls.

N Neutral

-1 Menu scroll down

RADIO Driver/pit radio toggle switch with light to show on/off

OIL Transfer oil from reserve tank to top up main oil tank

PC Pit confirm (I am coming in)

BBAL Display brake balance

DRINK Drink system (activates driver's drink pump)

RAIN Engine map for wet and rain light switch

MIX Fuel mixture

MULTI Various functions

F.WING Changes front wing angle

ENG Engine map

PIT Limiter for pitlane speed

+1 Menu scroll up

FAIL Deselects menu option

OK Selects menu option

WING Reduces front angle to reduce downforce and drag

REV Reverse gear selector

WARM Setting for max wheelspin mode to warm tyres (eg, on formation lap)

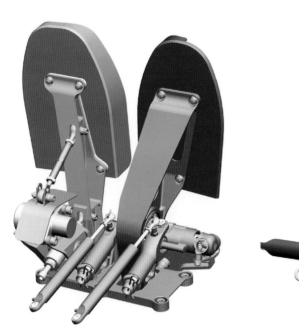

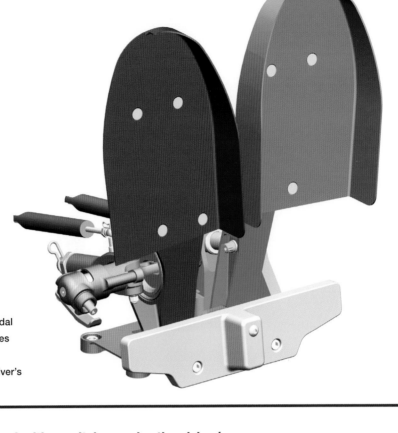

↑ A rear view of the pedal assembly, showing the linkages. In this view the throttle pedal is on the left.

→ A front view of the pedal assembly. Note the fences around the edges of the pedals to prevent the driver's feet from slipping off.

PEDALS

Only two pedals are fitted to an F1 car – the throttle pedal and the brake pedal. As previously explained, the clutch is operated via a lever on the steering wheel.

The driver brakes with his left foot, and uses his right foot for the throttle – he cannot move his feet between the pedals, as there is insufficient space, and the steering column runs between his feet.

On bumpy circuits, each pedal is fitted with a 'fence' around its edge to prevent the driver's foot from slipping off, as Mark Webber comments: "We use fences on the pedals for places like Monte Carlo, and other places where it might be a bit bumpy – it's just nice to make sure that your feet are in the right position when you come to apply each pedal."

OTHER COCKPIT-MOUNTED CONTROLS

Brake bias adjuster

The driver uses a lever on the left-hand side of the cockpit to adjust the front-to-rear brake bias. Refer to pages 155–156 for further details.

F-duct

Refer to pages 53–54 for details.

Ignition switches and extinguisher/ electrical cut-off switch

A panel of three switches is mounted on the right-hand side of the cockpit, beside the driver's leg. The lower switch, which is red, is the fire extinguisher/electrical cut-off switch, and the two above are the ignition switches.

The 'P_0-P_1' switch is similar to the 'auxiliary' ignition position on a road car, and energises all the car's systems except for the engine-related systems. The 'P_1-P_2' switch is the engine ignition switch, and this switch would be operated when the engine is about to be started using the remote starter.

↓ The switch panel on the right-hand side of the cockpit houses the 'auxiliary' switch (1), the engine ignition switch (2) and the fire extinguisher switch (3).

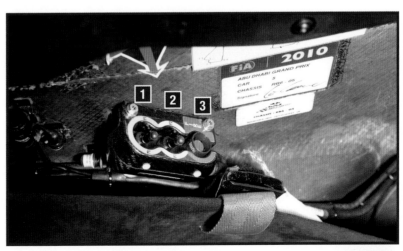

THE DESIGNER'S VIEW

'I do enjoy regulation changes – they allow me to sit back with a fresh sheet of paper and work out solutions from first principles.'

Adrian Newey – Chief Technical Officer, Red Bull Racing

INTRODUCTION

↑ Winning design. A studio shot produced for the launch of the RB6 at the beginning of the 2010 season.

F1 design is the fastest moving, most technologically advanced and technically challenging engineering process outside the defence and aerospace industries – indeed the pace of development in F1 design is significantly faster than in any other peacetime field of engineering. The recipe for designing a successful F1 car requires a complex blend of technical disciplines, unparalleled commitment from all those involved in the process, and a healthy helping of innovation.

The design process is very much a team effort, involving a number of groups of engineering specialists working together to create a winning package, but these teams need a guiding hand to provide inspiration, direction and motivation. In the case of Red Bull Racing, this man is Chief Technical Officer Adrian Newey. World Champion Sebastian Vettel gives his view on what makes Adrian one of the most successful F1 designers of all time: "Adrian is a passionate motor racer, a racing fan and he loves motorsport, F1, car –

➜ The RB6 runs for the first time, with Mark Webber behind the wheel, during testing at Jerez on 10 February 2010.

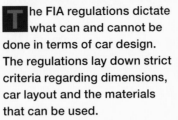

The FIA regulations dictate what can and cannot be done in terms of car design. The regulations lay down strict criteria regarding dimensions, car layout and the materials that can be used.

However, in recent years innovative engineers have found new ways to exploit the regulations to good effect, and clever new systems such as the double diffuser, blown diffuser, F-duct, tuned mass damper and instant-shift gearbox have all been developed.

REGULATION CHANGES FOR THE 2010 SEASON

For the 2010 season, a number of regulation changes were made, and these forced certain fundamental design changes from the cars raced in 2009.

The main regulation changes affecting the design of the car in 2010 can be summarised as follows (this is not an exhaustive list of all the changes):

- Refuelling during the race was banned, which meant that the car had to start the race with sufficient fuel to complete the full race distance.
- Major parts such as the survival cell, roll structures, impact structures and wheels had to be homologated by the FIA at the beginning of the season. Once these parts had been homologated, changes were only permitted if clear safety or reliability issues were involved.
- The minimum permitted weight of the car was raised from 605kg to 620kg.
- The width of the front tyres was reduced from 270mm to 245mm.

- The top 10 qualifiers had to start the race on the partially used set of tyres with which they completed their fastest lap in the final qualifying session (Q3).

WORKING WITHIN THE REGULATIONS

Before rules changes are implemented, the FIA makes the draft details available to the Formula One Teams' Association (FOTA) Technical Working Group (TWG) for discussion. The TWG includes senior technical representatives from each of the teams. Red Bull Racing's representative is Paul Monaghan, Head of Car Engineering. The teams then have the opportunity to discuss the proposed changes and provide feedback to the FIA. The TWG is kept up to date with proposed rules changes throughout the season.

Whenever a regulation change is implemented, a senior group within the Red Bull Racing design team will examine the regulations in detail to assess the impact of the change. Similarly, if the design team comes up with an innovation, they will study the regulations carefully to ensure that there are no conflicts with the rules.

If a new system or component is developed which the team feels may be viewed as an 'innovative interpretation' of the FIA regulations, then the team will discuss the relevant design details with the FIA to ensure that the concept or component will be accepted as legal. It is, of course, in the team's interest to ensure that any innovations will be accepted by the FIA: if a new concept is declared to be illegal, a significant amount of resource will have been wasted in developing a feature that cannot be used on the car.

so he is a petrol head. As it turns out he is very good at designing fast race cars. Obviously he is one of the key elements in our team and besides that a very nice guy. He is also very ambitious, and motivates the whole team and the drivers for a better performance, and this is also the reason why he is important for the team."

And there's nothing that Sebastian would change about the RB6: "At the end of the day we won the championship. We had a very good car and a very good team, and I don't want to change anything. We suffered some reliability problems, but they made us stronger for the second part of the season."

In the space of six years – a remarkably short gestation period in F1 terms – Red Bull Racing has risen from the ashes of the ailing Jaguar F1 team to win both the Constructors' and Drivers' World Championships in 2010. The Red Bull RB6 was consistently the class of the field during the 2010 season, and built on the success of its predecessor, the 2009 RB5, providing a masterclass in how to get it right in the complex and intensely competitive world of F1.

DESIGN TEAM

DESIGN TEAM

↑ The key team personnel at the launch of the RB6 at Jerez on 10 February 2010. From left: Rob Marshall (Chief Designer), Adrian Newey (Chief Technical Officer), Sebastian Vettel, Mark Webber, Christian Horner and Peter Prodromou (Head of Aerodynamics).

Invariably, all F1 teams have slightly different structures for their design teams, and at Red Bull Racing the design team includes groups responsible for specialising in the following disciplines:

MECHANICAL DESIGN AND DEVELOPMENT

■ **Composites** – chassis, wings, bodywork, impact structures, gearbox. The composites team at Red Bull Racing is also responsible for FIA homologation of relevant composite structures and components.
■ **Mechanical** – suspension and steering components, pedals, wheels, brake ducts, driver installation.
■ **Systems** – engine installation, fuel system, electrical system (including wiring loom design), exhaust system, cooling systems for engine cooling, oil and hydraulics.
■ **Transmission** – gearbox casing and internals, differential, clutch, driveshafts.
■ **Hydraulics** – gearchange actuation, power steering, adjustable front wing (2010).

■ **Stress analysis** – Finite Element Analysis (FEA) stress analysis and stress calculations for most components on the car.
■ **R&D** – 'design verification' of all systems and components using physical proof, fatigue, legality and impact testing at the factory.

AERODYNAMICS DESIGN AND DEVELOPMENT

■ **Aerodynamics development** – develop aerodynamic concepts and test them using the wind tunnel, CFD and race track.
■ **Aerodynamics design** – turn aerodynamic concepts into wind-tunnel model components. Develop mechanical systems for the model, design race car components and equipment for aerodynamic track tests.
■ **Aerodynamics production** – produce and fit wind tunnel model components in a range of materials including metal, rapid prototyping and carbon fibre.
■ **Aerodynamics performance** – develop strategies, tools and direction for the aerodynamic performance of the race car, provide the interface between the aerodynamics department and the race team.

- **Aerodynamics technology** – develop and maintain systems, software, technologies and techniques for aerodynamics development in the wind tunnel and on track.
- **Rapid Prototyping Group** – produce very short lead-time components in a range of materials for the wind-tunnel model and the race car.

In addition to the aforementioned design teams, there are numerous other technical specialists and engineers who contribute to the evolution and operation of the car. These specialists and engineers are all sited together in one large open-plan office at the team's Milton Keynes HQ. The departments include:

- Simulation
- Vehicle Dynamics
- Reliability Engineering
- Race Engineering
- Vehicle Performance Group
- Materials Science
- Technical Operations
- Management

All these teams interact constantly, sharing data and ideas throughout the design process to find the best possible solutions to produce a competitive car.

DESIGN TEAM STRUCTURE

At Red Bull Racing Chief Technical Officer Adrian Newey oversees both the aerodynamic and mechanical aspects of the design and development of the car. He will form an overall view of what he would like to achieve aerodynamically and mechanically for a new car. These concepts are then discussed and developed with Head of Aerodynamics Peter Prodromou and Chief Designer Rob Marshall. Peter and Rob then expand upon the outline of work and guide the aerodynamic and mechanical design teams, overseeing these teams and providing relevant feedback and discussion between them.

Various other groups, such as the Vehicle Performance Group, will already have collated a significant amount of data to analyse the strengths and weaknesses of the previous season's car, in order to assess which areas of the car need to be improved over the previous season's design.

Permanent groups exist for some areas, such as chassis design and suspension design, but if there is a specific new component or system under development, then specific working groups may be set up to manage the various projects.

Inevitably, all teams keep a close eye on what their rivals are up to during the season, and there may well be ideas seen on other cars that the design team feels are worth investigating and evaluating for possible adoption within the design for a new car.

Regular meetings between team members and between leaders of the various teams ensure that all teams are aware of any factors that may affect their own particular area of work.

↑ Chief Designer Rob Marshall oversees design and development of the mechanical aspects of the car.

↓ Head of Aerodynamics Peter Prodromou oversees aerodynamic design and development.

DESIGN PROCESS

As mentioned previously, the design process for a new car begins with Chief Technical Officer Adrian Newey forming his ideas and concepts for the new car. Uniquely in F1, Adrian drafts the lines (surfaces) for the entire car by hand on a drawing board, using traditional draughtsman's methods. These drawings are then digitised and fed into a 3D CAD (Three-Dimensional Computer-Aided Design) system by a team of dedicated engineers in the aerodynamics department. The CAD models produced from Adrian's drawings are passed to various specialist teams for CFD (Computational Fluid Dynamics) analysis, wind-tunnel model design, or for the design team to work on a full-size concept.

All F1 teams use 3D CAD systems for all aspects of the design process. The most commonly used CAD packages are Unigraphics NX and Dassault Systèmes Catia V5, both of which are used extensively in the aerospace industry. This CAD system is used for aerodynamic design, design of all aspects of the full-size car, tooling, jigs, rig-test equipment, garage and pit equipment and numerous other components.

Almost all components are manufactured directly from the CAD data, which can be used to control the various machines used in the manufacturing processes. A few components may be manufactured from drawings in the traditional way, and detail drawings are held for all parts in order that they can be used for inspection and assembly purposes, and for quotations if the manufacture of a component is sub-contracted.

Any new concepts or components are handled and manufactured in-house at Red Bull Racing, although a few non-sensitive components which do not justify the set-up costs of in-house manufacture, or which require highly specialised manufacturing processes and equipment, are sub-contracted out to specialist suppliers.

COST AND MANPOWER RESTRICTIONS

For 2010, the Formula One Teams Association (FOTA) came to an agreement regarding various restrictions on manpower and external spend, with a view to reducing the cost of running a competitive team. The agreement applies to the running of the entire operation – the race team as well as the design and manufacturing team – and includes limits on the number of personnel permitted to attend race weekends.

Essentially, this agreement involves the implementation of a sliding scale of a team's external spend versus its internal head count. So the more people in the team, the less the team is allowed to spend on external costs. A team can choose its own external spend limit, but it is unrealistic for any team to carry out all the jobs and processes necessary to develop and build a car totally in-house, so priorities must be chosen carefully according to which will give the greatest performance benefit on the car.

The agreement also stipulates a complete shut-down for all teams for a two-week period in August between grands prix. During this time, all team personnel directly involved with the design and running of the cars must hand in their laptops and all 'work' to the team HQ. No manufacturing machinery can be operated at the factory, and no external sub-contractors may work on components for the team.

↑ A view of the Red Bull Racing Design Office – a large open-plan area located at the team's Milton Keynes HQ, in which the team's technical specialists and engineers exchange ideas and carry out their design work.

⬇ A CAD view of a complete RB2 gearbox/differential assembly.

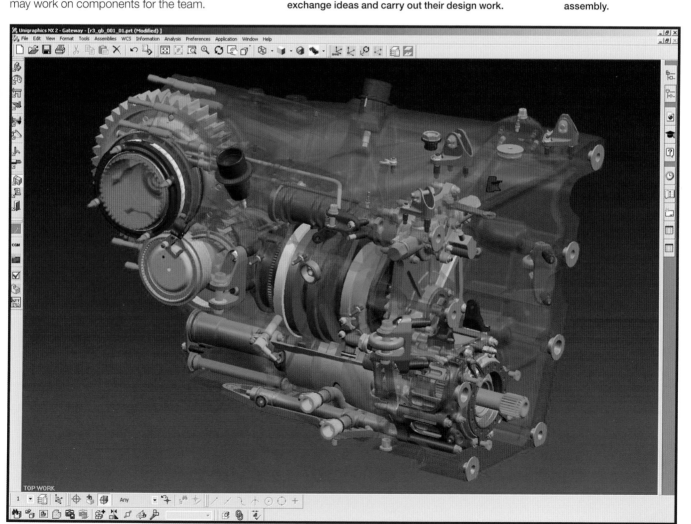

↑ The RB6 built on the strengths of the RB5, seen here at Silverstone in 2009 with Sebastian Vettel at the wheel.

THE STARTING POINT

At the start of the design process, there are a number of points that the designers will take into consideration:

- A good understanding of the previous car's good and bad points – the design team will aim to build on the good points and try to eliminate weaknesses.
- An idea of what other teams have been up to, gained by looking at how well other teams' cars perform and what they look like. There may be features to investigate or 'borrow' from other cars.
- Regulation changes, which usually force design changes on a team each season.
- New innovations of the design team's own that are germinating and that they may want to include.

All these points are analysed and discussed by the design team at the outset of the design process, and taken into account along with the operational parameters of the car. For example, from the start of the 2010 season the car had to start the race with a full fuel load (due to the refuelling ban), which resulted in a significant weight change to the car during the race. The designers had to bear this in mind to optimise the performance of the car with both a full and light fuel load.

The aim for the designers is to optimise all areas of the car as far as possible, building on the previous season's car (assuming it was a good car!) and ensuring that there are no significant weaknesses. The RB6 was a great example of this process working successfully, building on the strengths of the 2009 RB5 (excellent aerodynamics and mechanical grip) and reducing its weaknesses (the RB5 was not designed at the outset to work with a double diffuser), while taking account of rule changes (the ban on refuelling) and incorporating new innovations (a blown diffuser).

DESIGN PARAMETERS

There are two fundamental criteria to be considered in the design of an F1 car and they are critical to the car's performance – centre of gravity (C of G) and centre of pressure (C of P). The centre of gravity is the 'virtual' point at which the total weight of the car appears to be concentrated. The centre of pressure is the point at which the total aerodynamic forces acting on the car appear to be concentrated.

The location of the C of G depends on the weight distribution of the car and, similarly, the location of the C of P depends on the distribution of downforce on the car. For a stable car, the C of G ideally needs to be further forward than the C of P.

The C of G can be divided into two elements: longitudinal centre of gravity (LCG), which is the 'fore/aft' position of the C of G along the car's length, and the vertical centre of gravity (VCG), which is the vertical position ('height') of the car's C of G.

A great deal of effort is spent ensuring that the VCG is as close to the ground as possible. This provides a more stable car, as it will be less sensitive to the lateral forces acting on it during cornering. The higher the C of G, the more the car will tend to 'roll' or try to lift the inside wheels during cornering. In terms of the design, a low C of G is achieved by designing the lightest possible car structure. This allows the car to be ballasted up to the minimum weight limit by using as much ballast as possible (see page 32) as close to the ground as possible.

The location of the LCG defines the weight distribution of the car, and in design terms this is influenced by the positions of the front and rear axle centrelines in relation to the chassis, engine and gearbox. The optimum position for the LCG is not necessarily in the centre of the car – for example, if a relatively 'extreme' weight bias is favourable to suit the tyre-wear and handling-balance characteristics of the car, the designers may deliberately choose to design a car with a more forward- or rear-biased weight distribution than might be expected. Although the weight distribution can still be fine-tuned on the finished car by moving ballast, the fundamental weight-distribution characteristics have to be considered at the design stage. During 2010, the car's weight distribution could be altered as the team wished, but for the 2011 season, the weight distribution is restricted by FIA regulations, with a maximum of $46\pm0.5\%$ of the car's total weight permitted to act on the front wheels.

The location of the C of P depends on the design and location of the aerodynamic devices on the car. In simple terms, an increase in downforce at the front of the car will move the C of P forwards, and *vice versa*.

Although there are many other factors to be considered during the design of the car (a detailed explanation of the design process would easily fill this book!), two other important parameters are firstly tyre performance and secondly to provide the drivers with a car that has predictable handling in order to give them confidence behind the wheel.

Tyre performance is extremely important, as the car must be able to use its tyres effectively, keeping them within their optimum operating temperature range, while minimising tyre degradation (wear).

A driver will automatically be able to drive the car closer to the limit for more of the time if he has confidence that the car will respond accurately and predictably to his inputs.

Because the major components of the car (chassis, engine, gearbox) are extremely difficult to change once the parts have been homologated and manufactured, it is extremely important for the designers to get the basic 'architecture' of the car right before proceeding with the detail design. For example, the distance between the front and rear axle centrelines is a critical factor for the weight distribution of the car, and so this is one of the fundamental parameters considered at the outset of the design process. Although it is theoretically possible to move the axle centrelines slightly once the car is complete, it would be a huge task as a significant amount of re-design and re-homologation would almost certainly be required.

A good example of the thought that goes into packaging a car is the larger fuel tank that was required for 2010 due to the ban on refuelling. The packaging of the new, larger fuel tank on the RB6 was a straightforward packaging problem – a compromise between length and width, as Adrian Newey explains: "We have to get that extra fuel in by either making the chassis longer or wider. Wider would be preferable but you end up making the radiators smaller, and losing some cooling. The RB6 is a compromise – we've got a slightly smaller radiator and a slightly longer chassis."

By slightly lengthening the chassis, in addition to avoiding cooling problems, the Red Bull Racing design team was able to move the extra weight of the fuel tank backwards in the chassis, which helped to reduce the load on the front tyres and therefore helped handling balance.

⬇ A schematic of the combined aerodynamic loads that act on the car's centre of pressure.

Drag

Downforce

Centre of pressure

Rear Wing

Front wing

Diffuser

THE 'PACKAGE'

Drivers, engineers and commentators often talk about 'the package', and this term generally refers to the 'packaging' of the crucial elements required to make a quick car. The package is always a compromise, and the design team's aim is to minimise any weaknesses.

THE KEY ELEMENTS

In terms of design, four key elements can be considered to form the package, and the performance of each individual element needs to be optimised to produce a good car:

- Aerodynamic efficiency
- Mechanical efficiency
- Engine
- Driver

Red Bull Racing's Chief Designer, Rob Marshall observes: "If you have good aero and two of the remaining three, you'll have a good package; if you have all four you'll be unbeatable!"

In the past, tyres could be considered to be an additional element of the package, but since the introduction of 'control' tyres all cars have run on the same tyres, so no one team is able to develop the tyres as part of their package to improve car performance.

In reality, it is rare for all of the required elements to always be working at their optimum level, but if there is a significant weakness in any one of the four areas, the package will be uncompetitive.

A high level of downforce is key to a quick lap time, as Sebastian Vettel states in his summing of up of the RB6's qualities: "Obviously you always want a fast car. And I think the RB6 proved many times that it was the fastest. I think we got a lot of downforce out of the car, which allowed us very high corner speeds."

Reflecting on the performance of the RB6 during 2010, Adrian Newey comments: "RB6 seemed to have its biggest advantage at tracks with the longest-duration corners and the shortest straights... I was particularly impressed by it going through Barcelona Turn 9 flat. We just about managed to get Copse flat at Silverstone in 2009 and went one better at Barcelona Turn 9."

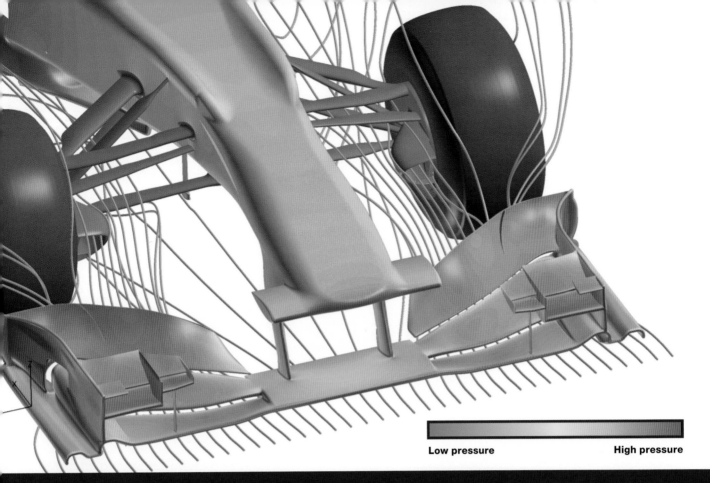

Low pressure   High pressure

CFD

CFD (Computational Fluid Dynamics) is a method of providing computer simulation and analysis of fluid flow – airflow in the case of an F1 car. CFD uses the enormous computational power of modern computers to enable complex mathematical calculations to be carried out to produce data and 'virtual' visualisations for airflow over the car. CFD is an essential tool in the car's design and development process.

The theory of CFD is beyond the scope of this book, but the important point is that it can be used to predict the behaviour of the air passing over the car by calculating the changes in the velocity and pressure of the airflow as it flows over the various surfaces.

In most cases CFD enables the prediction of the aerodynamic forces acting on the car to within a few per cent of the true values. CFD is not infallible, but it provides an extremely valuable predictive tool that is used in conjunction with wind-tunnel testing to design and develop the car.

One of the key benefits of CFD is its ability to provide visualisation of the data produced, which means that it's possible for engineers to actually 'see' the flows, pressures, velocities and animated 3D graphics of 'virtual air' flowing over the model.

THE CFD PROCESS

There are five key stages in CFD analysis:

■ A 3D CAD model is generated for the component(s) to be analysed – the aerodynamic design team produces this model.
■ The conditions for the analysis are set up – a 'virtual' box is put around the model to be tested, which defines the direction of the airflow, its velocity, etc.
■ 'Meshing' is carried out on the model – the 'mesh' is a three-dimensional grid containing a vast number (possibly millions) of cubic cells. The software carries out fluid dynamic calculations in each one of these cells.
■ 'Solver' software then performs calculations on the 'meshed' model – this enables the information from each of the cells in the mesh to be analysed in relation to all the other cells, and allows feedback of the results data between the

↑ A CFD image showing the streamlines (airflow) and static (air) pressures for a typical front wing assembly. The streamlines are the grey lines flowing over the components. The static pressure is denoted by the colour of the components.

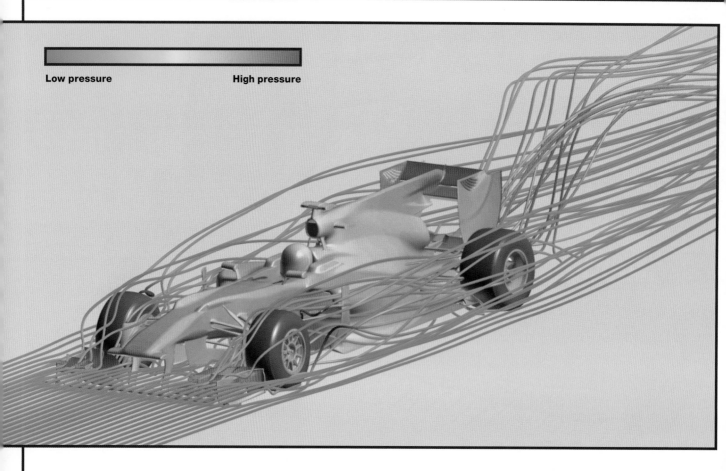

Low pressure   **High pressure**

↑↘ CFD images showing streamlines and static pressures for the whole car (above) and for the rear wing assembly in detail (below).

cells so that all the forces and flows can be balanced across the whole 'mesh'. Basically this step produces the 'big picture' of the airflow over the model.

■ 'Post-processing' enables final analysis of the results data – this can be used to provide force calculations and further analysis, and to enable 'visualisation' of the results.

CFD works hand-in-hand with wind-tunnel testing – both are important tools in the design process, and the two are complementary. CFD provides a better tool for evaluating new concepts, as it is easier to input unusual geometry into a CAD model than to make changes to a wind-tunnel model.

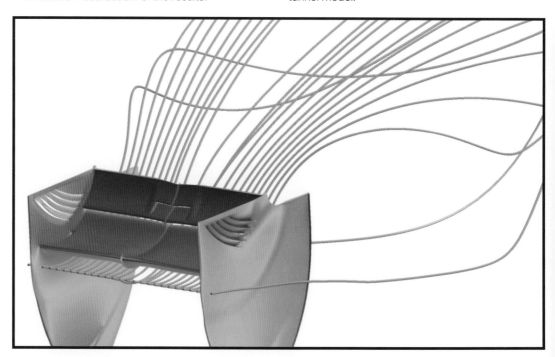

WIND TUNNEL

The wind tunnel is a very important simulation and development tool, and is used in conjunction with CFD to prove aerodynamic concepts and new components during the design and development process. Generally, wind-tunnel testing is used to prove and fine-tune concepts that have already been evaluated using CFD. Modifications take longer to make and analyse in the wind tunnel, but it provides a better tool for fine-tuning.

In the Red Bull Racing wind tunnel, located at Bedford, 60%-scale models are used. Very few teams employ full-scale models, as their use is heavily restricted under the Formula One Teams Association (FOTA) Resource Restriction Agreement (see pages 126–127), and in any case the use of full-scale models still does not guarantee accurate results that are repeatable on-track. For example a full-scale wind-tunnel model will not blow exhaust gas in the correct manner or at the correct temperature, and the density of the air emerging from the radiator area will not be consistent with that of a real car. Full-scale wind-tunnel testing tends to be more suited to road-car development, where the testing tends to look more at the overall airflow picture than at the very fine detail required for F1 development.

The FOTA agreement allows for six days of straight-line testing using a full-size car, on an airfield or proving ground for example, and these six days are used primarily for aerodynamic testing. Under the agreement, during the 2010 season teams were permitted to substitute one day of straight-line testing for four operating hours in the wind tunnel. For these additional hours, a full-scale wind-tunnel model could be used, but for all other wind-tunnel running models up to a maximum scale of 60% had to be used. Red Bull Racing use 60%-scale models for all their wind-tunnel testing work. The FOTA agreement also restricts the air speed used for wind-tunnel testing to 50 metres per second, or approximately 110mph.

At Red Bull Racing, a dedicated team of aerodynamicists run the wind-tunnel tests and collate and analyse the data produced to feed back to other groups in the aerodynamics team.

↑ Christian Horner at the Red Bull Racing wind tunnel in Bedford.

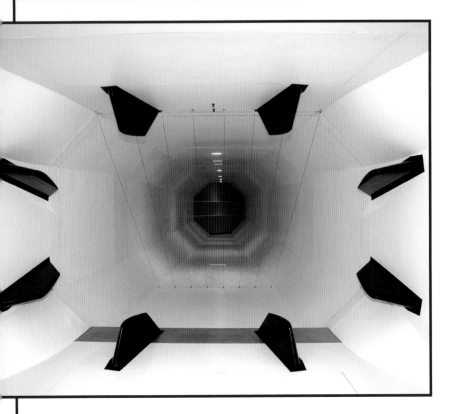

the air is passed over turning vanes and then through a screen that straightens the airflow before it passes into the chamber containing the model.

Inside the wind tunnel, the floor beneath the car must move at exactly the same speed as the airflow to provide a realistic simulation of the car passing over the track surface. The model's tyres rest on the moving wind-tunnel floor (a continuous belt), but the vertical strut that connects the model to the wind-tunnel roof supports the car's weight. This supporting strut allows the weight of the model to be set to 'zero' when aerodynamic testing is being carried out, so that the forces acting on the car are purely aerodynamic. The strut carries instrumentation to measure the aerodynamic forces acting on the model.

During wind-tunnel testing, regular checks are carried out on all equipment to make sure that the results recorded are consistent, and to eliminate any 'outside' variables. Repeatability of the data obtained from wind-tunnel testing is essential to avoid errors and possible 'wrong steers' with the direction of development.

Certain aspects of the airflow around the car are very difficult to replicate on a model in the wind tunnel – for example the airflow through a brake cooling duct, over the brake components and out through the wheel. A more useful analysis of the airflow over these tricky areas of the car can be provided by CFD, to supplement the results from wind-tunnel testing.

↑ Turning vanes help to smooth the airflow in the wind tunnel before it passes to the chamber containing the model.

WIND-TUNNEL OPERATION

The wind tunnel itself is a controlled environment, and the consistency and quality of the air passing through it is vital to ensure accurate, consistent and repeatable results. The air is not blown directly by the fan over the model, as the airflow generated by the fan is turbulent, and would not provide consistent results. To provide a smooth, consistent airflow,

➜ A wind-tunnel model of the 2008 RB4 on display at the team's Milton Keynes headquarters.

WIND-TUNNEL MODELS

Wind-tunnel models are works of art, and every detail of the model must faithfully replicate the full-size component. The level of detailing on a wind-tunnel model is astounding, and the model really is a scale replica of the full-size car.

Many wind-tunnel model parts are made via 'rapid-prototyping', which provides an accuracy of around ± 0.1mm.

Rapid prototyping is an automated process that produces faithful physical reproductions of 'virtual' 3D CAD models. The process works by dividing the CAD model into very thin virtual cross-sectional slices, and then laying down successive layers of liquid resin that fuse together as they are stacked up to accurately reproduce the contours of the CAD model. This process enables almost any shape – even shapes with complex curves and cut-outs – to be reproduced. Rapid prototyping enables parts that would take numerous hours or even days to manufacture by other means to be produced in a matter of a relatively few hours. The process enables faithful scale modelling of almost all the car's parts, including bodywork, aerodynamic devices, suspension components and even detailing such as brake ducts. Occasionally, rapid prototyping may be used to produce full-size parts for testing on a car, but this is relatively rare, and applies only to parts not subjected to significant loads.

The tyres fitted to wind-tunnel models are critical, as they must deform under load in exactly the same way as full-size tyres in order to provide

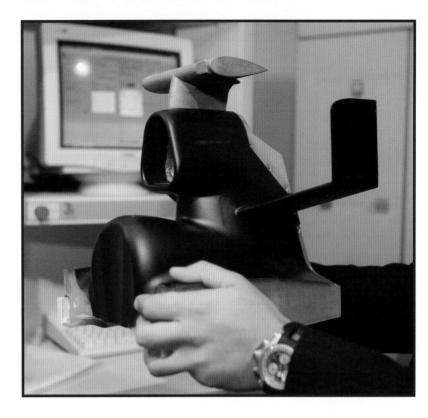

accurate simulation of the behaviour of the full-size car. To help to replicate the characteristics of real tyres, pneumatic tyres are used on wind-tunnel models, and when they are subjected to a scale load they behave like real tyres.

As in most F1 teams, the pace of development at Red Bull Racing is such that a full-time team of model makers is constantly working on producing new components for wind-tunnel testing.

↑ An airbox for an RB2 wind-tunnel model manufactured by rapid prototyping.

← An RB4 wind-tunnel model ready for testing. Note the vertical strut connecting the model to the roof of the tunnel.

SIMULATION

SIMULATION

↑ The Red Bull Racing driving simulator provides a very useful development tool.

Various forms of simulation can be used to good effect when designing and developing the car, and also to aid the driver. The main resources used for simulation are CFD and the wind tunnel, but rig-testing and driving simulation are also employed. Although none of these forms of simulation can predict or perfectly replicate what happens to a real car on the circuit, they are being constantly developed to provide increasingly accurate predictive tools.

RIG TESTING

Test rigs are used extensively to check components and systems, both during the design process and during development.

Various rigs are used, from 'simple' rigs for destructive testing of suspension components, to seven-post rigs on which a complete car can be mounted.

Test rigs can be used to accurately simulate the cycle of forces that a component, or a complete car, is likely to encounter on-track, and can therefore be used to verify the strength and durability of components before they are used on the car.

During the destructive testing of components,

rigs may be used to apply a steadily increasing load to a component until it breaks, or may be used to simulate 'load cycles', where the load varies through a number of repeated cycles until the component fails. During these tests, the components can be fitted with instrumentation, such as strain gauges to monitor the forces acting at various points, and measuring equipment to record the movement or distortion of a component. The data collected from these tests is analysed to provide vital information on how well the component is likely to perform in service.

The seven-post test rig has become a very important simulation tool for most F1 teams. This substantial piece of test equipment allows a full-size car to be mounted with each of its four wheels supported independently by a hydraulically actuated pad. The four such pads move vertically to simulate the vertical suspension forces acting on each wheel. The rig is also fitted with three tension struts (making seven 'posts' in all), which can pull the car down to simulate loads such as aerodynamic downforce, pitch and roll, and – as a result – weight transfer during braking, acceleration

← The seven-post test rig is an important simulation tool that assists the design and development of the car.

and cornering. Using data collated during races from the car's on-board data-logging system, a seven-post rig can be programmed to simulate an entire race in terms of the various forces acting on the car during a lap and over a race distance.

DRIVING SIMULATION

Driving simulators are now used by most of the major F1 teams, including Red Bull Racing. While they don't provide a perfect simulation of the driving experience, over the past few years driving simulators have been developed to act as very useful development tools for both the team and

drivers. They can help a driver and team learn the characteristics of a new track, and give a new driver an idea of how the car operates and handles before he drives a real car on track.

The data obtained from the race car's on-board data-logging system can be used in conjunction with complex mathematical models defining aerodynamic, tyre and suspension characteristics, and Newton's Laws of Motion, to programme the driving simulator, providing a very realistic driving experience for a specific circuit. Data obtained from the simulator enables analysis of the driver's driving style and the performance of the car.

↙ Chief Engineer Vehicle Dynamics Mark Ellis and his team are responsible for developing the simulation tools that are used throughout the engineering team, and assessing the performance (lap time) benefits and compromises of any new systems or concepts.

↓ The control station for the team's driving simulator.

TESTING

↑ Winter testing of the RB6 at Barcelona in February 2010.

Testing is a vital part of the development of a new car. Since a ban was introduced on testing during the season (the intention being to cut costs), pre-season testing has become critical, as it is the only opportunity to test on-track other than the limited testing that can be carried out during the Friday practice sessions of race weekends. Once a new car has been designed and built, the next phase in the process is pre-season testing.

In addition to pre-season testing, under the FOTA Resource Restriction Agreement, in 2010 teams could also run 'straight-line' aerodynamic tests for six days – see 'Wind tunnel' on page 133.

During testing, data logging and driver feedback are both important tools. Data logging can tell the engineers the state of whatever parameter they are measuring, but it cannot tell them what is good or bad, or what is right or wrong. It is therefore important for the engineers to be able to interpret the driver's feedback (what he likes and what he does not like) in order to put the data into context. Data from one driver's test laps can be overlaid on similar laps from the other driver, which can help

interpretation. If a driver provides feedback that completely contradicts the data – this is rare! – then the engineers need to sit down and decide how to interpret the information.

PRE-SEASON TESTING

In 2010, pre-season testing consisted of four four-day test sessions, all in Spain, at Valencia, Barcelona and Jerez. The teams therefore had 16 days of on-track testing to prove new concepts, optimise the car's systems and identify any weaknesses before the first race of the season.

The aims of pre-season testing are to confirm that the car behaves as expected mechanically and aerodynamically, to ensure that the main structures and systems are reliable, and to identify and successfully resolve any problems before the car races in anger. Testing also provides a team with the first opportunity to improve its 'base' design for the car.

The normal pattern is for a team to launch their new car to the press before or at the first test (this varies from team to team), before working on mechanical and aerodynamic upgrades during testing prior to the first race in March. For the last few years, Red Bull Racing has launched its new car in Spain at one of the early pre-season test sessions.

Because the team has the previous season's car as a reference point, within a day or two of testing a new car for the first time, it will know if it has a competitive car or whether it is likely to struggle. However, it is difficult to assess how a new car compares with those of rival teams, as Mark Webber confirms: "Sometimes it's difficult because we have heavy regulation changes. You get a good idea if the car is basically doing the fundamental things for you, and whether it has any big vices or problems, or is doing uncharacteristic things that are surprising you. You know pretty quickly if a car is doing the basics, and quickly after that we interrogate the performance."

One of the problems with pre-season testing since the refuelling ban came into force (at the beginning of 2010) is that it is almost impossible to know how much fuel other teams are running in their cars. Cars now have a fuel tank capable of carrying 160kg of fuel, and in testing a car may be running with 160kg, or 30kg, and setting lap times accordingly. This makes it difficult to determine how a new car is performing compared to the opposition, and places more emphasis on the comparative performances at the first race of the season to show the true picture.

TESTING DURING FRIDAY PRACTICE

Teams are free to carry out testing and evaluation of new components during the two Friday practice sessions of a race weekend, but the cars must be 'legal' for these sessions. This restricts the testing of any radical new components, and also means that teams cannot use any sensors or data-logging equipment not normally fitted to the cars for racing. During pre-season testing, teams can run with the cars in any configuration they wish, and are also free to fit special sensors, data-logging equipment and test rigs to aid development.

During race weekends, most test and evaluation work is done during the Friday morning session, as in most cases teams will be concentrating on car set-up work during the afternoon session and during Saturday morning practice. When testing on a Friday, it is important to strike a balance between running consistently to evaluate new 'tweaks' and allowing the driver to run flat-out to 'get his eye in' for the weekend.

↑ Sebastian Vettel and Mark Webber unveil the RB6 to the world's press at Jerez prior to testing on 10 February 2010.

← Testing is every bit as intense as the racing season, and the development process begins right from the first day the car hits the track.

DEVELOPMENT

↑ A new front wing assembly awaits its starring role in the garage during the 2010 Brazilian Grand Prix weekend.

Once the season is underway, the pace of development is relentless, particularly aerodynamic development. For the RB6, from the 2010 season-opening Bahrain Grand Prix until the season finale in Abu Dhabi, each race was accompanied by a significant aerodynamic upgrade.

UPGRADES

For each race, a typical aerodynamic-upgrade package consists of detail modifications, or even fundamental redesigns of a combination of the following components:

- Front wing
- Rear wing
- Floor
- Upper bodywork

Additionally, numerous minor modifications may be made to aerodynamic devices such as turning vanes and strakes.

With aerodynamic developments, the components being tested in the wind tunnel are usually a step ahead of what is concurrently running on the car. Wherever possible, development is timed so that, for example, a complete new bodywork package does not coincide with a 'flyaway' race, as this would be logistically hard to handle. One of the limiting factors in development is the quantity of parts being developed (and manufactured) at any one time, as the factory has a finite capacity. When deciding on the best development course for new parts, the engineers must weigh up the likely magnitude of the gain against the practical difficulty of achieving it.

So, when an aerodynamic upgrade is fitted to the car, is it possible for the driver to actually feel the difference when he tries it for the first time, or is the difference only visible from the car's data? Mark Webber explains: "Oh yes, you can feel the difference, and that comes with an increase in grip and performance, but we need to feed back to the engineers what we're actually feeling – the areas we feel have improved against what they think has improved – and look at this in relation to what actually happened."

All teams are constantly working on new developments, and each will keep a close eye on its rivals to see if there are any new ideas appearing on other cars that might be worth adopting. A good example of this in action during 2010 was Red Bull Racing's development of the blown diffuser, which first appeared in pre-season testing. Several other teams developed a similar system during the season, although it took time, and the other teams met with varying degrees of success, as the system could not be fully integrated into their cars' designs, as it was with the RB6.

To optimise the blown diffuser, the RB6 made use of a specifically designed new gearbox casing and the pull-rod suspension developed previously for the RB5. In terms of scheduling, a team could develop a blown diffuser and associated revised exhaust system in a matter of weeks. However, to adopt a pull-rod suspension system would have been impractical due to the long lead times (months) involved in development and manufacture.

Conversely, like other teams, during 2010 Red Bull Racing adopted the F-Duct system that first appeared on the McLaren. Although Red Bull Racing was not able to integrate the system neatly within its chassis, as McLaren had done, it was still able to devise a system that worked to good effect – see pages 53–54.

THE DEVELOPMENT PROCESS

As with all things F1, speed is of the essence when developing new components, and once a modification or redesign is identified that provides a potential performance gain, huge effort is put in by the design, R&D and composites departments to ensure that the updates appear on the car as soon as possible.

The following steps provide an example of the process involved in developing an aerodynamic upgrade:

- **Conception** The aerodynamics department, led by Adrian Newey and Peter Prodromou, arrives at a new concept, or a worthwhile modification to an existing component.
- **CAD modelling** The aerodynamics department translates the concept into a 3D CAD model.
- **CFD and/or wind-tunnel evaluation** The concept is analysed using CFD and/or wind-tunnel testing to evaluate its potential benefits.
- **Release of CAD model data to composites design group** The definitive CAD model for the new components is released so that the composites department can start work on translating the design into a full-size physical component.
- **Composite design** The composites department designs tooling, mouldings, any jigs and fixtures required for bonding and assembly, assembly and installation details and procedures, and any documentation required – both internal (laminate documentation for composites assembly staff, etc) and external (any legality documentation required by the FIA).
- **Stress analysis** This will usually run in parallel to the composite design.
- **Manufacture** Usually in-house, but occasionally by external suppliers. Certain aspects of the manufacturing process run in parallel with the composite design.
- **Design Verification Process (DVP)** Structural verification (if required) of the component(s), including proof, fatigue testing and legality checks.
- **Destructive testing (if required)** The components will be tested to destruction on appropriate test rigs, and the data collected will be fed back to the stress-analysis team to check that the results correlate with their predictions.
- **Fit component(s) to car** Usually for assessment during a Friday practice session in order to carry out a final evaluation before fitting for qualifying and the race.
- **Race or bust!** Occasionally (though rarely) developments that have shown promise do not translate to improvements in lap times on the track, in which case the components are literally binned! If the package, or part of the package, proves to be an improvement, then it will appear on the car for the race.
- **Retirement** Often the components become obsolete within two or three races as improved parts progress through the preceding process.

As a result of this ongoing development, the car that finishes the season is often significantly different from the one that appeared at the first race, particularly from a driver's point of view, as Mark Webber explains: "If you take the car from the start of the year to the end of the year, it's a completely different beast. We're looking for two or three tenths [improvement] in testing, which for the driver is a lot, so when you're talking about a second-and-a-half, two seconds [gain], or even more over the course of a season, the car's completely different. Obviously from a design point of view it hasn't changed a huge amount structurally – chassis, etc – but there have been some sensational subtle changes which increase the performance massively."

THE RACE ENGINEER'S VIEW

'If a driver trusts his race engineer 100 per cent, what he says goes.'

Paul Monaghan – Head of Car Engineering, Red Bull Racing

← Mark Webber shares
a light-hearted moment
with his Race Engineer
Ciaron Pilbeam.

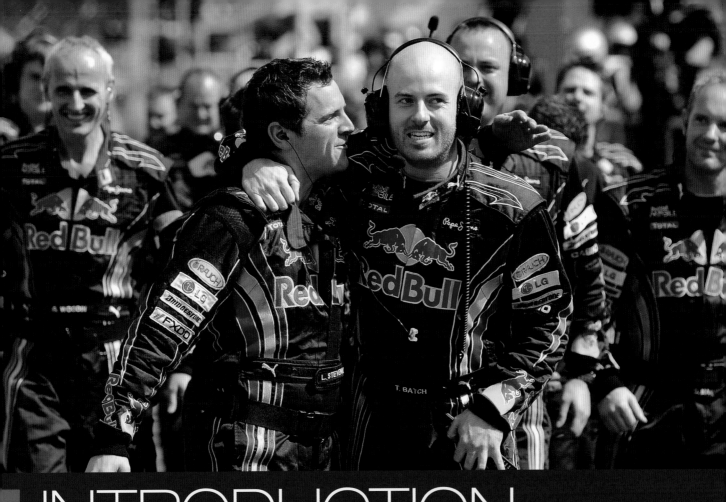

INTRODUCTION

Strictly speaking, the job description of Race Engineer applies to a driver's 'personal' engineer – the man who works closely with the driver to help him maximise the potential of the car during a race weekend. Each driver has his own race engineer, and the close bond between them is an essential factor in getting the best from both car and driver. The race engineer requires an intimate knowledge of the car and its systems in order to exploit its potential, but he must also build a good relationship with the driver in order to understand what the driver needs from the car. The race engineer is the man who delivers good and bad news to the driver, often via the pit-to-car radio, and if the driver trusts his race engineer 100 per cent, what he says goes!

The race engineer's job is to work with his colleagues in the engineering team, and with the driver, to get the best out of the car over a race weekend. This involves setting up the car for qualifying and the race, managing tyres, fuel, and strategy during the race, and acting as the 'engineering conduit' between the team and driver.

However, in this chapter the term 'race engineer' is used in a more generic sense to describe the numerous technicians and engineers in the team, all of who have vital roles to play in preparing the car – both at the factory and at the circuits – and running the car in anger.

Race engineering is essentially the exploitation of the assets available to the engineers – the car and driver, and all the team's resources – with the ultimate aim of winning races.

Each engineer/technician/mechanic has their own particular area of responsibility, and will be fully familiar with all the components and associated working practices and procedures relevant to his particular area. Teamwork is essential and every team member working in the garage has a good general knowledge of all the car's systems and can help his colleagues with general work on the car.

Probably the finest illustration of F1 teamwork in action is a race pit stop. Although pit stops follow a well-rehearsed routine, every member of the crew has to perform his job perfectly, under extreme pressure, and any error or delay could cost the team a race victory. In 2010 the Red Bull Racing pit crew was the class of the field.

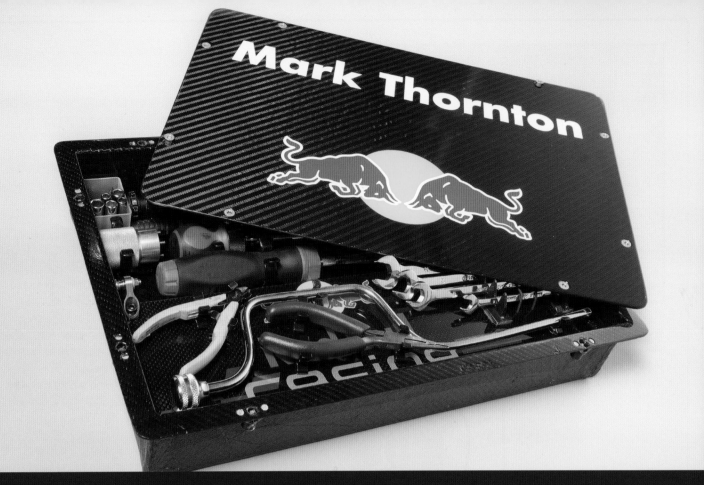

WORKING ON THE CAR

Working on an F1 car requires a great deal of care and attention, but is not significantly different to working on any other car. Anyone permitted to work on the car must be familiar with its systems and with the special precautions necessary to avoid damage to the car's components and the risk of personal injury, and scrupulous cleanliness is observed at all times. An F1 garage resembles an operating theatre rather than a typical car repair workshop.

SAFETY FIRST

It goes without saying that the F1 pitlane and garage can be a dangerous environment if not managed correctly. Fuel, hot coolant, hot oil, hot tyres, hot brakes – all are potentially serious hazards. And for the 2011 season the additional hazard of KERS joins the list.

For protection, at relevant times all team members working on the car wear fireproof overalls, gloves and – when necessary – goggles or visors. The garage, or workshop, is considered to be a controlled environment in which skilled, trained technicians all know where the potential hazards lie. Anybody who is allowed near the car knows

what they are doing, and everyone has a specific job to do, so all team members know the dangers associated with their particular area of responsibility, and can take appropriate precautions.

TOOLS AND WORKING FACILITIES

Where possible, during the design process the design team will try to bear in mind the ease of working on the car, but this is not always possible. Performance has to be the number-one priority, and so there are sometimes challenges for the mechanics!

⬆ Mark Thornton's 'home-engineered' carbon-fibre toolbox would be the envy of any DIY mechanic.

⬅ A place for everything, and everything has its place.

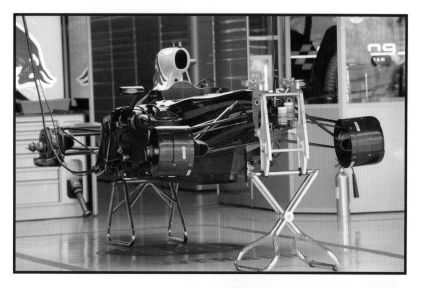

Most work on the car can be carried out with standard tools that would be found in a normal automotive tool kit – sockets, spanners, screwdrivers, etc. A few specialist tools are required for certain jobs, such as removing gear ratios.

Each mechanic has his own personal tool kit, so that he knows where everything is, and can have tools set up ready for the common jobs that he has to do. For example, certain sockets may be pre-fitted with appropriate extensions to reach a specific component, ready to snap onto a suitable ratchet. Because each mechanic is responsible for a particular area of the car, he has sufficient tools to cover that area, plus a few more 'standard' tools in case he has to help colleagues with other jobs.

Given the dominance of aerodynamics, the aerodynamic performance of the car is never compromised to make the mechanics' lives easier, and because aerodynamic seals (often in the form of small cover panels) are sometimes required in awkward areas, access can sometimes be tricky. The mechanics are inevitably ingenious, and are sometimes able to contribute to the design process to improve the car in certain areas.

↑ With its floor removed, an RB6 is supported on a trestle at the rear and a lifting frame and trestle at the front.

A single tool partner supplies all the team's tools, and the quality of the tools would be the envy of the average DIY mechanic! Only the highest-quality tools are used – all tools must fit the relevant fasteners and components perfectly to avoid damage and to save any unnecessary time-wasting.

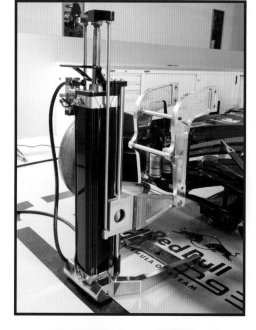

→ A pneumatic jack and lifting frame positioned ready to lift the front of the car.

JACKING AND VEHICLE SUPPORT

Like any other car, an F1 car has specific recommended jacking points to avoid the risk of damage and to provide the mechanics with better access to certain areas of the car.

In the workshop and garage, mechanical and pneumatic jacks are used, but in the pitlane only mechanical jacks are permitted.

When work is being carried out on the car in the workshop or garage, the nose/front-wing assembly will be removed before any other work is carried out. Once the nose has been removed, a frame is bolted to the front of the chassis, locating on the four nose mounting lugs. A front lifting jack is then attached to the lifting frame.

↘↓ A pneumatic jack positioned ready to lift the rear of the car using the rear crash-structure jacking point. The rear lifting point is painted yellow to ease identification during pit stops.

At the rear of the car, the jacking point is under the crash structure on the rear of the gearbox, and the jack is placed directly under the jacking point.

With the front and rear of the car raised on jacks, the wheels can be removed. A-frames can then be fitted, one to each axle, to support the car. The A-frames engage with the uprights and are secured by wheel nuts on the stub axles. Depending on the work to be carried out, the floor can now be

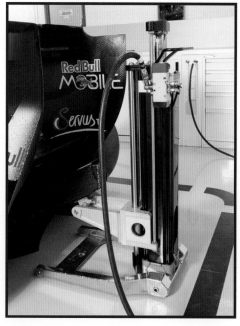

removed, and wheeled trolleys and/or trestles can be placed under the car to support it.

When work is being carried out in the pitlane, or during a pit stop, 'quick-lift' mechanical jacks are used, one at the rear of the car beneath the jacking point on the rear crash structure, and one at the front of the car under the nose.

OBTAINING SPARE PARTS

During race weekends, the team will carry sufficient spare parts to build a third complete car. Various sub-assemblies of components, such as pre-assembled gearbox/rear suspension assemblies, are carried to avoid the need to build up assemblies from scratch. For particularly vulnerable components, such as suspension wishbones, extra spares will be carried.

Nuts, bolts and fasteners are usually aerospace-standard components, and all external component suppliers are chosen because they can be relied upon to produce and deliver components to the required quality and on time – all components must be absolutely reliable.

Five gearboxes are normally taken to each race – two for use on each car during the weekend and one spare (see page 155 for details of gearbox use) – and two of these would be installed in the cars during transport. Similarly, six engines would normally be taken to a race – a 'Friday' engine and a race engine for each car, plus a spare for each car.

MAINTAINING THE CAR AT THE TRACK

Maintenance of car at the track during a race weekend is an ongoing process, and details are given as part of the 'Race weekend' information beginning on page 158.

MAINTAINING THE CAR BETWEEN RACES

Because the cars are completely rebuilt between races (although the engines and gearboxes cannot be worked on internally, as they are sealed by the FIA), maintenance as such between races is not applicable.

However, new developments and modifications are almost inevitably incorporated on the car during rebuild work between races. The fitting of any newly developed parts will involve a briefing with the relevant personnel so that they are fully aware of any related changes in operating procedures, and access to components, etc.

Almost every component on the car is 'lifed' according to mileage, and so numerous parts will be replaced as a matter of course between races.

Certain parts may be subjected to Non-Destructive Testing (NDT) in between races to determine whether they can be reused, and also to analyse any weaknesses in the design. NDT is usually carried out using ultra-violet (UV) light and fluids that will highlight problem areas such as cracks.

ACCIDENT REPAIR

If the car suffers an accident, the damage must be carefully assessed to determine which components need to be replaced. The policy is always to replace rather than repair components, unless spares are unavailable.

The decision on which components require replacement is based on data from the accident. It is possible that certain parts that do not show any obvious visual signs of damage may have suffered damage or deterioration due to the forces involved in an impact. For example, a front push-rod that may not appear to have been damaged in an accident could have been subjected to a very high load as the car crashed over a kerb, and so that push-rod, and perhaps all the other suspension parts on the relevant corner of the car, will be replaced. The front push-rods and rear pull-rods are fitted with sensors (strain gauges) to monitor the loads to which they are subjected.

The team will always err on the side of caution, and no chances will be taken where safety is concerned.

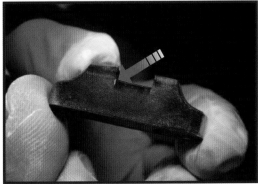

←← One form of NDT testing involves spraying a component with a special fluid that glows under UV (ultra-violet) light. Fluid will be retained in any flaws or cracks, which appear as luminous highlighted areas (arrowed) under the UV light.

SETTING UP THE CAR

↑ Chief Mechanic Kenny Handkammer oversees final checks on the car before Mark Webber straps in and heads out on to the track.

→ Sebastian Vettel walks the track with his Race Engineer Guillaume Rocquelin ('Rocky') and engineering team prior to the 2010 Chinese Grand Prix.

At every grand prix, the aim is to optimise the performance of the car for qualifying and the race, to ensure that the car's lap times are as quick as possible. This is a complex process, and a large number of factors come into play. The race engineer will work closely with the driver to develop the optimum set-up, and will relay the driver's feedback to the engineering team. This feedback is used in conjunction with data collected from the car's telemetry to enable the engineering team to provide the driver with what he needs to do his job.

To hone the car's set-up, the driver needs to be confident in the car's handling – he needs the car to behave as he expects, particularly at the limit of its performance. If the driver is confident in the car, he will be able to extract the maximum from it.

For each circuit on the calendar, data records from the team's previous visits are used for reference in setting up the car, along with various predictive tools (simulation software and simulator equipment) and an understanding of how the current car compares with its

predecessor. The engineering team will prepare a logical list to work through in order to optimise the car's set-up, as Red Bull Racing's Head of Car Engineering, Paul Monaghan, explains: "If a previous car was unsettled over the kerbs, and you believe that the new car can cope better with kerbs, you may go into the weekend not worrying about a kerbing problem, and so move to the next item on the list."

During a race weekend, the data for both cars will be shared and analysed between the engineering teams and the drivers. Comparisons can be invaluable in improving the performance of both the car and the driver, as Mark Webber confirms: "We're constantly comparing each other – it's a great tool for us to use, the engineers and drivers, because generally someone can always do a slightly better job on certain sections of lap, so you try and bolt both of your best areas together and that way the car performance improves as well."

With the 2010 regulations and car characteristics, the most important phase of the weekend was the final qualifying session (Q3) on Saturday afternoon, and the aim was always to put the car in pole position. To this end, the strategy was often to aim for pole position at the expense of optimum set-up for the start of the race.

From the beginning of the 2010 season, with the ban on refuelling, the cars had to start the race with a full fuel load, and ideally finish the race with an almost empty tank. This means that the weight of the car can change by up to 160kg during the race, but does this have an effect on the car's set-up? Again, Paul Monaghan explains: "Lightening fuel load is not really something that can be catered for within set-up – it's really too late by that point! If the car is fundamentally good, it should be able to operate in a range of circumstances – light fuel, heavy fuel, windy day, still day – without having a significant impact on set-up. The set-up would only be changed to fire-fight. What you are really trying to control is the centre of pressure (see pages 128–129). If the centre of pressure position is so ride-height sensitive that you can't go from heavy fuel to light fuel and still have a driveable car, then that probably isn't something that can be rescued via set-up. If the car is benign to the fact that its weight changes by 160kg, you're OK. If it is very sensitive to weight change, you're going to struggle at some point, and you would choose to struggle at the start of the race, not in qualifying."

To set up the car for the race and qualifying, any adjustments to its mechanical set-up, or major aerodynamic adjustments, must be carried out during the weekend's three practice sessions, which take place on Friday morning (P1), Friday afternoon (P2) and Saturday morning (P3). The instant the car leaves the pitlane for the first qualifying session (Q1) on Saturday afternoon, its specification is effectively frozen. So, it is very important to optimise the set-up of the car during the final practice session.

HANDLING CHARACTERISTICS

There are two main handling characteristics for which drivers tend to have their own personal preferences – understeer and oversteer. The terms understeer and oversteer are used to describe the car's sensitivity to the driver's steering input.

Understeer occurs when the car steers less than the driver's steering inputs – the car wants to carry straight on when the driver turns the wheel to enter a corner. Understeer is a stable condition. The car can be turned more by increasing the steering input and/or stepping on the throttle.

Oversteer is exactly the opposite, when the car steers more than the driver's steering inputs – the car tends to want to spin when the driver turns in to a corner. Oversteer is an unstable condition, as the car will spin unless the driver takes corrective action by applying 'opposite lock' to the steering or lifting off the throttle.

Mark Webber gives an insight into how he likes his car to be set up: "I'm pretty much in the middle in terms of I do like to have the car pretty stable on the way in [to a corner], but not too stable. We've had some drivers in the past who could deal with a car that's incredibly neutral on the way in, so the rear is very, very unstable on the way in, and that's what they find is the right way for them to get round the track. Other drivers like a little bit more understeer, so more slipping of the front tyres through a corner. It sounds completely obvious that you'd like a perfectly balanced car, but I'm probably a little bit more towards the understeer side, but not too much. It's always a compromise – you'll never, ever have the perfect, perfect car through every corner and through every speed range, and certainly not for every lap of a grand prix – you're going to have to put up with problems here and there."

↑ The two Red Bull Racing drivers compare notes during a briefing before the 2010 Abu Dhabi Grand Prix.

ADJUSTMENT PARAMETERS

In order to get as close as possible to the performance potential of the car, it is necessary to achieve the best compromise of mechanical and aerodynamic set-up to suit track conditions, tyre characteristics and driver preference.

Generally, low-speed handling performance is governed by mechanical parameters, whereas high-speed handling performance is dictated by aerodynamic downforce and balance, although in practice there is a great deal of crossover between the two areas.

Optimising the set-up of the car is a complex process that relies heavily on the collation and interpretation of data (both from telemetry and from driver feedback). This is not always an exact science, as it is dependent on the driver's preferences, the fundamental handling characteristics of the car, and the changing circuit conditions during the weekend.

MECHANICAL ADJUSTMENTS
Anti-roll bars

The anti-roll bars are used to adjust the 'roll stiffness' of the car – its resistance to the tendency to roll around its longitudinal axis when cornering. The degree of roll during cornering has a direct effect on the weight transfer between the inside and outside wheels.

The anti-roll bars themselves are not adjustable, and the bars are changed to adjust roll stiffness. A selection of anti-roll bars is available, and bar choice is circuit-dependent. Often, anti-roll bars are changed when working on set-up during a lapping session – low-speed balance can be tuned by anti-roll bar changes. Softening the rear anti-roll bar can reduce oversteer and improve traction, whereas softening the front bar will reduce understeer.

Camber, castor and toe angles

Camber, castor and toe angles are all adjustable, although castor is rarely altered because the procedure involves changing major components such as wishbones and uprights.

Camber and toe adjustments are made primarily to keep the tyre working effectively – to present the tyre at the most appropriate angle to the tarmac all around the lap. Adjustments are always a compromise.

Once a basic toe setting has been established, small adjustments can be made to sharpen or dull the car's turn-in, to increase stability under braking, or to influence tyre temperature.

Toe adjustments are made using shims of varying thickness at the track-rod connections to the uprights. A bolt can be slackened to change the shimming on each side as required, providing a quick and easy means of adjustment.

Camber angles are always negative on an F1 car (negative means that the top of the tyre is leaning in towards the car), in order to maximise the contact patch of the tyre as the car rolls during cornering, and to try to provide an even temperature across the tyre tread. The camber angle used depends on the circuit, speed and the load on the tyres.

At Monza, typically a low rear camber angle would be used due to the high-speed nature of the track and the resulting high longitudinal loads and tyre temperature. As a result of the high loads and temperatures at Monza, blistering of the inside shoulders of the tyres is quite common.

Typical static camber angles would be 0–4° negative for the front and rear, although the front negative camber is always higher than the rear.

Typical toe angles are 0.5° toe-out to 0.5° toe-in for front and rear. Usually the front wheels will toe-out a little, and the rear wheels will toe-in.

At a low-speed track such as Monaco, a relatively high rear camber angle would be used, as the circuit imposes relatively lower loads and temperatures on the tyres.

Increasing the camber angle increases lateral grip at the expense of longitudinal grip (braking and traction).

Camber adjustments are made using shims of varying thickness at the upper wishbone connection to the upright.

← Camber adjustments are made using shims (arrowed) at the upper wishbone connection to the upright.

← Mark Webber's mechanics prepare to send him out of the garage for another lapping session.

↑ The performance of the car over kerbs is an important factor in overall lap times.

↓ A view of the inside of the team's 'tree house'. This room is mounted on stilts over the race transporters in the paddock, and acts as the team's operations centre at the circuit.

Springs and dampers

Spring and damper settings can be adjusted as part of the car set-up.

Although an F1 car has extremely stiff suspension, it is not completely rigid. The typical range of movement for the suspension, measured at the uprights, is around 20mm at the front, and 50mm at the rear – extremely limited compared with a road car. These figures exclude tyre squash, which is dependent on temperature and pressure. At the front of the car, tyre squash allows for more movement than suspension travel, but this is not the case for the rear.

The relationship between suspension movement and aerodynamics is very important, and this is another area where ride height comes into play, as Paul Monaghan explains: "If the aero team can create a front wing, or a rear diffuser, which is reasonably insensitive to ride height, that essentially means that you can allow the car to move up and down a lot, because the aero is not sensitive to vertical movement. This in turn means that you can soften the suspension to enable the car to run over kerbs well. If the car has to be nailed to a particular ride height because the aerodynamics fall apart if the car moves about, then you have to run very stiff springs, which means that the car clatters over kerbs and flies in the air. If you can have a car that can be run soft enough to benefit from running over kerbs to shorten the circuit, but still not lose all its downforce when running on the [smooth] track, then it will help lap time, and you're in pretty good shape."

Ballast

The position of ballast can be adjusted to tune weight distribution, and hence the position of the car's centre of gravity. This is a major tuning aid to balance the car and optimise tyre performance and life.

AERODYNAMIC ADJUSTMENTS
Ride height

Altering the ride height has a significant effect on the aerodynamic balance of the car. The closer the car's floor is to the surface of the track, the more downforce is generated, and the aim is always to run the car as close as possible to the ground. Generally, the lower the ride height, the quicker the car will go. However, there is a compromise to be struck, as the lower the car is to the track, the more it will bottom out – the bottom of the car hitting the surface of the track. This affects the car's controllability, and erodes the FIA regulation plank under the car; the plank is 10mm thick at the start of the race, and must be a minimum 9mm thick at the end.

It is impossible to keep the ride height constant, as the aerodynamic load on the car increases with speed, pushing the car further down on to the track the faster it goes, so the ride height must be optimised to give the best compromise for a specific circuit.

The other major factor in determining the ride height of the car is controlling the position of the centre of pressure (C of P – see pages 128–129). This is a critical factor in the car's aerodynamic stability. If the C of P is too far forwards, it can cause directional instability (usually oversteer).

Bumps in the track can be a significant problem, and so ride height may be raised to avoid problems at a point on the track where the driver needs the car to have good stability, such as under heavy braking at the end of a fast straight with significant bumps in the braking zone. This is a situation where there's a risk of the car spinning if it bottoms out under braking.

The car is normally set up with the front ride height lower than the rear, giving a slightly nose-down attitude known as 'rake'. This rake allows the floor and diffuser to work efficiently to produce downforce. Changing the attitude (angle) of the floor has a significant effect on aerodynamic performance (see 'Floor' on page 43).

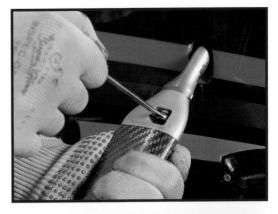

← To change the front ride height, the push-rod top bolt is slackened.

← The push-rod is pulled away from the chassis so that shims can be added or removed as required.

So, essentially, by fine-tuning ride height at the front and rear of the car, the aerodynamic balance of the car can be changed. A tiny change in ride height can have a significant effect on the balance, and adjustments are made in increments of just a few millimetres.

Ride-height adjustments are made by using shims of varying thickness at the push-rod mounting to the chassis at the front of the car, or the pull-rod mounting to the gearbox at the rear. With push-rod suspension the shimming thickness is increased to raise the ride height, whereas with pull-rod suspension the shimming thickness is *decreased* to raise ride height.

↓ In this view of Mark Webber's car at Silverstone, the rake of the floor, with the front ride-height lower than the rear, is very apparent.

↑ Sebastian Vettel talks to his Race Engineer, 'Rocky', on the grid as the mechanics jack the car up to fit tyre warmers prior to the start of the European Grand Prix.

→ Fine adjustment of the angle of the front wing main flap can be made by using a key.

Wing angles

As we have already seen, both front and rear wings are constantly evolving over the season. Generally the wings can be divided into three distinct sets – for low, medium or high downforce. Low-downforce wings will be used at a circuit such as Monza, high-downforce at Monaco and medium-downforce at circuits such as Silverstone or Montréal.

On the front wing, the main plane is normally set at a fixed angle, but the main flap is adjustable. During 2010, the front wing main flap on the RB6 was adjustable by the driver during the race, and this system and its use are described in more detail on pages 38–39.

The rear wing has two elements, and the angle of both elements, and the gap between them, can be changed to provide the downforce characteristics required. Sometimes the elements themselves may be changed. The downforce characteristics for the rear wing can be 'mapped' using CFD and wind-tunnel simulations, and the race engineer can then select the best rear wing set-up (in terms of the two elements and their angles) to achieve the required downforce/drag compromise that gives the lowest lap times or desired End of Straight (EoS) speed. It is rare to adjust wing element angles during a weekend for set-up reasons, and more usual to change a complete wing assembly.

Any change made to the rear wing must be balanced with a change to the front wing, and *vice versa*.

Both front and rear wings may be fitted with various 'gurney' flaps and trim tabs to provide fine adjustments. These flaps are used for various purposes, but generally they create turbulence at the rear edges of a wing element. This helps to reduce the pressure behind the wing element, and therefore speeds up the airflow over it, providing a small increase in downforce.

Once the base set-up for the car has been established for a specific circuit, adjustment of the wings is normally used only to fine-tune the balance of the car to suit the driver's preferences. The steeper the wing angle, the more downforce (and more drag) the wing will generate. Wing

adjustments can be used to move the car's centre of pressure forwards or backwards, which in turn can alter the handling characteristics by changing the bias from oversteer to understeer. For example, if the driver's preference was for less understeer, the wings can be adjusted to move the centre of pressure forwards to reduce understeer. To achieve this, the front wing could be adjusted to provide more downforce, or the rear wing could be adjusted to give less downforce, or a combination of the two.

GEARING

As part of the set-up process, the gearing must be set to suit the circuit. The optimum gearing will depend on the mix of low-speed and high-speed corners, and the top speed achieved by the car on the fastest part of the circuit.

At the start of each season, the team must declare 30 pairs of gear ratios to the FIA, from which to select gears to suit all the circuits visited during the season.

Gear ratio selection (the gearbox has seven forward ratios) is an important part of the car set-up process for each race. The general philosophy used to select gear ratios is to select the lowest gear ratio to provide the best acceleration out of the slowest corner on the circuit, and to select the highest ratio to ensure that the car is approaching the engine's rev limit at the end of the longest straight (allowing for the fact that the revs will effectively rise if the car is following closely in the slipstream of another car). The intermediate ratios are adjusted so that they are evenly spaced between the lowest and highest gears to ensure that the engine can be kept in its optimum power band. The engineers also aim for the minimum practical rev drop between gears, as the higher the rev drop, the higher the impact loading on the gears during gear changes, leading to increased stress and wear on the components.

Gear ratio selection is complicated slightly for the 2011 season by the introduction of the adjustable rear wing and the reintroduction of KERS, which means that the highest ratio must be selected to cater for the temporary increase in speed (and revs) when the rear wing and/or KERS is activated.

Although the gearbox is sealed by the FIA, the seals can be broken once during each race weekend, 'at any time prior to the second day of practice, for the sole purpose of changing gear ratios and dog rings (excluding final drives or reduction gears).' Because the gearbox has to be removed to change the ratios, it takes around two hours to carry out a ratio change, so this is a procedure that can be carried out between practice sessions, though it is not practical during a session.

Teams will not run a race gearbox during Friday practice, as this would put unnecessary mileage on a gearbox which, during 2010, had to last for four full qualifying days and races (five from the beginning of the 2011 season).

The standard procedure is to run a non-race gearbox on Friday and then, after Friday practice is completed, break the seals on the race gearbox (if it has been used at a previous race) in order to change the ratios to suit the relevant circuit. For example, the ratios used in a gearbox at the Canadian GP would be wrong for the next race at Silverstone, and so they would need to be changed before fitting the gearbox to the car. The gear ratios to be used for qualifying and the race must be selected and declared to the FIA no later than two hours after the second Friday practice session (P2). The gearbox is filled with fresh lubricant when the new ratios are fitted.

The differential ratio cannot easily be changed for a specific race, because it is an integral part of the gearbox, which had to be used for four consecutive races during 2010 (five for 2011).

BRAKES

The two main brake set-up parameters are brake cooling and brake bias. Red Bull Racing uses the same brake pad materials for all circuits, although they are tailored to suit the drivers' preferences.

As explained on page 70 ('Brake wear' panel), brake cooling is critical to keep the brakes within their optimum operating-temperature range. To provide optimum cooling for the circuit characteristics and ambient temperatures, a range of brake cooling ducts is available, and numerous different brake duct configurations will be

⬇ A selection of brake ducts. Various configurations are used, depending on the circuit and ambient temperature.

→ A typical front brake duct assembly.

↓ The driver's brake-bias lever (arrowed) is located on the left-hand side of the cockpit.

used during the season. It is not uncommon for brake-duct modifications to be made at the circuit over a race weekend if the conditions differ from those expected.

Although the 'base' brake bias is adjusted on the car as part of the set-up procedure for each race, fine-tuning of the brake bias can be carried out by the driver. A mechanical brake-bias adjustment system is used, and on the RB6 the driver controls this using a lever on the left-hand side of the cockpit.

Brake bias is not only circuit-dependent, but also corner-dependent, and the driver will often adjust the brake bias between corners during a lap,

as Mark Webber explains: "The brake bias control can be used during a lap because for some corners the car will perform a little differently, even though they might be the same speed. A corner might be a second-gear left-hander or a second-gear right-hander, but sometimes some tracks give different characteristics for each corner, and we need to be able to adjust our brake balance around the lap. There will generally be a trend or a pattern that will unfold, and certain corners require different brake balance. So, we would just quickly flick the lever with our [left] hand, forwards or rearwards to adjust the brake balance before we hit the brakes, and reset it at a set point on the track. So there will be a pattern emerging, but that pattern could go forward or back.

"Let's say that you have a specific brake balance that you might start the race with and you hover two or three clicks pre- and post- that position, and then as the race goes on the car gets lighter, and there's more grip on the track, and the tyres wear, then that position might need to change again. It's something that has a reasonable influence on the balance of the car on the entry to a specific corner."

ENGINE AND TRANSMISSION

Engine mapping and the setting of the gearshift points are used extensively as part of the car set-up for a particular circuit. Engine mapping can be used to improve driveability, giving the driver more confidence in the car, and aiding lap times by providing the maximum possible engine power when the driver requires it.

The FIA regulations permit five engine maps. The mapping of the engine can be adjusted for both drive and overrun conditions, but the main area of concentration is the transition from 'neutral' power to full power – effectively the adjustment of how progressive the throttle is (the throttle is a 'drive-by-wire' system, with no mechanical connection between the throttle pedal and the engine).

The aim is always to enable the driver to pick up the throttle to obtain maximum power as quickly as possible, but from the point of view of car control and providing maximum acceleration, there are certain times when it is useful to be able to adjust the throttle response. For example, when cornering, once the driver has finished braking, he will turn in and balance the car on the throttle, with the aim of accelerating as quickly as possible to maximum power through the exit of the corner. When the car is under a high lateral load during cornering, especially on a bumpy track, and the driver is moving from a 'neutral' throttle – balancing the car – to full throttle, it is useful to have a progressive throttle 'action' (with a linear response to the driver's right foot). Once the driver is accelerating hard out of the corner, with the

← Paul Monaghan, Head of Car Engineering, is reponsible for the build spec of the cars, and ensures reliable and safe operation of the cars at the circuit.

⬇ Brake cooling fans ready for action outside the pit garage at the Spanish Grand Prix.

lateral load decreasing, he needs to be as close to maximum power as quickly as possible, and so the power delivery can be more aggressive. Then, if there is a kerb or a rumble strip on the exit of the corner, ideally the driver again needs a more progressive throttle (with the engine already much closer to maximum power) in order to avoid the risk of sudden changes in power unsettling the car as the driver's foot vibrates on the throttle pedal over the kerbing.

TYRES

Tyre temperatures are critical, as are tyre pressures, and the tyre temperature must be kept within the manufacturer's recommended operating window. The most fundamental set-up parameter for adjusting tyre temperature is altering the weight distribution. An F1 car has a rearward-biased weight distribution, but this must be optimised to suit the tyre requirements. Camber adjustment is also used to control tyre temperature.

When setting up the car for a specific circuit, the engineers will aim for equal tyre temperatures at all four corners of the car, with an even temperature across each tyre contact patch. If the tyre temperature moves outside the specific temperature window for the compound being used – too hot or too cold – the level of grip can drop dramatically, resulting in slower lap times. If the tyres are too hot, blistering can result, which can exacerbate grip problems and lead to increased tyre wear.

The car is fitted with tyre temperature and pressure sensors for each wheel, to enable the team to monitor tyre performance and condition during a race. This system enables the team to inform the driver, via the radio system, if there is any issue with the tyres and to advise him on how best to deal with the situation, perhaps by making adjustments to the differential settings or changing driving style to minimise the impact of the problem.

Optimum operating temperatures for the tyres vary according to the tyre manufacturer. During 2010, the optimum operating temperatures windows for the Bridgestone tyres were often somewhere around 80°C for a dry-weather tyre, anywhere between 50°C and 80°C for an intermediate tyre and between 30°C and 50°C for an extreme-wet tyre.

RACE WEEKEND

↑ The calm before the storm. An RB6 lies under the covers in the garage awaiting action in Valencia at the 2010 European Grand Prix.

➜ The middle label in the cockpit shows that the car has been passed as fit to race by the FIA scrutineer. This is the car in which Sebastian Vettel clinched the Drivers' World Championship in Abu Dhabi.

A race weekend usually starts on a Wednesday, when the teams arrive and set up at the track. The cars are scrutineered on Thursday, and will run on the track for the first time on Friday, when two 1½-hour practice sessions are held. A further one-hour practice session is held on Saturday morning, followed by qualifying in the afternoon. After Saturday's final qualifying session, the cars do not run on the track again until the

'reconnaissance' lap(s) on the way to the grid for the race on Sunday afternoon.

Various meetings will be held over a race weekend, and a schedule of engineering meetings will have been put together before the weekend starts. A general engineering meeting will be held at the beginning of each day, and as a result of this there will be spin-off strategy meetings, a tyre meeting, car-build specification meeting, etc. Over the weekend, the team will follow a set plan of action, and all the engineers and mechanics will be kept constantly busy.

SCRUTINEERING

On the Thursday of each race meeting, the cars are scrutineered by FIA-approved scrutineers to ensure that they conform to the regulations. Each car's chassis number is verified, and checks are made to ensure that FIA seals are fitted in the required positions. Checks are made on safety-related items such as the harness and the driver's helmet to ensure that they are of the correct specification. On a rotation basis, samples of fluids may be taken for analysis, or a fire extinguisher bottle may be disconnected to check its contents. The scrutineers may decide to carry out a random test such as a front-wing deflection test or a tea-tray deflection test (see pages 37 and 45). Local scrutineers will carry out simple checks such as harness and paperwork, but permanent FIA scrutineers carry out more complex checks.

At any time during a race weekend, the scrutineers may check the dimensions of the car's bodywork and wings, etc. To ensure that the car is legal in this respect, standard FIA templates are used, and the car is checked on a flat reference platform called 'the bridge', on which the car can also be weighed. On Thursday, each team will normally use the scrutineers' templates to check their own cars, to ensure that they will conform to the regulations if checked at any point during the weekend.

Cars may be called at random at any point during the race meeting for checks, and the top three finishers are usually scrutineered after the race.

START-UP

Details of the start-up procedure for the car are given on page 83.

THE INSTALLATION LAP

The first time a car runs on any given day, the driver will exit the pitlane, drive a single lap at a relatively leisurely pace, and drive straight back to the team's garage. During this lap, the driver may be asked to check specific systems or follow certain procedures. This is known as the installation lap.

The installation lap is used to check that all the car's systems are functioning correctly before the driver takes to the track for full-speed running. When the car returns to the garage after the installation lap, the team will check for visible leaks and signs of any damaged or loose components. During the installation lap itself,

the team will be checking data from the car's telemetry system, and when the car returns to the garage the 'umbilical' will be plugged in to carry out a complete systems check.

After the installation lap, oil samples will be taken from the engine and gearbox. The oil supplier (Total in the case of Red Bull Racing) will take these samples for analysis at its mobile trackside testing facility. Data on any contaminants found in the oils will be available very quickly, often during the relevant track session. From this analysis, it is possible to determine if any unusual wear or contamination is taking place that may indicate a problem. For example, high iron or aluminium content may indicate to the engineers that unusual wear is taking place. This analysis is particularly important during the Saturday morning practice session, as the specification of the car is frozen from the start of the first Saturday qualifying session (Q1) and no components can be changed without incurring a grid penalty.

It is rare for any set-up adjustments to be made after the installation lap, as the driver will not have a feel for the car at this stage. One of the most important checks made at the end of the installation lap is a tyre-pressure check. Any unexpected rise in tyre pressure may indicate a problem with the starting pressures (even though the tyres are pre-heated using tyre warmers, the tyre pressures will rise significantly from the 'cold' static value once the car is running at speed).

Once the installation lap is completed, and assuming that there are no issues arising from the checks made afterwards, the team will send the driver back out on to the track to follow a predetermined running programme. Often, the first run will be relatively short, say five laps or so, and small set-up adjustments may be made afterwards depending on the driver's feedback and data.

← With helmet visor still up, Sebastian Vettel heads out on the track for the first time during the Malaysian Grand Prix weekend to carry out an installation lap.

↑ A Renault engineer monitors data in the garage during the Abu Dhabi Grand Prix weekend.

↓ Sebastian Vettel in conversation during a pre-race briefing.

PRACTICE

There are three practice sessions over the race weekend (in 2010 and 2011): the first on Friday morning (P1), the second on Friday afternoon (P2) and the third on Saturday morning (P3).

The set-up of the car for Friday-morning practice can be tricky, as the track conditions at some circuits can change dramatically between the first Friday practice session and the final qualifying session (Q3) on Saturday afternoon. In these circumstances, an experienced team will learn not to change the set-up to react to the track conditions on Friday morning, when the track is likely to be 'green' and quite possibly very 'oversteery' (giving the impression of low rear-end grip). If set-up changes are made on Friday morning, by Friday afternoon, when the track has 'rubbered in', a team may find itself in trouble if it is chasing a set-up to suit the changing conditions. This is where data and

experience from previous visits to the track is invaluable. In this situation an experienced team will probably elect to carry on lapping without making any major changes to suit the conditions, on the assumption that all will be well by the time qualifying takes place on Saturday afternoon. This may give the impression that the team is not competitive in terms of lap times.

Mark Webber gives a driver's perspective on the track 'rubbering in' over a 2010 race weekend: "When you go somewhere with a green track and there's not much rubber been put down, the compound on the tyre is actually left on the track, and that increases the grip as the weekend goes on. You have more rubber on the track, so the rubber on the tyres loves that and their grip increases, so your lap times will improve. Then you get more and more confident in how the car behaves. You need to stay on top of that, particularly at a place like Monaco or Budapest where the tracks aren't used that often. They're very green when we arrive there, and so the 'ramp-up' of the track can be much more severe."

With the ban on in-season testing, Friday practice can be used as a test session, though the time spent changing components, and hence the reduced opportunity for time on track, must be weighed up against the likely benefits. The car must be 'race-legal' during Friday practice, so no parts or data-logging systems can be fitted that do not conform to FIA regulations.

Set-up changes such as anti-roll-bar changes, ride-height changes and front and rear wing changes are relatively quick and easy to carry out, but fitting an item such as a new floor or diffuser can be a time-consuming job, and so the team might choose to carry out this work between the two Friday practice sessions.

After the second Friday practice session, the car will be dismantled in order to set it up for qualifying on Saturday. The engine, gearbox and rear suspension assembly are usually changed ready for qualifying and the race. Non-race units will be run on Friday to avoid putting unnecessary mileage on the units used for the race.

Various engineering and strategy meetings will take place after the second Friday practice session, in order to make significant decisions on the configuration of the car for Saturday. For example, during Friday practice a new floor, front wing or rear wing may have been tested, and the car may have been run in various different configurations during the day – for example, with high and low ride heights. It is possible that there

may have been significant aerodynamic and/or mechanical changes, possibly involving new parts. Changes may have been made to software, such as new differential maps.

On Friday evening all these changes are evaluated to give the optimum 'cocktail' of changes for Saturday. The configuration in which the car finished Friday running may not be the best option. When there has been time to analyse the data from Friday in detail, previously unseen patterns may emerge. For example, a rear wing configuration that was tried during the first Friday practice session (P1) may have been taken off at the end of the session because it was perceived not to be as effective as expected with the car configuration being run at the time. It may be that further analysis shows that this particular wing configuration needs to be combined with other options tested during the day, in order to provide the best overall package.

Often, new brake discs and pads will be fitted on Friday evening, in addition to other components, ready for the final practice session on Saturday morning. A new exhaust is always fitted when the race engine is installed.

The period between P3 and Q1 is the last chance to fit new components and make changes to the car's set-up before qualifying and the race without incurring a penalty. Once the car leaves the pitlane at the start of Q1, its specification is effectively frozen for the weekend. The 'Post-qualifying *parc fermé* regulations' section on the next page details the work permitted on the car between the start of Q1 and the start of the race.

QUALIFYING

The set-up for qualifying is determined at the end of P3. Based on data collected from this session, the team will usually make a decision on how many qualifying laps they think is optimum for the tyres with which they are intending to finish the final qualifying session (Q3).

There are a few points to bear in mind to gain a better understanding of the strategy used for qualifying:

■ The regulations stipulate that each car that takes part in the final qualifying session must start the race using the same set of tyres with which the driver set his qualifying time.
■ In 2010, and for 2011, cars can qualify on a light fuel load, as they are topped up with a full fuel load after final qualifying, ready for the start of the race.
■ In 2010, and for 2011, the eight slowest cars are eliminated from qualifying after the first, 20-minute, session (Q1). Another eight cars are eliminated at the end of the second, 15-minute, session (Q2), leaving the 10 fastest cars to participate in the final, 10-minute, session (Q3).

↑ The team's senior management and engineers monitor the performance of the cars and refine race strategy from the pit wall during the race.

The FIA regulations state that only the following work is permitted on the car between the beginning of Q1 and the start of the race:

■ Engines may be started.
■ Fuel may be added or removed and a fuel breather fitted.
■ Wheels and tyres may be removed, changed or rebalanced and tyre pressures checked.
■ Spark plugs may be removed in order to carry out an internal engine inspection and cylinder compression checks.
■ Permitted heating or cooling devices may be fitted.
■ A jump battery may be connected and on-board electrical units may be freely accessed via a physical connection to the car.
■ The main electrical battery and radio batteries may be changed.
■ The brake system may be bled.
■ Engine oil may be drained.
■ Compressed gases may be drained or added.
■ Fluids with a specific gravity less than 1.1 may be drained and/or replenished, however, fluids used for replenishment must conform to the same specification as the original fluid.
■ If the FIA technical delegate is satisfied that changes in climatic conditions necessitate alterations to the specification of a car, changes may be made to the air ducts around the front and rear brakes and radiator ducts. These changes may be made at any time after the message "Change in climatic conditions" is shown on the timing monitors, from this point the choice of air ducts around the front and rear brakes and radiator ducts is free, subject always to compliance with the relevant Technical Regulations.
■ Bodywork (excluding radiators) may be removed and/or cleaned.
■ Cosmetic changes may be made to the bodywork and tape may be added.
■ Any part of the car may be cleaned.

■ On-board cameras, marshalling system components, timing transponders and any associated equipment may be removed, refitted or checked.
■ Any work required by the FIA technical delegate.
■ Changes to improve the driver's comfort. In this context anything other than the adjustment of mirrors, seat belts and pedals may only be carried out with the specific permission of the FIA technical delegate. The addition or removal of padding (or similar material) is also permitted but may only be carried out under supervision and, if required by the FIA technical delegate, must be removed before the post-race weighing procedure.
■ Drinking fluid for the driver may be added at any time, however, the capacity of the container for any such fluid must not exceed 1.5 litres.
■ Repair of genuine accident damage.
■ Any parts which are removed from the car in order to carry out any work specifically permitted above, or any parts removed to carry out essential safety checks, must remain close to it and, at all times, be visible to the scrutineer assigned to the relevant car.
■ Any work not listed above may only be undertaken with the approval of the FIA technical delegate following a written request from the team concerned. It must be clear that any replacement part a team wishes to fit is similar in mass, inertia and function to the original. Any parts removed will be retained by the FIA.
■ However, if a team wishes to change a part during the qualifying session and/or on the grid before the start of the race, this may be done without first seeking the permission of the technical delegate, provided it is reasonable for the relevant team to believe permission would be given if there was time to ask and the broken or damaged part remains in full view of the scrutineer assigned to the car at all times.

The team will determine whether the car configuration is better suited to one long qualifying run, or two short runs, and whether there is time to do two short runs on low fuel. This would involve doing a qualifying run, pitting to take on new tyres and more fuel, and going out again for a second run before the end of the session. There may not be time to refuel, in which case the driver can do two runs, with a change of tyres between runs, but on the first run the car will be heavier than ideal, as it will be carrying sufficient fuel for two runs and the in- and out-laps. This means that the car will be less competitive, but the driver will be able to get in a 'banker' lap, in case the second lap (with optimum fuel load) does not go as planned. This is all part of the strategy, and by this stage the team may have been able to glean a good idea as to what their rivals are doing in terms of qualifying strategy.

The strategy may be affected by events at the previous race. For example, if a driver was held up in qualifying at the previous race, and was unable to fulfil the car's potential as a result, the team may decide to send the driver out early in the final qualifying session, knowing that the tyres will last, or they might choose to go out in the final seconds of the session, with the aim of being the last car on the track. All these decisions have usually been made beforehand.

Within 3½ hours of the end of Q3, the cars enter parc fermé overnight, at which point the teams are not allowed to carry out any further work on them. The only work allowed on the cars before this overnight cut-off is that described in the section 'Post-qualifying parc fermé regulations' on the facing page.

SEBASTIAN VETTEL'S RACE PREPARATION

Sebastian Vettel provides this insight into his personal preparations on race day:

"Usually something light for breakfast, muesli and fruit in the morning and some combination of pasta or rice and chicken plus some mixed vegetables for lunch. Very basic – no secrets. Basically Sundays are routine. We go to the drivers' parade, after that I have some time for myself where I lie down and relax, listen to some music, then I get ready, which means changing and getting into my suit. Around 40 minutes before the start I go into the garage and get strapped into the car. I drive the car onto the grid, go for a quick pee, then get strapped into the car again and get ready for the race. I always get into the car from the left side. And I carry a few lucky charms with me, such as a lucky coin and a lucky pig."

THE RACE

On race morning, the cars are released from overnight *parc fermé*, but the restrictions on working on the cars still apply (see 'Post-qualifying *parc fermé* regulations' on the facing page).

The pitlane is opened 30 minutes before the start of the race, and the cars are allowed to complete a 'reconnaissance lap' on their way to the grid. Each car can complete more than one reconnaissance lap, but in this case the car must drive down the pitlane at reduced speed, rather than proceeding to the grid.

When the car leaves the garage for its reconnaissance lap(s), each lap is treated as

← During final qualifying (Q3) rapid tyre stops may be made if a two-run qualifying strategy is being used.

As the race start approaches, the regulations state that the following procedure must be followed:

- Fifteen minutes before the start of the race, the pitlane is closed (warning signals are given). Any car left in the pitlane at this point cannot make its way to the grid, and must start the race from the pitlane.
- The approach of the start is indicated by signals (visual and audible) ten minutes, five minutes, three minutes, one minute and then fifteen seconds before the start of the formation lap.
- When the ten-minute signal is given, everyone except for drivers, officials and team technical staff must leave the grid.
- When the three-minute signal is given, all the cars on the grid must have their wheels fitted. After this signal, wheels may only be removed in the pitlane, or on the grid if the race is suspended. A ten-second penalty is imposed on any car that does not have all its wheels fully fitted at this point.
- When the one-minute signal is given, the engine must be started, and all team personnel must leave the grid by the time the fifteen-second signal is given, taking all equipment with them. If any driver needs any assistance after the fifteen-second signal, he must raise his arm, and when the other cars have left the grid, the marshals will push the car into the pitlane, from where it must start the race.
- When the green lights illuminate, the cars must begin the formation lap.
- When the cars return to the grid after the formation lap, they must stop in their correct grid positions with engines running.
- Once all the cars have come to a halt, the first red light will be illuminated on the starting-light gantry indicating five seconds until the start of the race. The four-, three-, two- and one-second lights will follow this. At any time after the one-second light illuminates (all red lights now illuminated), the race starts when all the red lights are extinguished.

an installation lap. During each lap all the car's systems are checked, exactly as described on page 159 for an installation lap.

Once the car arrives on the grid, tyre warmers are fitted, and the umbilical is connected to monitor all systems. Electric cooling fans will usually be placed in the radiator ducts and often in the brake cooling ducts, to ensure that 'heat soak' does not cause overheating of the engine, gearbox and brakes. Temperatures will be monitored continually, and if any temperatures drop close to the lower end of the recommended operating range, the relevant cooling fans will be removed. If the engine temperature drops significantly, due to a long wait on the grid, the engine may be fired up to circulate fluids and maintain the temperatures.

For a wet race, suitable tyres will be fitted, and certain software settings will be changed on the car – gear upshift and downshift points, differential settings, etc – to suit the lower level of grip available.

For details of the race start procedure, refer to the 'Race start' panel on the left.

Once the race is underway, the engineers will constantly monitor all the car's systems. A separate team of Renault engineers will be watching the engine telemetry, while other engineers will be monitoring the circuit timing data and TV coverage to keep an eye on what rivals are doing in terms of strategy and track position.

The team has a real-time data-link with its factory in the UK, and during a race weekend the team's 'mission control' room in the Milton Keynes factory will be constantly manned, with specialists analysing the data transmitted back from the track. This data analysis enables the team to develop race strategy as the weekend progresses, and to check for any signs of potential problems with the car. The team in Milton Keynes works in parallel with the engineers at the track to optimise the performance of both of the team's cars throughout the weekend.

The pit crew responsible for carrying out work on the car during pit stops will be ready for action at any time during the race, in case the unexpected happens, for example a puncture or accident damage. Often, the pit crew will watch the race on monitors in the garage until they are called into action.

Pit stops are well-drilled, slick operations, and with the ban on refuelling from the start of the 2010 season, unless there is a problem with the car, pit stops are made purely for tyre changes. In 2010, the rules stated that at least one pit stop had to be made, as each car had to use two different compounds of tyre during the race.

When the driver is on the way into the pits, he will reset any adjustments he has made to the car's systems as a result of tyre performance issues to their default values, so that the car is set up for the fresh tyres.

When a decision is made to bring a car in for a pit stop, the pit crew spring into action. The driver is guided into his pit 'box' by the 'lollipop man'. The driver will stop in a predetermined position, and two mechanics will instantly move into position to jack up the front and rear of the car.

PIT STOP

During a 2010 Red Bull Racing pit stop, 17 crew members worked on the car. Each pit stop is absolutely critical to the outcome of the race, and any mistakes could have serious consequences, both for the result of the race, and from a safety point of view.

Race Team Manager Jonathan Wheatley drives the development of equipment and procedures to speed up pit stops and other trackside activities. He supervises frequent pit-stop practices in the continuing effort to knock another tenth of a second of the pit-stop time. The role of each member of the crew is as follows:

- Lollipop man – responsible for stopping and releasing the car safely.
- Three mechanics for each wheel – one working the air gun to remove and replace the wheel nut, one to lift off the old wheel, and one to fit the new wheel.
- Front jack – operates manual jack under front wing jacking point.
- Rear jack – operates manual jack under crash-structure jacking point.
- Fire extinguisher – stands by in case of problems.
- Air bottle top-up – replenishes Renault engine pneumatic-valve reservoir if necessary.

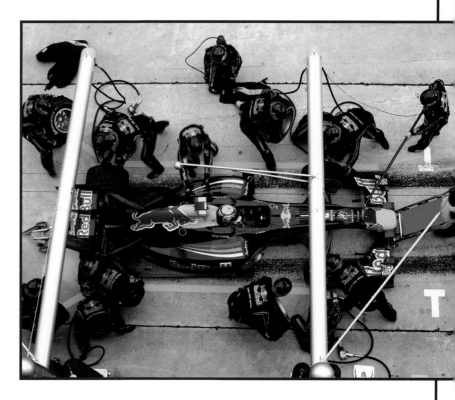

↑ The pit crew go to work on Mark Webber's car during the 2010 Malaysian Grand Prix.

Each of the four mechanics operating the wheel guns will raise a hand when his wheel is securely fitted, and the 'lollipop man' watches in order to lift the 'lollipop' once all four wheels are fitted, signalling the driver to rejoin the race.

During 2010 Red Bull Racing were astonishingly quick at carrying out pit stops, and the time taken from the point at which the car stops, to change all four wheels and leave the pit box was often less than four seconds!

AFTER THE RACE

At the end of the race, there is still plenty of work to do as the cars must be prepared for transport back to the team HQ in Milton Keynes or to the next race. In either case, there is plenty of packing up to do. If there are two consecutive 'flyaway' races, then the cars and the team's equipment will usually be transported straight to the next race. If the cars have been called in for post-race scrutineering, there will be a wait before they are released back to the team.

If the cars are being transported by air, fluids will be drained for safety reasons. Usually the two cars are transported more-or-less complete, with all components in place, although sometimes certain components may be removed. All the team equipment is designed to fit into either the team's trucks for European races or in air-freight containers for the 'flyaway' races. When all the equipment arrives back at the team's HQ, or at the next race, the whole procedure begins again...

← 'Mission control' at the team's Milton Keynes HQ. This room is a hive of activity during a grand prix weekend.

THE RACE DRIVER'S VIEW

'The driver is the biggest sensor in the car, and he's the one who's got to be in charge of most things.'

Mark Webber – Driver, Red Bull Racing

↑ The RB6 cockpit is a tight fit, with just enough space for the driver to sit.

FROM THE COCKPIT
An insight into how the world looks from the cockpit of an F1 car.

"The first thing that strikes you is the seating position. What's in the cockpit is very limited, and there are no comforts for the driver. It's pretty raw, and everything's in there to do a job and no more. We have an amazing set of seat belts, and the steering wheel is pretty tiny, and only two pedals. There's a lot which is completely alien to most people who have only driven road cars.

"We lie down in the car, a bit like lying in the bath, with our feet up, strapped in very, very heavily to the back of a carbon-fibre seat, which is very hard and very lightweight and strong in construction. You then have the main chassis, which is very close to you, with your elbows very close to it. It's very compact, your knees are together and your ankles are together down in the footwell area. All braking is done with the left foot – you can't get across from one pedal to the other, because the steering column is in the way. It's built for the minimum the designers can get away with to package the driver in the cockpit.

"You can see the tops of the tyres – that's important because when we're talking about feedback and modulating the inputs, particularly under braking. Sometimes we'll lock a front tyre, which means that we've over-applied the brake pressure slightly and if we were blindfolded we could probably feel that through the pedal. Instinctively we'd probably eke out a little brake pressure or, even within that braking phase if you leave the same brake pressure [applied], with speed coming off, time will probably get that tyre turning back again. This all happens in a split second. It's useful to be able to see the tops of the tyres so that we can see instantaneously what's happening to the tyres.

"The driver needs to have very good forward vision for lots of reasons – for racing, for wheel-to-wheel combat. For racing at somewhere like Monte Carlo we need to be able to see the edges of the front tyres. We know where the rear tyre is – we can't see the tyre, but we've got a good idea of where it is, and obviously that's important on a street circuit where we're brushing barriers.

"We can't see the front wing, but we've got a good idea of where it is. We need to be careful, it's not that easy. I think we can get within 30cm pretty easily, but after that – 20cm, 10cm – it's quite difficult to know exactly where it is."

Although the fundamental principles involved in driving an F1 car are no different from any other car, it does require a unique set of skills and only a handful of drivers in the world possess the ability to take such a car to the limit to explore its full potential. On-board TV footage provides a good impression of how the world looks from the driving seat, but the perspective is distorted. TV pictures cannot give an impression of what it *feels* like to experience the acceleration, braking and cornering forces, the sounds and smells, and the emotions of driving an F1 car at the limit while racing wheel-to-wheel with equally committed rivals.

Mark Webber provides a flavour of how it feels to drive the best F1 car in the world during 2010, the Red Bull Racing RB6.

PERFORMANCE

A comparison between driving an F1 car and driving a typical road car.

"The car is very stiff – you can't really compare it to a normal road car. As soon as you leave the garage, there's not much suspension movement, and the clutch is on the steering wheel, so there's a lot which is completely different to what you'd probably have on a road car, and yet has the same function. We still have a clutch, we still have to put the car in first gear, but once we've left the garage things are very different.

"Performance comes from the fact that the car is incredibly stiff and rigid and that will ultimately give the car more grip and performance. Another thing that hits you is how direct the steering is; the car is incredibly precise. Horsepower and braking are incredibly violent – nothing like a road car.

"If you have the skill and the talent to put the car on the limit, and get the brakes hot and the tyres hot, the car gives you a lot more back, because that's how the car is meant to be driven – an F1 car is not a very nice thing to drive slowly. It doesn't like being driven slowly – the tyres get cold, the brakes get cold, it's not a very pleasant experience at all, as there's a very low feeling for what the car's doing. In the right hands, it gives you feedback."

SENSING THE CAR'S RESPONSES

Putting a car on the limit.

"Our job is to control the slip of the tyre. Obviously not on the straight, but when we're braking and going around the corner. When we're braking we're trying to control the slip of the tyre, so that the tyres, front or rear, don't lock up. We're trying to get the maximum adhesion possible, then we turn the steering wheel, and we start to interrogate the lateral performance and try to judge the slip, both front and rear again, then we get on the power, and switch more to the rear in terms of balance, judging how much power to put on. So we're testing the edge of the tyre, and that's the difference between someone who can drive a car fast and someone who can't."

↑ Sebastian Vettel at speed during the 2010 Malaysian Grand Prix, *en route* to his, and the RB6's first victory of 2010.

← Driving on a damp track requires a very delicate touch.

↑ Mark Webber goes through some mental imagery to prepare for a qualifying lap.

PRECISE CONTROL INPUTS
The need for precision and finesse.

"We're very, very precise with our inputs – you might question how we do that with the brakes, but we hit the brakes incredibly hard. We have carbon-fibre brakes, we have incredible grip from the aerodynamics, and from the tyres, so the grip we have is very, very high, but we need to be able to modulate that brake pressure. If you think of your left foot pressing the pedal to the tune of 60 or 70 kilos initially, then we need to be able to modulate that, to be as precise and as delicate as we can, but yet hitting the pedal very hard.

"Driving in the wet, for example, we have to be extremely delicate, because we have a huge amount of performance at our disposal, and we need to be very smooth and precise with our inputs. It's very different to perhaps how people would expect, how aggressive we can be at certain times, and yet there's an element of being precise as well with both feet and hands."

A QUALIFYING LAP
The mindset required for the ultimate lap.

"There's some imagery. Mentally I use some techniques which put me into the situation of what I might expect in terms of what the grip might be, in terms of how the car's going to behave, and get really focused down on what I'm going to expect from the car when it really counts. It's different for the race, there are so many things that can happen. Qualifying's a bit more like a downhill ski race – you've got more control over your own performance. There are a lot more unknowns in the race, and questions about what's going to happen."

We asked Sebastian Vettel for his view on a few of the sensations experienced during a race.

■ **Is there time to relax at any point during a race?**

"We are busy all lap and you don't really have time to relax, but it also depends on the race situation, whether you are fighting for a position or the positions are set and you have some room around you, which means big gaps to the front and back. Then you have a bit of time to relax but this is more towards the end of the race when positions are set. Throughout the majority of the race you have to stay focused and try to use the straight to regain your breath and relax as well as you can."

■ **Can you hear other cars' engines during a race, or feel the heat when running close behind?**

"It depends how close you are to them. Obviously if they are far way you cannot but if you are racing somebody then, yes, you can hear their engine especially when you are alongside. You can smell the fumes but not necessarily feel the heat because generally it is quite hot in the car anyway. But you can definitely make out the difference when you run behind a car, because of grip and because of fumes, but it's not bad."

■ **How does it feel in the cockpit during a wet race?**

"Most of the water doesn't get to us because the speed is too high, but in low-speed corners we do get wet. After a long race in the wet, usually the upper body becomes wet, whereas your feet and legs, which are stuck in the cockpit, deeper in the tub, stay drier."

■ **Can you suggest three elements required for a perfect lap?**

"Commitment, joy and a bit of the unknown ingredient."

↑ The look of a World Champion. Sebastian Vettel focuses as he prepares to do battle.

← The ultimate driving experience – Sebastian Vettel puts the RB6 through its paces during pre-season testing.

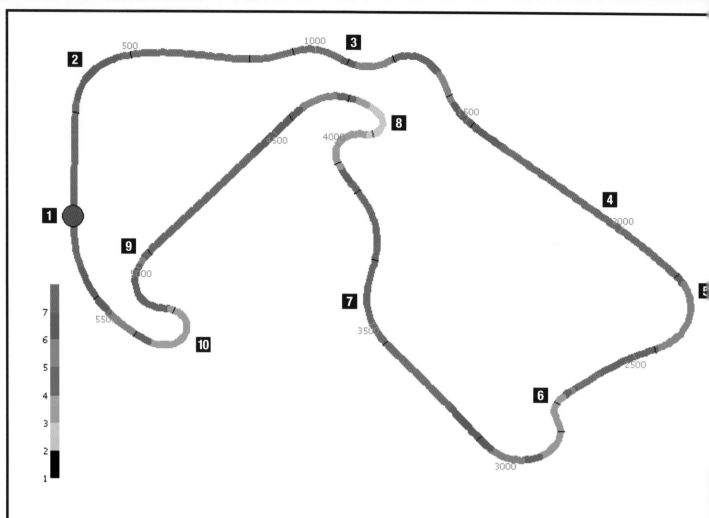

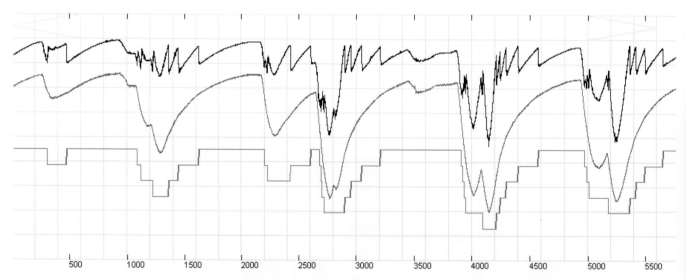

↑ A data plot for a lap of Silverstone by Mark Webber in 2010.
The plot shows a typical flying lap, so begins in top gear (seventh) at
the 2010 start/finish line. The colours on the map denote the gears.

Key to traces

Black – Throttle

Blue – Road speed

Red – Gear position

Mark Webber talks us round a lap of a typical grand prix circuit, in this case Silverstone in its 2010 British Grand Prix configuration – a race that Mark won, taking his third victory of the 2010 season.

1 "At Silverstone, if you start the lap where we used to start on the old grid (2010), obviously the track's changed a little bit [for 2011] where the new [pit] facility is.

2 "The first corner, Copse, is sixth gear, completely flat-out, very, very fast. You'll arrive there, and what's very important to me as a driver is making sure the ride height's not too low. If we have slightly too low a pressure in the tyres, or the car is set up a little too low in terms of its overall height off the ground, the plank will be kissing the ground – the plank always touches the ground the quicker you go because the car's being pushed into the ground with the aerodynamics. The faster you go, the harder it's being pushed into the ground, so at what we call EoS, which is End of Straight, the car will be at its lowest point front and rear. So, turning into a corner like Copse, we need to make sure that the car is kissing a little bit, but not too much because you're unloading the tyres, and that means you're not getting the most grip out of them either. I need to be very accurate with my turn-in, making sure that I've got full trust that the car is on its tyres, which it will be, because my engineers are great and they know what they're doing, so we work on that together. Clipping the apex kerb, sixth gear, very, very fast, high g-loading through there.

3 "That's over very, very quickly, then we head down to Maggots and Becketts, which is a very fast section of corners where there's an incredible change of direction, and this is where an F1 car is at its absolute peak. That you can flick the car from left to right, and then right to left again, through such an aggressive sequence of corners is really an incredible feeling for the driver to go through and feel what the car's performance can do. So, through that section, again you've got to be accurate, clipping the kerbs and making the track as wide as possible to get through there in as quick a time as possible, straight-line the corners, and downshifts as well, so we'll be going down a few gears through those corners, accelerating hard out on the Hangar Straight.

4 "Again, the touching will probably be at its worst on this part of the lap. It's very bumpy at the end of that straight, so you'll probably be able to smell the plank a little bit – you can smell the wood sometimes, that happens every now and again, particularly when the plank is new, or it's early in the race when the car is heavy with fuel.

5 "Turning hard into Stowe Corner, it's a fourth-gear, very fast corner, bumpy on the way through again. Use the kerb on the exit so the car can run wide through there. Again, the cars can be abused within reason – you can hit things pretty hard with them, as long as it's not with the chassis. With the tyres, you need to be able to use all the road and use the kerb.

6 "Then, out of that corner, down to the section called Vale and Club. So this is the first heavy braking point on the track, over a crest, so you're going to have some rear locking potentially, initially, because that's what generally happens on that type of corner over a crest, so you need to make sure that you've got a good feel for the rear tyres initially on the brakes. Then, use a bit of the inside kerb, down to second gear, it's a slow corner. Around the long Club Corner now, which is a very long right-hander, accelerating hard through that corner.

7 "You're coming back towards the pits [new for 2011] now, and you go through a very, very tricky right-hander, which was very challenging for all the teams last year, including us. Our car was probably one of the best through there in terms of controlling the bumps. It's very, very fast, but bumpy, so ride is important, sixth gear again through there.

8 "Then you come in to the Village-complex section, with a tight right-hander again, braking heavily. With this section it's very important to position the car for the following corner, so it's all about rhythm and setting the car up to run through these tight corners. Right-hander, then a left-hander, accelerating hard through there.

9 "Then you're coming right back down in front of the BRDC suite, finishing the lap, heavy, heavy braking – fast on the way in, but heavy braking into a tight left-hander, using the flat kerb on the inside, short acceleration and back another gear into Luffield.

10 "Luffield is the last corner and takes forever to get round – one of the most painful corners in F1! The car doesn't really like it round there, there's a lot of understeer that builds up, so you've got to do your best in terms of set-up to combat that with the differential. Then, across the line to finish the lap. Around a lap like that, you might adjust the brake balance maybe once or twice, very rarely would you be adjusting the diff too much."

EPILOGUE

Sebastian Vettel takes the flag to win the 2011 Malaysian Grand Prix – two wins from the first two races of the season for Sebastian and the Red Bull Racing RB7.

'As a sportsman you're always looking forward. Now, though, 2010 is behind us. It's a very proud memory, but now it's 2011 and there's another job to do, so we move to the next challenge, which is trying to do the same again.'

Sebastian Vettel – 2010 F1 Drivers' World Champion

FIA CRASH TESTS

T he chassis for any new car must undergo a series of FIA crash tests, all of which must be passed before the chassis is homologated and the car is allowed to race. The impact tests are usually carried out at the Cranfield Impact Centre, near Bedford, with an FIA witness present, but certain of the other tests can be carried out at the Red Bull factory, again with an FIA witness present.

Various tests are carried out, divided into impact tests, roll-structure tests and push-off tests as shown in the table opposite.

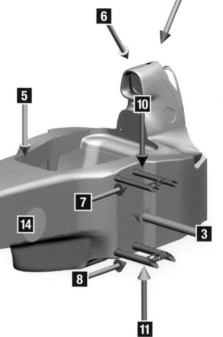

← A schematic showing the various FIA crash tests that the chassis and crash structures must pass for homologation.

■ Crash test
■ Squeeze test
■ Push-off test
■ Calculated result

FRONT IMPACT TEST 1 (SEE TABLE)

NUMBER	NAME	TEST	COMMENTS	REQUIREMENTS FOR PASS
1	Front impact 1	Impact at 15m/s, trolley ballasted to 780kg	Fuel tank empty, nosebox fitted	Various max/mean deceleration/energy requirements. No damage to monocoque for a pass
2	Front impact 2	Impact at 15m/s, trolley ballasted to 900kg	Nosebox removed, impact wall fitted with impact tubes	No damage to monocoque for a pass
3	Side impact	Impact at 10m/s, trolley ballasted to 780kg	Fixed sideways to strong wall	Various max/mean deceleration/energy share proportions in four load-cell areas. No damage to monocoque for a pass
4	Rear impact	Impact at 11m/s, trolley ballasted to 780kg	Gearbox and rear impact structure on strong wall	Various deceleration/energy requirements. No damage to gearbox for a pass
5	Front roll structure	75kN vertical load	Fitted in FIA squeeze frame	No damage to monocoque 100mm below load point for a pass
6	Rear roll structure	120kN (x-60kN, y-50kN, z-90kN)	Fitted in FIA squeeze frame	No damage to monocoque 100mm below load point for a pass
7/8	Push-off side-impact structure horizontal test	Horizontal load of 20kN	Calculation, no physical test	No structural failure
9	Rear-impact structure push-off test	Transverse load of 40kN	30 seconds	No failure of attachments between structure and survival cell
10/11	Push-off side-impact structure vertical test	Vertical load of 10kN up/down	Calculation, no physical test	No structural failure
12	Rear roll structure 2	120kN (x-60kN, y-50kN, z-90kN)	Calculation, no physical test	No structural failure
13	Nose push-off	Transverse load of 40kN	30 seconds	No failure of attachments between structure and survival cell
14	Side intrusion test	Force truncated cone through test panel at 2mm/s	For 150mm	Various load and energy displacement requirements

SPECIFICATIONS

CHASSIS

Composite carbon-fibre monocoque structure, carrying the Renault V8 engine as a fully stressed member

ENGINE

Renault RS27–2010

No. of cylinders	8
Capacity	2,400cc
Maximum rpm	18,000
Number of valves	32 (4 valves per cylinder)
Vee angle	90°
Power output	Approximately 700–750bhp
Engine construction	Cylinder block and heads in cast aluminium alloy
Engine management	FIA (McLaren Electronic Systems Limited) 'standard' ECU – TAG310B
Oil	Total group
Weight	FIA minimum weight of 95kg

TRANSMISSION

■ Hydraulically operated AP Racing multi-plate carbon clutch.

■ Seven-speed gearbox, with composite carbon-fibre casing. Longitudinally mounted with hydraulically operated gear selector mechanism.

■ Hydraulically operated differential with variable locking action.

SUSPENSION

■ **Front** Aluminium-alloy uprights, composite carbon-fibre wishbones and push-rods. Torsion springs and anti-roll bar with Multimatic dampers.

■ **Rear** Aluminium-alloy uprights, composite carbon-fibre wishbones and metal pull-rods. Springs and anti-roll bar with Multimatic dampers.

BRAKES

Brembo calipers, with Brembo discs and pads. Front/rear hydraulic system split, with adjustable bias.

ELECTRONICS

12-volt electrical system.
System under control of FIA standard ECU.

FUEL

Total group

WHEELS

OZ Racing, 12.7x13in front, 13.4x13in rear

TYRES

Bridgestone

PERFORMANCE

Top speed (Monza)	214mph (345kph)
0–100mph (160kph)	3.8sec
(typical of all circuits and tyre compounds)	
100–0mph (160kph)	4.0sec
(typical of pitlane grip levels, as this is the only instance when the car stops aggressively)	
Maximum longitudinal acceleration	1.5g
(peak traction)	
Maximum braking deceleration	5g
(peak braking)	
Maximum lateral acceleration	4g
(typical of car operation throughout the season)	
Fuel consumption	Typically 4–6mpg
(circuit-dependent)	(47–70l/100km)

DIMENSIONS, WEIGHTS AND CAPACITIES

Width	1,800mm
Height	950mm
Wheelbase	3,200mm
Front track	1,800mm
Rear track	1,800mm
FIA-specified minimum weight	620kg
(including driver and camera)	
Fuel tank capacity	Approximately 165kg
Engine oil capacity *(typical)*	4 litres
Engine coolant capacity *(typical)*	8 litres

INDEX